USER-CENTERED WEB DESIGN

JOHN CATO

 Addison-Wesley

An imprint of **Pearson Education**

Harlow, England · London · New York · Reading, Massachusetts · San Francisco
Toronto · Don Mills, Ontario · Sydney · Tokyo · Singapore · Hong Kong · Seoul
Taipei · Cape Town · Madrid · Mexico City · Amsterdam · Munich · Paris · Milan

PEARSON EDUCATION LIMITED

Head Office: London Office:
Edinburgh Gate   128 Long Acre
Harlow CM20 2JE   London WC2E 9AN
England   Tel: +44 (0)20 7447 2000
Tel: +44 (0)1279 623623   Fax: +44 (0)20 7240 5771
Fax: +44 (0)1279 431059   Website: www.informit.uk.com
                                       www.aw.com/cseng

First published in Great Britain in 2001

© Pearson Education Limited 2001

The right of John Cato to be identified as Author of this Work has been asserted by him
in accordance with the Copyright, Designs and Patents Act 1988.

ISBN 0 201 39860 5

British Library Cataloguing in Publication Data
A CIP catalogue record for this book can be obtained from the British Library.

Library of Congress Cataloging in Publication Data
Applied for.

The programs in this book have been included for their instructional value. The publisher
does not offer any warranties or representations in respect of their fitness for a particular purpose,
nor does the publisher accept any liability for any loss or damage arising from their use.

Many of the designations used by manufacturers and sellers to distinguish their products are claimed as
trademarks. Pearson Education Limited has made every attempt to supply trademark information about
manufacturers and their products mentioned in this book.

10 9 8 7 6 5 4 3 2 1

Typeset by Pantek Arts Ltd, Maidstone, Kent.
Printed and bound in Italy.

The Publishers' policy is to use paper manufactured from sustainable forests.

ABOUT THE AUTHOR

John Cato is Managing Director as well as a practicing designer of Software Design & Build Ltd (johncato@softdesign.co.uk), a software consultancy specializing in designing interactive systems.

John's involvement in the software business began in 1973 and since then he has enjoyed a wide range of roles within major blue chip companies. He is actively involved in a variety of professional bodies, in particular the British Computer Society HCI SIG, the OOPS SIG and BCS Bristol Branch activities. He is also a member of the ACM and the UPA.

He is a popular speaker on user-centered design at international conferences such as HCI 93, HCI 95, Object Expo 97, HCI 97, OT 97, OT 2000 and Application Development 2000.

Software Design & Build is recognized for its work on design and useability on multimedia kiosks, websites, graphical user interfaces and telephone systems such as WAP and secure telephony. They were involved in the design and useability of the award-winning Nationwide Building Society project, "Interact" – a ground-breaking multi-media kiosk – as well as input into the design of their website. John Cato's clients have included Nationwide Building Society, Nuclear Electric plc, Andersen Consulting, Datastream International, Brann Direct Marketing, Renishaw plc, Serco plc, National Health Service, Westinghouse Signals, Hewlett Packard Research Labs, Open University, Admiral Computing and Eloan, amongst others.

John provides consultancy on design and useability evaluation, as well as running multi-disciplinary workshops on "Design for Use." His interest lies with excellence in design, so as to empower the individual at work, particularly interaction design, multimedia systems design, visual design, useability evaluation and object-oriented design. He is excited by practical ideas that may help with design strategies for interactive systems – and fascinated by solutions that give him the leverage to produce excellent design that is effective in a commercial environment for the client and the user.

John's most recent work has included the user-centered design and useability evaluation of the most recent Internet WAP phones, the first UK PDA interfaces, and Internet TV for a major financial institution.

ACKNOWLEDGEMENTS

Thank you, my friends for helping me get this book written – much more work than you'd think, more help than you'd think one way or another.

This book was written with you in mind Tim, even though you are now travelling another path in the Himalayas, and honours you Ruth with your love and integrity and David with your search, my children, with my love.

Special thanks go to:

Katherin Ekstrom
Steve Temblett
Bob Hughes
John Teire
Luke Hayman
Jonathan Earthy
Mike Rehberger
Koko
David Parkin
Ruth L
Chris McEvoy
Don Norman
Jakob Nielsen
Kevin Lynch
Edward Tufte
Don Koberg and Jim Bagnall

My mother and father, and a million others along the way, all conversations and communications since the day I was born gave me the thoughts that I have now – I thank you for your generosity.

PERMISSION ACKNOWLEDGEMENTS

The publishers wish to thank the following for permission to reproduce images, screenshots or text in the book.

Page(s) 171 Courtesy of Palm, Inc

Page(s) 75, 99, 100, 102, 117, 121, 126–127, 131–134, 174–176 Amazon, www.amazon.com

Page(s) 142, 143 CBS Marketwatch.com, www.bigcharts.com

Page(s) 116, 122, 146–147, 241, 242–255 Blackwells Online Bookshop, www.blackwells.co.uk

Page(s) 71, 119, Frances D K Ching, *Architecture, Form Space and Order*, Required by permission of John Wiley and Sons, Inc

Page(s) 112, culture finder, www.culturefinder.com

Page(s) 165–167, 168–169 E-LOAN Limited, www.uk.eloan.com

Page(s) 128, 129, 156–158 Labaratorio Farmaervas Ltda, www.farmaervas.com.br

Page(s) 110–111, 121 The Solomon R. Guggenheim Foundation, New York, www.guggenheim.org

Page(s) 112, howletts, www.howletts.co.uk

Page(s) 159–160, 161–164 interactive investor international, www.iii.co.uk

Page(s) 116, The Internet Bookshop, www.bookshop.co.uk

Page(s) 257, Crisp Publications, Inc.

Page(s) 171 Ionic

Page(s) 113 www.kreskytv.com

Page(s) 149, 150, 186, 225–234, 236, Primark Financial Information Division, www.marketeye.co.uk

Page(s) 193, Nationwide Building Society

Page(s) 194 Jakob Nielsen, Nielsen Norman Group, www.useit.com

Page(s) 294, 297–299 Nokia

Page(s) 4, From *The Psychology of Everyday Things* by Donald A. Norman, reprinted by permission of Basic Books, a member of Perseus Books, LLC.

Page(s) 135–137, 167–168 PriceWaterhouseCooper Ltd, www.pwc.com

Page(s) 109, 138–140 San Francisco Museum of Modern Art,
www.sfmoma.org
Page(s) 108, 122, Tate Britain, www.tate.org.uk
Page(s) 144–145, 152 Edward R Tufte, *The Visual Display of Quantitative
Information*, Graphics Press, 1983, Visual Explanations, Graphics
Press, 1997.
Page(s) 106, Washington Post, www.wpni.com
Page(s) 107, Lycos, Inc. www.wired.com.

CONTENTS

INTRODUCTION

Websites are for *people*; people like you and me. Some we might use every day and others we take occasional brief rambles through.

Using a website, we get to know the organization and feel their character. We decide if we want to have a relationship with them and whether we will come back.

So, think of your website *as an extension of yourself.* It is a reflection of you in the role you have and the context of your world. As a business, you need to convey the style of your corporate culture, and visions for the future of the company, its customers, staff and suppliers. The whole message is on your website; you and your website are not separate things.

Whatever you do, it will create an effect on the person who enters it and interacts with it. As Thoreau said "it is the mark of the special man to raise the quality of the day." As designers, we might try to do this when we create a website.

When you think of a website, you might think of many different things, including information, e-commerce and shopping, or enjoyment and advertising.

There are two main aspects of use.

- What use is it to the visitor (the user)?

- What use is it to you as an organization?

VISITORS' PURPOSE	ORGANIZATION PURPOSE
● to purchase (air tickets, books, toys, CDs)	● selling (e-commerce)
● to look at (leisure, reflection, visual entertainment)	● obtain involvement

VISITORS' PURPOSE	ORGANIZATION PURPOSE
● to live in (regular daily business, transactional)	● reduce daily overhead costs
● to communicate (group space)	● relationship, marketing, communication
● to visit occasionally (examining bank balances, stock prices)	● provide more cost-effective financial services
● to explore (information, education)	● sell information

Although the needs of the user and the organization are connected, each has a different point of view. Each point of view must be honored and satisfied. It must be a mutually satisfying relationship.

Some sites have changed since writing this book but the lessons from these sites still apply.

I encourage you to treat this book as a personal workshop. This gives you an opportunity to do design and explore how to meet the needs of the *user* and the *organization*. By taking small components, and working with them, you can experience design in a microcosm.

I | DESIGN FOR USE

What is "design for use," and why bother with it in the first place?

Design for use is wide-ranging and multi-disciplinary. Insight comes from areas as far apart as architectural design and graphic design, art, psychology, film craft and animation. Designing for use provides products which are comfortable, powerful, useful, creative, constructive, intuitive, relevant, sensitive, used immediately and learned without tears.

Perhaps the most easy-to-use products are the ones you don't notice.

I don't claim to know all the answers, and you wouldn't believe me if I said I did. Even if I knew all the answers and I could tell you what they are, it is unlikely you would understand. This is not because I doubt your intelligence but because...

Understanding comes through doing.

Throughout this book I invite you to practice, to try out the ideas; don't believe me without finding out for yourself. Use what works for you in your environment and your work culture.

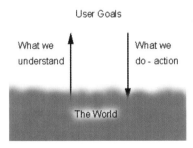

AWARENESS, UNDERSTANDING, ACTION (AUA)

The "awareness, understanding, action" model is so important to user centered interaction design that I am introducing it now. Its greater significance is explained in more detail in Chapter 4, Designing the system.

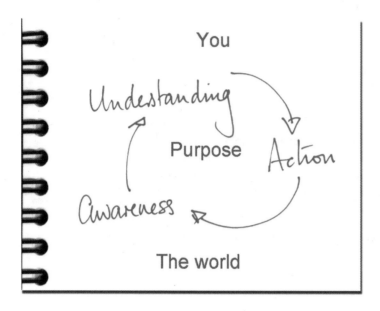

Everything you do in your relation to the world is an ever-evolving attainment of purpose, based on awareness, understanding and action. This is as true for interaction design as it is to developing your skills.

Keep your mind open with *awareness*. This book is a framework to explore and develop an *understanding* of key areas of software interaction design. Give yourself 100 percent to *action*; this level of involvement, exploration and questioning will help you to discover things about design for use which are not in the standard textbooks.

WHAT IS DESIGN?

"Design is solving problems that cannot be formulated until they have been solved. The shaping of the answer is part of the question."

from Francis Ching's wonderfully illustrated book *Architecture: Form, Space and Order*

This definition is one of great insight; it is so right, and points to the need to design *iteratively*. A dictionary definition of design is as follows.

"Design is: (i) to work out the structure or form of something, as by making a sketch, outline, pattern or plan; (ii) to plan and make something artistically or skilfully; (iii) to form or conceive in the mind, invent, create; (iv) a plan, sketch, or preliminary drawing; (v) a

coherent and purposeful pattern, as opposed to chaos; (vi) a finished artistic or decorative creation."

It turns out that design is the process of creating an artefact with structure or form which is planned, artistic, coherent, purposeful and useful.

So, by inference, try a simple test right now. For each statement below, please score it between 1 (strongly disagree) and 7 (strongly agree).

STATEMENT	SCORE
My project is lacking a clear purpose	
My project is lacking a clear usefulness (to the user)	
My project is lacking a clear structure or form	
My project is un-artistic	
My project is inconsistent or not coherent	
My project is not planned	
My project is delivering after one design, build, cycle	

How well did you do? The higher the score, the greater your need to focus on "What is the use?" "What is good design?." If you scored less than 8 or greater than 42, tell me about it.

I would guess that you have seen projects that score badly on this simple measure, and you may even be working on one now. This book will help you score better on this test.

But what of the use?

WHAT IS USEABILITY?

Useability refers to how useable a system is from a user's point of view. It has many definitions but for me the guiding principle is:

Useability is being able to do the things you want to, not the things you have to!

When you see someone struggling to use a product, doing things they have to in order to do things they want to, you are witnessing bad design. Don Norman gave a number of examples of this in his popular book *Psychology of Everyday Things* (POET).

just doing it

and
an example of a user **having** to read a sign to open a door...

At left and below are photographs of hardware for doors that open by being pulled. The large plates at the left are a signal to push, but in fact the door is supposed to be pulled: no wonder the door needs the signs. The simple U-shaped brackets below is a much better design, but they are ambiguous enough that a sign still seems to be needed. Contrast with the two handles at the top, neither of which needs a sign yet is always operated properly. If a door handle needs a sign, then its design is probably faulty.

Source: *Psychology of Everyday Things*, Norman, D.

Useability concerns are not only about presentation, but a whole gamut of exchanges that form human–computer communication.

The quest for useability is the search for ways of creating excellent communication and dialogs between two "actors"; the multimedia web application (created by the minds of designers) and the human user. The aim is to provide efficient, effective and satisfying outcomes for all concerned (the "stakeholders," anyone who has a "stake" in the design, i.e. customers, business, designers, marketing and so on).

It is concerned with identifying and understanding both the *users'* psychological, physical, social and activity requirements and the *organization's* objectives, and designing a useable and useful system for both.

A useable product is one which is conceived and produced to be easy to learn, easy to use, and useful. This is easy to say, but harder to achieve.

Useability can be measured against a number of attributes. Schneidermann, in his book *Designing the User Interface*, defined five attributes of useability.

- *learnability*. The system should be easy to learn, so the user can quickly get some work done.

- *efficiency*. Once users have learned the system, they should be able to use it productively.

- *memorability*. The system should be easy to remember, so the casual user is able to use the system again without having to re-learn everything.

- *errors*. The system should have a low error rate, so the user feels they are making positive progress and are in control, and if they do make errors they should be able to recover from them easily. Catastrophic errors should not occur.

- *satisfaction*. The system should be pleasant to use, so users are subjectively satisfied when using it.

Since then, other key attributes have been suggested.

- *control*. Users feel they are in control rather than the system controlling them.

- *skills*. Users feel that the system supports, supplements and enhances their skills and expertise – it has respect for the user.

- *privacy*. The system helps users to protect information belonging to them or their clients.

The International Standards Organization (ISO) model
(ISO 9241) defines useability as measures of the following.

- *efficiency*. The accuracy and completeness the user achieves with
  respect to the goals.

- *effectiveness*. The user effort required to achieve the user and
  domain goal.

- *satisfaction*. The measure of user satisfaction on a number of
  attributes.

And last, but by no means least

- *usefulness*. The measure of the value the user places on the product.

See also pages 211–213 for the user perception metrics I use –
usefulness, effectiveness, efficiency, satisfaction, respect, presentation,
and learnability.

WHY DESIGN FOR USE?

The Interact '90 Conference[1] showed one of the first results of formal
studies of cost-benefit analysis with respect to iterative prototyping and
evaluation throughout the design process. At IBM, $20,000 was
invested in user-centered design over seven months of development to
return $40,000 savings in three days of running live. On another
project, it was shown that for each $1 invested in these studies early in
design, in the order of $100 was saved in cost of end user time with
respect to work effectiveness.[2]

In some recent consultancy, I carried out 15 days of useability
evaluation and 12 days of re-design. The number of "sales" of $800
gross profit items increased from 35 per week to 250 per week.

See also *Cost benefit* in Chapter 6, where Nielsen also suggests a
return of 100 to 1 from useability evaluation.

If we want to be effective, it is our responsibility to pay greater
attention to interface and interaction design.

The benefits of user-centered design include the following.

- *increased usefulness*. The more evidently useful a product is, the greater
  the acceptance and the greater the desire the user has to use it.

- *increased efficiency.* Helps users work in the way they prefer so they can be effective and efficient rather than being ineffective wrestling with a poorly designed user interface.

- *improved productivity.* Because the user is more effective and efficient, concentrating on the job in hand rather than the user interface.

- *fewer errors.* Much of human error can be the result of a badly designed user interface. Really understanding the way the user is aware of what they see, how they understand it and how they will act can significantly reduce human error.

- *reduced training time.* Consistency, support and reinforcement in a user-sensitive manner can reduce learning and competency time.

- *improved acceptance.* A quickly accepted interface leads to a system the user will trust and enjoy using. Enjoyment reduces stress and reduces the chance of rejection.

A PRAGMATIC VIEWPOINT

Good design:
- is the process of making visions come true
- makes the business visible to its customers
- satisfies business needs and visions
- satisfies the user needs and visions
- satisfies the customers' needs and visions.

Every project is different. Judgments must be made on a project-by-project basis concerning the financial investment and depth of detail you give to issues raised in this book. Also, you need to decide whether to do them yourselves or to employ a consultancy to do them for you. This is also a cost-benefit decision.

Notes

1 "Cost-Benefit Analysis of Iterative Useability Testing"; Karat, C. M., In Proceedings of Interact '90.

2 For a comprehensive approach to cost-benefit analysis, see Bias, R. G. and Mayhew, D. J. (eds) 1994, *Cost-Justifying Useability*, London: Academic Press, ISBN 0-12-095810-4.

2 | DISCOVER, DESIGN, USE

Following any design framework is better than being haphazard. While this should be self-evident, it is often forgotten in our haste to produce a product.

This chapter contains the basis of a framework and subsequent chapters develop on this. Use it and you will succeed.

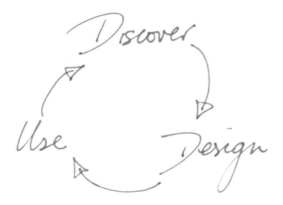

First, let's look at other design frameworks.

I found the following process framework in *A Technique for Producing Ideas* by James Webb Young, and have modified it a little with my note on step 6.

According to Young, the process of design is as follows.

1. Gather facts and information.
2. Examine and explore.
3. Incubate.

4. Give design its birth.
5. Examine and refine.
6. Iterate (probably 6–8 times).
7. Deliver the designed product.

Others have written similarly on design models. For example, in the 19th century, Helmholtz, the German physiologist and scientist, defined his own process of creation as being:

- saturation

- incubation

- illumination.

> "I can remember the very spot in the road, whilst in my carriage, when to my joy the solution occurred to me."

from the life and letters of Charles Darwin, 1887.

Poincaré, the French mathematician, supplemented Helmholtz's list in the early 1900s by adding a further stage, that of *verification*. Then in the 1960s, American psychologist Jacob Getzels added a stage at the beginning which can be thought of as a pre-analytic vision, the stage of *first insight*, or finding and formulating the initial thought that it might be done, the initiating creative vision. This all seems obvious now.

- first insight

- saturation

- incubation

- illumination

- creation

- verification.

We now have the following three stages.

1. *discovery.* – Includes pre-analytic vision, gather facts and information, examine and explore, incubation, illumination – the "Ah ha" moment.
2. *design.* – Give design its birth.
3. *use.* – Market testing, useability, verification, validation.

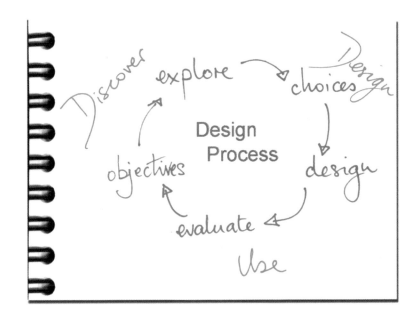

The over-frequent reality of design is: dabble in discovery, go almost immediately to design, followed by a dabble in functional testing with no useability testing, and then deliver the designed product. This often results in an ill-thought-out design and a poorly tested solution; then users test it in *"ANGER."*

Marc Rettig comments in "Hat Racks for Understanding," *Communications of the ACM*, October 1992:

> *"I'll sit down to work on an assignment, start sketching screens or composing an outline, then suddenly stop and say to myself, 'these are all "hows!." What is the "what?" What am I really trying to deliver?'"*

We get so caught up in creating things that we jump to stage 2 of the process almost immediately, and give the stages of *discovery* limited attention to detail at the right time. This is one of the major causes of poor design, perhaps because this doesn't feel like design at all.

You cannot just jump in to creating a design; you have to give a reasonable and appropriate amount of time to *discovery* (saturation and incubation) stages if you are going to come up with quality insights.

The concept of the incubation stage is interesting; that time where the mind works on the problem when you are doing something else. If you can, give yourself time during the *discovery* and *design* stages to take time out doing something completely different. Go to the theater, take a team outing somewhere – even if for a short space of time, it will pay off.

Then there is what we might think of as a bardo[1] state somewhere between discovery and design, the instantaneous moment of insight when everything clicks into place, after which you just have to write down what it is and how it all works.

What Young and the others *omit* to emphasize, is the user and the importance of use in design:

Use IS Design

You have to involve your users very early on so they can give regular insight and input into the use they will expect from the product throughout the design process.

Too often, the worthwhile work of useability testing and market testing are largely carried out after product delivery. Now labelled "maintenance" rather than design and development, it corrects all the things that should have been right in the first place. Unfortunately, this just wastes resources, although it does have the advantage of putting it into another budget.

THE ITERATIVE PROCESS OF DESIGN

The process of design is one of creativity in problem solving. It is a process which explores facts and feelings, identifies design objectives and goals, generates possible solutions, chooses a solution, creates a design, evaluates the design and repeats. And so, to "repeat."

> **"Design is solving problems that cannot be formulated until they have been solved. The shaping of the answer is part of the question."**

This is from my variation of a quotation found in Ching's wonderfully illustrated book, *Architecture: Form, Space and Order* which I highly recommend. The quotation is attributed to the Danish poet and scientist, Piet Hein. The original form is

> *"Art is solving problems that cannot be formulated until they have been solved. The shaping of the question is part of the answer."*

It is unusual to get a design adequately correct the first time.

The design cycle often repeats 6–10 times.

So, think of developing the system iteratively at first as prototypes and then as fully working systems, building successive refinements of useful and reuseable components at different levels of refinement.

Why should you do this? Often you get it wrong first time, but learn a great deal and have good material to take forward to the next cycle. You can only really know how good or bad the design is by *using* it. It often happens that the fourth or fifth iteration heralds a breakthrough in understanding the misunderstood – suddenly, the blindingly obvious hits you, so far missed by everyone. It is then that the design becomes good and is iterated until it is excellent.

Throughout the development process, assess the system to understand:

- key critical high-risk areas *(for example, on a financial information site, the details of the data feeds and the use of them in the interface might be critical and high risk)*

- areas of activity or information where the issues are representative of other areas of the site *(for example, on the Amazon site "books," "music," "videos" and the like are essentially areas of similar activity; once you have cracked the design problem for one, you have cracked it for them all)*

- components which are ubiquitous and complicated, and so will be high gain once they are right *(for example, on air ticket booking sites, entering a date or selecting an airport are ubiquitous and require careful design)*.

Get leverage and safety margins by focussing your attention on key critical high-risk areas first (see *Controlling Software Projects* by Tom de Marco, an essential and highly readable book), then move on to areas where the issues are representative of other areas of the site, then to components which are ubiquitous and complicated.

Don't try to build the whole site in one go. Don't try and deal with all these problem areas at once unless you have a large team of people working, and then you might deal with all of these in parallel.

Go for a "low fidelity" prototype initially, concentrating on the scope, structure, user process, function, useability. This can be done simply with paper prototypes. In later iterations, successively refine the design into "high fidelity" with all the code, graphics and details highly refined.

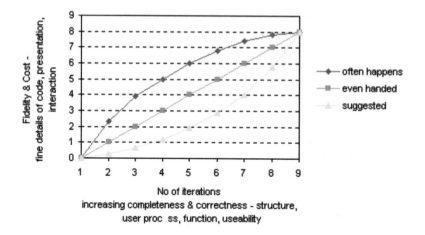

There is a large financial advantage to this approach. It will cost you less to learn more about the issues and you will get it right for less cost overall. (The area under the curve is the cost.)

Low fidelity initial iterations have the added benefit of less resistance to making the changes indicated by the evaluation. Developers hate to change things which have taken a long time and deep involvement to create, and managers are highly reluctant to support changes to improve the site if they have already spent a large amount of their budget and are then being shown that it has to change. Both groups fear ongoing high commitment and cost. If there has been less "emotional" and financial commitment, the changes are easier to accept and the outcome is more effective.

Also, low fidelity prototypes can even be better for initial user testing since the users will focus on the real issues and not feel obliged to comment on or criticize colors and details of graphic quality (which should be nearly the last thing to focus your attention on). This was pointed out by Brenda Laurel at the CHI 92 conference in Monterrey.

It is most important that iteration is *planned*, to be effective with each cycle and to recognize the value of prototyping in its various forms. If you are lucky, or very good (or both), you might not need all the iterations, but don't bank on it.

OVERVIEW OF THE DESIGN PROCESS

So we can see the design process is relatively straightforward. Given that you have a pre-analytic vision, you *discover*, you *design* and you *use*... and then you repeat the loop until you've done it.

That's all there is to it, and you have to trust in the "Ah ha" moment or moments that occur along the way. And, the more you can trust, the more that it happens.

It seems fairly simple and yet there is a lot to it. While the process seems ordered and linear, in reality, it is a non-linear process which keeps iterating and interleaving in order to get it all together.

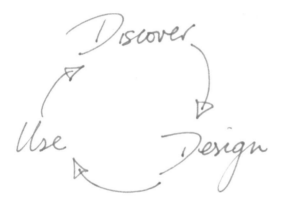

However you choose to weave these threads of development together, have and use a design process that works for your organization; it's better than having none.

Scaling up from small to large projects is a skilled management task. It requires greater attention to framework and method and detail. Most crucially, have the best people at all levels on the project. Combine this with excellent teamwork, mutual respect and understanding.

THE MINDSET YOU BRING TO DESIGN

"Design is the process of making dreams come true."

Don Koberg and Jim Bagnall in *The Universal Traveller*

There is no point to making a dream come true, unless it fulfills a use. Dreams have a use.

So, back to the big question "What's the Use?' How is this useful and how is it used?

You need *weltenshaum*, a world view of the use. And then, with the use, we are back to dreams. Whose dreams? Your dreams, your customer's dreams, your funder's dreams, your user's dreams, and your developer's dreams. Learn to make your mindset the same as the dreams that matter.

Design takes place within a context. This context is jointly a business environment and a consumer culture. Software design is to do with the process of creating a software system to meet a business need and to satisfy customers.

The central objective in user interface design is that of "meeting the users' needs in the performance of their activities within their operational context." To meet the user's dreams, we must bring the right mindset to design. We must focus on the user's-eye-view of the system. We must understand and meet our users' needs and make it easy to learn and easy to use.

The design mindset should:

- take a user's-eye-view

- involve users throughout

- focus on the user's needs and expectations

- encourage openness to ideas from users

- minimize criticism of suggestions from users

- respond to all criticism of design.

WHEN TO INVOLVE USERS

We are aiming to design for use, so you must make sure you involve the users from the very beginning to make sure you do not get too far adrift. You need them as soon as you can get them, as soon as you have any understanding of what kind of people they are. This is discussed in Chapter 3, *The users – roles.*

Many companies – if they involve users at all – only involve users during the final testing; perhaps carrying out useability evaluation (finding out what doesn't work) but more often during user acceptance testing (getting users to sign it off as OK) and they fall into the *sanction trap* (see *Useability evaluation* in Chapter 6, Use).

If you don't involve users until very late in the project, you will be miles adrift. Perhaps 80 percent to 90 percent of the work will have been done and only then will you know it is wrong.

Users are an essential part of the discovery stage.

Note

1 The word *Bardo* is from buddhist teachings and is commonly used to denote the intermediate state between death and rebirth. Sogyal Rinpoche considers a bardo as being like the moment when you step towards the edge of a precipice (which looks fearful) yet heralds the birth of some new insight, such a moment when one is introduced to the most essential, original or innermost nature of one's mind. There are a number of different kinds of bardo, and one of the most important to me is the sipa bardo, the bardo of becoming. Sipa also means "possibility" and "existence" and so the mind is in a state where the possibilities are infinite for new existence. This is the state where true creativity exists. This is where one releases the old (a kind of death) and is reborn with new knowledge, insight and commitment to the creative vision.

3 | DISCOVERY

Discovery is the process of finding out everything you can about what you are going to design, and defining the design requirement. I call this "discovery" because it is a much more active exploratory word than "analysis," the term usually used to describe this stage. An essential part of design is the deep understanding which comes through active discovery and knowledge.

You cannot carry out design without going through this part of the process, although many people actually skip large parts of what I think is essential to this stage, understanding users and their needs.

I was asked to redesign a website by a company which specializes in software tools, tools to manage the process of software development and creating models of design. These tools are sold for the benefit of doing the whole process and modelling properly. They require the designer to describe in minute detail the objectives of the project and the system design using class diagrams, state charts and so on; as well as the business and technical specification of a project and the design.

Naturally, I asked a number of questions.

- Could you describe the product's purpose, from the organization's and the customer's viewpoint?

- What are your users like?

- What are your customers like?

- What do the users like?

- What do the users expect to be able to do with it and what benefit does it give them?

- How do you see the cost benefits for the organization?

Interestingly, despite their own business being based on selling the whole idea of detail understanding and modelling, there was no clear answer.

These are simple questions. The answers must surely be known and written down? This is often not the case. It exists in the dreams and visions, but remains unclear. It remains at the pre-analytic vision stage even when the draft or finished designs have been produced. In practice, many projects are completed without the developers being clear about the needs and the use. None of these project people would dream of driving over a bridge built this way, or driving in a car built without the designers having explored the issues. Yet, they would not carry out these "safety checks" on their own website project, saying it would take too much time, and wasn't worth it. They could not answer the above questions with clarity. They were falling into the *creation trap*.

The creation trap

The creation trap is the mindset that says, "We know what we want; don't waste any more time exploring and understanding, just get on and create it."

Why? There is a collective perception of poor cost benefit of spending time clarifying what is wanted to the designers and developers. There is lack of appreciation of the benefits of user-centered design. Time pressure, budget pressures, management and political pressures all conspire to getting something visible immediately. So a jerry-built bridge is at least visible, "We can show progress."

As discussed in Chapter 2, *Discovery, design, use* we all want to get into the creation stage; then it feels like we are doing something, and detail discovery seems unproductive. But no-one ever designed anything good without becoming absorbed in the discovery stage first.

If you don't know what your organization wants to achieve, who your users are, what their usage needs are or what information they need, nor what makes the users and the organization satisfied, you are not going to be very successful. You cannot afford to be lazy on this, and yes, it takes time, and you won't see the "bridge" being built for a little while – but it is *essential*.

Paralysis by analysis

Now a word of warning; while you must spend time soaking in the discovery stage, an opposite syndrome can rear its head. This happens when people spend so much time in discovery they get stuck in it, continually raising problems and not finding objective sensible solutions.

If you do become stuck in the discovery stage, it is usually because:

● you are trying to achieve too much first time

● the problem can't be solved right now however much time you give it

● you are not following a development framework, just being haphazard.

Either way, some clear, objective decision making is required.

The foundations of excellent design

There are a number of *discovery* foundations for excellent design, and each is discussed in more depth here.

The big question you should apply to *everything* you do

What is the use?

So, what is the use of a designed product?

A website is not something in isolation. Don't think only of the site itself, while giving little real attention to the context and the other people who have a stake (the stakeholders) in the design. It is like going to a theater and only having the drapes pulled back a foot or two and assuming that is the whole set and the whole play.

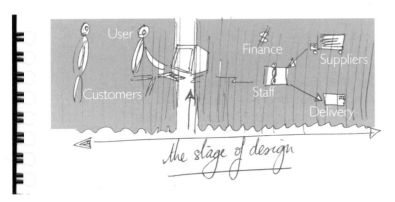

That idea is now changing. The website may be observed from many different viewpoints. It may be observed from afar, or over the shoulder, it may be interacted with at the front end or the back end of order fulfilment, supplies and deliveries and finance. We need to investigate the whole theater of action and interaction.

The purpose of the designed product is a useful, useable, effective, efficient and satisfying system for *users* that meets the *organization's* business objectives.

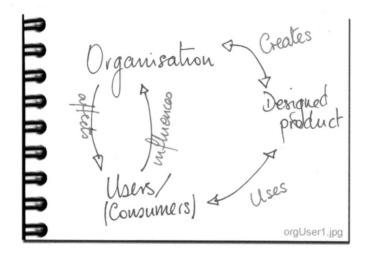

What we want to do, as an organization, affects those we design the system for – our users and customers.

What we find out about users – their needs and objectives – influences what we design, and what we provide as an organization.

There are therefore two primary discovery issues in user-centered design which influence each other – the visions, needs and objectives of the *organization* and those of the *users*. The needs of the *users* should be considered as a user-centered triad.

The user-centered triad

1. *The users.* Who they are, their roles, what they want, their objectives, what they are like, what they know, what they like and dislike, what do they think is useful, effective and efficient; what satisfies them. This clarifies and defines the use, the task.
2. *The use.* What the users' functional needs are, what they want to do to meet their objectives, where they use it from, what they consider success. This defines and clarifies the information.
3. *The information.* What information is needed to support the use, what information do they bring to the use; these components become key interface and design components.

Discovery is design

Even discovery is design. Why? Because even in discovery, since you can collect so much information which you explore and tease around, you build models to get a handle on it all. This means you are synthesizing, classifying and structuring. This puts your own frameworks on the facts, which is, of course, design.

It is difficult to avoid pre-judgment or prejudice – all I can say here is to be aware of this problem and notice whenever you have crossed the boundary between discovery and design. It is not wrong; it's very natural – but every time you do it without sufficient awareness or knowledge, you may be creating something which won't work well for the user.

> **There is no tight distinction between discovery, design and even use. Things some do in discovery, others defer until design, and still others defer until use.**

Now, let's take a look at the organization and its needs.

THE ORGANIZATION

What you need to know

Objectives

When any project starts, it begins as an idea in someone's mind. This vision may have had little detailed analysis, but it is the basis for the project.

It is important to be clear about what the organization wants to achieve. It could be your answer is:

- marketing – brochures, products, company

- sales – doing business, process, e-commerce

- internal experience – experimenting, skills development

- because the CEO wants it

- business support.

Your own idea might be even clearer than these.

You would not play skittles blindfold, or play cards without being told all of the rules, so why design without clear objectives? Without them, it is very easy to try out many ideas or create lots of interesting things on the site; but you will still end up developing a purposeless site.

Try this: write down – *NOW* – before turning the page, the answer to this question. What are we trying to achieve?

Now consider the following questions about your response.

- Does it describe your primary *intentions* and *focus?*
- Does your definition define the *scope* and *constraints* of the project?
- Does your definition give a *quantifiable measure of success* for the organization?
- Does it say anything about the *timescales* you intend to meet?
- Does it describe your intentions with regard to how people feel about you?

Stakeholders

Stakeholders are not just the people who have a direct financial stake in the success of the system. Stakeholders are all those who are influenced in some way by the system. They can be customers, users, programmers, consultants, managers, accountants, project sponsors, other parts of the existing business, etc. This is illustrated in the case study later in this chapter.

Target market/users

The software system (website or any other) must be designed for the usefulness of a target group of people. You cannot achieve a good design without knowing:

- who it's for – your target audience
- what the users are like
- the user's use context
- what users want to achieve.

The detail of this comes later, but first, identify who you think are the target users – make a list.

Scope of the project

It is important to define the scope of the project. For a website, your objective may be to create an interactive brochure and sales vehicle for your company, or a company intranet as a form of communication and dialog with employees, an e-business site or a worldwide company information system.

You are likely to have an enormous amount of information to communicate, and you will have a range of products or items to sell.

In developing the system, it is unwise to attempt to deal with it all at once, because this often results in failure. However, you will want to define the total scope as well as the primary delivery scope, because the whole system will need to have a coherence about it.

The scope document is a living document that evolves into the requirements specifications describing the users, the use and the objects. In the early stages, it is the management definition of what key functionality will be delivered, describing the top-level processes. This is not the same thing as a definition of the site structure – that can only be developed during the *design* stage after all the *discovery* tasks have been carried out.

Try writing what is a *mandatory objective* and what is an *optional objective*. This gives you flexibility in the delivery schedule and makes sure you know what the real objective is.

Constraints

You should define constraints for the project. These constraints will define:

- timescales
- costs
- software environments
- style
- operational
- other issues.

This is illustrated in the case study later in this chapter.

Measurable objectives

Objectives must be set up front, so designers can ensure the system meets them, and you can be sure the designers have met them.

To ensure the objectives are right, a representative sample of users must be involved throughout the design process, from the very beginning. You have to fully understand "What is the use?" before you can achieve a good design.

Quantifiable measures of success are the only way of determining whether or not you have met your objectives. Objectives should state explicitly what you are trying to achieve.

> *"Rational, competent men and women can work effectively to maximize any single observed indication of success."*

De Marco, in *Controlling Software Projects*, p. 58, "The Metric Premise."

Whatever you set as objectives will be what you get. What you get most will be the metric your people *perceive* as most important. If you don't set any, then assumptions will be made. These will be based on what is most obviously measured in the company, and you will get what best meets those assumptions.

BUSINESS

Get some clear and measurable business objectives. For example:

- sales must be made to at least 10 percent of the site visitors

- the number of users who obtain the image we want to present exceeds 80 percent

- we will sell 100 widgets and 250 gidgets in the first month

- we will have a sales growth rate of 5 percent per month

- we will have no more than 1 percent unsatisfied customers

- we will have a 20 percent ROI in year 1.

USE

The business purpose is more likely to be fulfilled if the user is satisfied, and this has much to do with useability. A site can only be defined as being sufficiently useable if it meets your useability goals – quantifiable measures of useability. So how do you do that?

The ISO standard ISO 9241 Pt 11 describes useability and useability measures remarkably well. It defines useability as a combination of learnability, effectiveness, efficiency and satisfaction.

In brief, both for the website as a whole, and for each primary user activity, you should define quantifiable targets for each of the following.

- *Learnability.* The time taken to get accustomed to the system and its operation and how easy it is to remember operational details. Set time objectives and memory objectives after that period of time. This measure may be less of an issue for some websites, especially those populated by people who are regular users and which have fewer one-off users.

- *Effectiveness.* Accuracy and completeness. This measures the number and nature of *pauses, hesitations* and *errors*; the number and nature of places user got stuck and any showing of *misunderstandings* or uncertainty during use or afterwards; the *degree of user success.* Essentially, this is the degree to which it meets the mindset, expectations and objectives of the user. For example, *90 percent of users must make no more than three hesitations, make no errors and correctly understand the degree of completion.*

- *Efficiency.* How much is the user effort reduced. This measures the *time* to meet a specific user objective, the *cost* and *resource* usage. If the site is not efficient, your customer will leave. People will stay on site while they feel the effort they spend is worth the payback, but not a second longer. For example, *the customer will know how to make contact with sufficient information for that contact to be useful and meaningful within five minutes.*

- *Satisfaction.* User satisfaction is subjective. Even so, it can be measured using carefully crafted questionnaires. These questionnaires ask the user to score the system based on quantitative useability measures. For example, *90 percent or more of the users must score more than 80 percent on the quantitative questionnaire scales.* (See *Useability questionnaires* in Chapter 6, Use, for more details of these measures.)

OTHER TARGETS

As well as the above, you should also set targets for the position your site is ranked in the major search engines and for the activity volumes on your site. For example:

- number of visits made per day must exceed 400 and increase by 5 percent per month

- number of customer contacts by e-mail must exceed 40 per day and increase by 5 percent per month

- number of enquiries made on site must exceed 30 percent of visitors

- number of times a person has visited must average 60 percent "more than once" and 40 percent "more than twice."

Visions, values and issues

If you are very early into the project, or if you want to try a quick validation check comparing what your team feels now against what you decided earlier in the project, this is a way to get started.

Take each of the categories of "what you need to know" and do some brainstorming under each of them. (See *Brainstorming* in Chapter 7, Side trips. This can be quick and extremely useful.)

However, we also need to understand the dreams, values and organizational issues behind the reality of making this vision work. Any issues that arise must be dealt with, and ideas that come out must be considered for inclusion in the design requirement.

One way of getting to the information is to carry out a "six hats brainstorming," and this is described in more detail in the *Six hats technique* in Chapter 7, Side trips. The output from this should be studied in detail to ensure that any problems are addressed early on.

Here is an example of the organization's project brief.

FINANCIAL INFORMATION WEBSITE — ORGANIZATION BRIEF

OBJECTIVE

There is a demand for financial information on equities, available on demand by a wide range of users with worldwide access.

The opportunities for the business come through increasing business volume and profits by developing trusted long-term relationships, charging customers for a greater range of up-to-date information and marketing of other related companies and products on the website. More can be made of this if the business can provide a dealing service on the web and by phone. Thus the site acts as a one stop shop for investors. The quality of information on the site and the ease of use will encourage investors to visit regularly, and thus the company can build a long-term relationship with investors, both existing clients and potential clients. The information provided will need to be:

CASE STUDY

- dynamic, regularly changing information such as share price
- irregular information such as company news and analyst reports
- infrequent changes such as company results and dividend details
- more static information on the company, such as the purpose, directors, and other background company information.

The site must ensure that changes take place without impact on customers who may access the information from any part of the world at any time of the day or night.

The point is to inform and provide effective services to develop trust and confidence so customers can feel it is worth their while to use our services. The site must communicate strongly that we can be trusted for quality information and an effective service for them.

INTENTIONS

- To project an up-to-date image.
- To project an image of us as a major player for everyday financial investment needs.
- To reinforce our brand and the association with our products.
- To project an image of a successful and socially responsible company.
- To provide quality, up-to-date information.
- To make users want to tell their friends about it.
- To provide concise, pertinent, clear information.
- To sell products – sales closure.
- To increase the user population's awareness of us.
- To make sales online.

PRIMARY FOCUS

We particularly want customers to be attracted to:

- our equity information service
- our share dealing services
- our pay to view financial information.

STAKEHOLDERS

- Private investor – getting information cost-effectively.
- Corporate marketing – using it as a business expansion tool.
- Business futures – envisioning the future possibilities.

- Site developers – producing new versions that work.
- Information providers – updating the databases.

TARGET AUDIENCE

Our target market is anyone who is a private investor.

SCOPE

Mandatory
To provide equity information:

- dynamic, regularly changing information such as share price
- irregular information such as company news and analyst reports
- infrequent changes such as company results and dividend details
- more static information on the company, such as the purpose, directors, and other background company information.
- To provide for dealing by telephone.
- To provide customer-driven portfolio management.
- To advertise other related companies which are not competitors.
- To provide information about investment events and seminars.
- To provide information about our company, corporate culture, management structure, history, relationships with other companies, track record, how to contact us, etc.

Optional
- To provide for dealing by internet.
- To provide a company newsletter.
- To provide a site download facility.
- To provide an open forum for customer comment.

CONSTRAINTS

Timescales
The site must be live within five months, providing the essential services.

Costs
The cost of the project must be less than the projected profit from the site from one year's operation, i.e. the project must repay all costs within one year.

Software environments
- The project must be capable of running on 90 percent of the currently most installed PC environments.
- *Browsers.* In practice, this means Netscape 5.0 or IE 5.0.
- *Screen resolution.* 800 × 600 and 14-inch monitor is the base line.
- *Colors.* 8-bit color images will be employed, web safe colors should be used. (The issue then is one of image quality across 90 percent of user displays and performance (image size).
- *Languages.* Javascript, Java, Database (SQL?).

Style
The corporate style and feel must be consistent throughout the site. The site must be in keeping with all our other company material.

Operational
The site must ensure that changes take place without impact on customers who may access the information from any part of the world at any time of the day or night.

Other issues
Copyright issues must be respected without exception.

MEASURABLE OBJECTIVES

Business
- To make a business profit on the venture within one year.
- To reduce our cost per customer in the year by 30 percent.
- To reduce the cost for the customer in the year by 15 percent.
- To increase the profit per customer in the year by 15 percent.
- To increase the number of customers by 30 percent a year.
- To develop trusted long-term relationships with our customers.

Use
- Ninety percent of users must be able to obtain useful information from any page within ten seconds; an assumption of 56k lines is made.
- Ninety percent of users must be able to reach their objective within two minutes.
- Ninety percent of users must score greater than 80 percent on each scale of the useability "satisfaction" questionnaire.

Other targets
- We want to be in the top 20 references for our field on hotbot, altavista, webcrawler, yahoo, yellow pages.

- We are aiming for 800 people to be visiting the site by the end of the first month, growing exponentially over time so that by the end of the third month we have 1500 people visiting a month.
- In three months' time:
  - more than 3000 people within our target audience will have visited our site
  - more than 50 percent of those will go beyond the first page
  - more than 20 percent of those will have indicated an interest in our "product"
  - more than 10 percent will have purchased one of our products as a direct result of the site
  - the profit gained from these sales will be greater than $45,000.

- In a year's time:
  - more than 20,000 people within our target audience will have visited our site
  - more than 50 percent of those will go beyond the first page
  - more than 20 percent of those will have indicated an interest in our "product"
  - more than 10 percent will have purchased one of our products as a direct result of the site
  - the profit gained from these sales will be greater than $240,000.

What we have

You will notice, this exercise has forced you to:

- outline your organization's objective
- clarify your focus
- define your target audience and their needs
- question how the target audience are going to find the site
- scope the site
- define constraints
- define measurable objectives
- know what your financial expectations are
- understand what your financial budget is.

You can explore and refine this statement of purpose until you decide that it is appropriate. It may lead you to decide not to have a website yet, or you may be able to define "intangible" benefits that support your investment. Otherwise, you may as well stop now.

THE SYSTEM

Websites are discretionary use systems. They must be even more carefully designed than regularly used, compulsory organizational systems. With those, training can be given to overcome design inadequacies; this is not the case on a website.

Users use a system to meet their objectives. We need to understand users' requirements from their point of view.

User requirements

We need to know about three things to create a design.

- *The users* – who they are, what they are like, what they know, what they like and dislike, and what they think is useful, effective and efficient; what satisfies them.

- *The use* – what they want to do, where they do it from, what their functional needs are, what they consider success.

- *The information* – what information they need and what information they give to support their use objectives.

   Know your user.

The users – roles

All *users* are different. They use a website or any other computer system with their unique knowledge, skill set and objective. If you don't know what they are like, you cannot design for them. The users are like actors' performance, a *role*. So, we can classify users into roles and profile these roles as "classes" of user.

You must understand what all the user roles are and what they are about.

"The users – understanding their roles" later in this chapter provides the framework for recording the detailed information. As new roles are identified, build up a dossier of information about them.

The use – actions

They use the system for some purpose, a purposeful action. This is the use, the task, the function, the action. The way this is designed can be useful, effective, efficient and satisfying, or just the opposite. This is the designers "choice." The use is a set of *actions* to fulfil an objective.

People at work carry out a variety of actions. These actions are part of a person's role. They are the means by which a role reaches their objectives.

The information – objects

The information is what they do it with. How this is structured and presented makes as much difference to the user's understanding and effectiveness, as the way the "task" or "action" is structured. In object-oriented terminology we would think of the information as objects. The information is a collection of objects which have value or purpose.

An action cannot take place in isolation. It must operate on some object and it might relate, communicate or connect with some other actor or role's needs.

This makes up a triad of components which relate to each other.

The RAO model

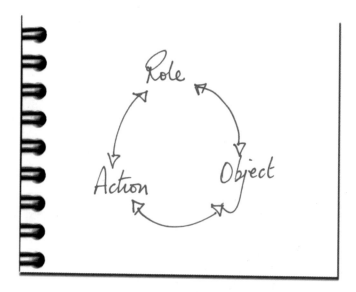

Roles carry out actions on objects, roles use objects to perform actions.

Actions are carried out by roles on objects, actions need and affect objects to meet a role's objective.

Objects have actions performed on them by roles, objects are used by roles to perform actions.

Wherever you start looking at the RAO model, you can use it as a questioning framework to tease out the other components, and as a completeness checking framework – discussed in principle below.

The process is iterative and forces all undiscovered information out simply by logically questioning until all the relationships are complete.

Later in this chapter we get to the detail of each aspect of the roles, actions and objects.

At this point, we are just making a start, getting a high level feel for the system.

Identifying roles, actions and objects

We can use "PostIt brainstorming" to get a team collective view. Brainstorming gets a load of thoughts and facts down fast. PostIt brainstorming on a shared workspace such as a desk, a wall or a whiteboard is a useful and effective technique.

The people involved in this process should be all the "stakeholders" – management, designers, developers, marketing, and all the others.

Begin by brainstorming into the three categories of roles, actions and objects.

This will get you a collective understanding of what everyone thinks about who the system is for, what actions are to be supported and what information is in the system. This is particularly useful for drawing out a wide range of high level material. Equally importantly, it raises opportunity for shared discussion, debate and understanding about all the team members' points of view, differences in terminology and views on degrees of importance.

Identifying roles

There are two *other* ways of identifying roles. Both add to the foundation knowledge gained from the brainstorming.

- **From "what the organization wants to achieve."** The first way is to re-read the brief of what the organization wants to achieve. In the case study, we can easily identify three such roles – those of private investor, marketing and business futures.

- **The system as an object.** The second way is to consider the information system as an object. We know from our knowledge of life, let alone object orientation, that all objects can be:

– created
– destroyed
– changed
– used.

With these thoughts in mind, we can consider what roles would take part or contribute in these activities on the information in the system. So, thinking about any and all of the objects in the system, we can reason as follows. At the highest level, system information is:

● created by information providers (data feeds)

● destroyed by information providers (data feeds)

● changed by information providers (data feeds), site developers

● used by private investors, marketing, business futures, information providers, site developers.

You will notice that one of our roles is a computer system in the form of a data feed. Just because this is not a person does not exclude it from the role.

Continue, using the same process on all objects in the system.

Identifying actions

Similarly, there are two *other* ways of identifying actions.

● **From "what the organization wants to achieve."** We can identify actions the roles will carry out by studying what we have so far from "discover the organization" and picking out all the user's objectives (an objective is, in effect, a top level action) and all indications of user activities.

● **The system as an object.** In the same way we identified roles by considering the objects in the system, we can question what actions would be carried out on the objects in order to create, destroy, change or use the object. We also find ourselves identifying more roles as a result of this questioning.

Identifying objects

Similarly, there are two *other* ways of identifying objects.

- **From "What the organization wants to achieve."** We can identify objects from studying what we have so far from "discover the organization" and pick out all the information and things (noun phrases) we can find, identifying all the things the user carries out some action on.

- **The system as an object.** We have used the idea of the system as an object to create more information about the roles (users) and the actions (the use). Now we can re-examine all the actions and pick out all the other information implied by that activity. Again, this will be all the noun phrases you can find which are not roles. Some noun phrases will be roles and they can be added into your list of roles.

   You can keep going back to the RAO model as a questioning framework at subsequent stages and deeper levels of understanding the users, the use and the information.

WEB-BASED FINANCIAL INFORMATION — ROLES, ACTIONS AND OBJECTS

From our earlier case study, following this approach, we begin fleshing out the roles (users), the actions (use), and the objects (information).

CASE STUDY

Roles

For the roles, we have (amongst others):

- private investor – getting information cost-effectively
- related company representatives
- customer support staff
- data administrators – updating the databases
- information providers (data feeds) – updating the databases
- system developers – producing new versions that work
- marketing – using it as a business expansion tool
- business development – envisioning the future possibilities.

Actions

The actions of a private investor role are to:

- identify an equity to invest in
- find an equity price

- examine equity price graph
- update equity prices
- update equity news information
- update equity analyst reports
- update equity dividend information
- update equity results information
- update equity corporate information
- examine equity news information
- examine equity analyst reports
- examine equity dividend information
- examine equity results information
- examine equity corporate information
- get dealing phone number
- find other financial information
- set up a portfolio
- track a portfolio.

Objects

The objects here are:

- equity
- equity price
- equity price graph
- equity news information
- equity analyst reports
- equity dividend information
- equity results information
- equity corporate information
- dealing phone number
- other financial information
- portfolio.

We are now ready to move on to the next stage – knowing who the website is for.

Knowing who it is for

From work on the system and roles, actions and objects, we already have an idea about who the system is for. Often, however, people within the organization masquerade as "users," taking control of and driving the design. These "users" may be any of these groups of people:

- marketing and corporate image makers – since they feel it is an image thing

- sales – because they are focussed on making the site sell

- users' managers – since they think they know what their staff want

- developers – thinking they know best

- budget holders – because they control the purse.

Any of these may hold a position of influence so they can insist on calling all the shots, "hiding" the real users. You, reading this book, may be one of these. There is a degree of validity to their input, as they all have something useful to contribute. These people are "users" in the sense that they are "using" the system to market, sell, etc. Knowing who these "users" are and what their needs are will help you design the system. Their needs must be met also and their contributions add to the definition of objectives and the formulation of quantifiable measures of success.

> **Remember, your real user is the person who is interacting with your system, the person who "buys," the customer.**

As a designer, you must help these people of influence contribute to defining who the real users – the customers – are. Help them think from the user's point of view and work with you to keep users satisfied. Help them be involved or in some other way to commit to supporting you and your work. If the customer users are not satisfied, it is likely neither these people of influence nor you will achieve success.

Knowing what the 'real' users are like

You must know what the users are like, if you intend to satisfy them.

Keep your user satisfied

As we have seen already, most systems have more than one kind of user (role). (If you are familiar with UML (Unified Modelling Language) and want to use it in the detail design model specification, individuals acting out roles are actors.)

Each role must be understood to ensure their needs are met. The first step is to create *user profiles*.

The user profile

A user profile should be created for each class of user (role). These documents are living documents and we will improve on them in the light of what we learn after further research.

The user profile comes in four parts:

- a person profile
- a web use profile
- a "context of use" profile
- personalizing the "user."

The profile should be as accurate, clear and realistic as possible. Collect facts if you have them, or make reasonable guesses because even a reasonable guess provides a focus. It can always be refined as the work develops. (For a good formal description of this, I refer you to Part II of ISO 9241.)

PERSON PROFILE
.The person profile should describe:

- what the users are like, such as gender, status, employment, age range, culture, social group, education, experience of the domain (financial resources, financial awareness), relationship with you, nationality, interests, motivation (interest and involvement, what encourages them), what they understand
- what represents their viewpoints
- what makes them happy, such as being in control, being guided, quality, aesthetics, efficiency expectations.

WEB USE PROFILE
This should consider how they use the medium – the web such as web experience, web awareness, site use frequency, site use pattern, finding the site, etc.

CONTEXT OF USE PROFILE
The context of use profile is concerned with knowing the user's "context of use." We must understand where the user will be accessing the site from. The main aspects of this are:

- what environment they use the medium in, such as location (work or home)

- their hardware and software systems, e.g. machine, screen resolution, modem, operating system, browser

- all the concepts the user relates to in the context of their use, such as background reference material.

We make a preliminary assessment of this. Later, when carrying out user involvement activities such as useability evaluations or market research, you can obtain more accurate information.

PERSONALIZING THE USER

It is good to make it personal and real. The way to do this is to become more specific, give this user a name and characterize them.

By personalizing the user and giving him or her an identity, we can use "shorthand" on the project whenever we are referring to that user. We can ask hypothetical questions when thinking about design, like, "What do you think Jo would think about this?" The more real we make the user, the easier it is to become user-centered about the design. You could even take a photo of someone who typifies this user. This summary, along with the "user's" photo (or even a collage of photos of his or her interests and lifestyle) should be put up on the design team's wall, as a constant reminder.

We can now have a characterization, each class of user, and get a sense of who they are and what they are like.

This characterization gives a one or two paragraph synopsis of the person, so we can get a sense of who they are. We have given them a name so we can relate to them and talk about them. We can discuss in design discussions what "Jo" might think about this. The information about users is on the project team wall, so everyone understands who they are building for.

Involving users

Users, a representative sample, must be involved throughout the design process, *from the very beginning*. They can help you with these and all the next stages.

We "recruit" representative users who seem to fit the user profiles of our roles and have an active need for such a system. (See *Recruiting users* in Chapter 6, Use.)

The user is king. They must always be treated as right, even if later you choose to decide they are not.

FINANCIAL INFORMATION SITE

Continuing the earlier case study, we can now go into more detail. The table below shows a "person profile" of private investors.

CASE STUDY

PERSON PROFILE

Gender	MALE	FEMALE					
%	70	30					

Status	Married	Single	Cohab	Sep	Wid	Div	
%	63	17	7	1	6	5	

Employment	Full time	Part time	Self emp	Student	Retrd	Not	Unable
%	43	15	7	4	20	10	2

Age range	<25	<35	<45	<55	<65	65+	
%	8	16	26	22	13	16	

Social group	A	B	C1	C2	D	E	
%	4	27	37	20	8	4	

Education ended	<=14	<=16	<=18	19+			
%	9	46	20	25			

Household income (annual)	<6500	<11500	<15500	< 20000	< 25000	<35000	>35000
%	6	8	9	14	17	21	25

Product experience	Low	Medium	High				
%	20	60	20				

Relationship	Non-Cust	Past Cust	New Cust	Lasting	Staff		
%	25	5	10	60			

Interest/motivation	Low	Medium	High				
%	15	65	20				

Ethnic origin	White	Caribbean	African	"Indian"	Chinese	Asian	Other
%	94	2		3	1		

Nationality	UK	USA	Europe
%	60	30	10

Private investor – person profile

You may wish to capture other statistics in this table, but this is a pretty good start. This tells us that the "generic" private investor is male, married, in secure employment, between 35 and 55 years old, well educated, with reasonable finances and with a good financial ("domain") awareness, highly motivated, and interested in UK markets.

Design implications
The site must be professional, clean and tidy – designed to meet the expectations of this group of people. It should be efficient and effective, not patronizing them in any way. It should provide further financial awareness information on demand, but should not force it on them. It must ensure they feel in control rather than being controlled or forced to do things. The fact that the web is international will need to be taken into consideration; the site should be clearly identified as dealing with the UK markets with links to US information and dealing sites.

WEB USE PROFILE

Web experience	<6 mths	<1 year	<2 yrs	<3yrs	3yrs+
%	6	14	32	28	20

Web awareness	Low	Medium	High
%	12	38	50

Site use frequency	Daily	Bi-weekly	Weekly	Bi-monthly	Monthly
%	40	6	30	8	16

Site use pattern	Browsing	Focussed
%	10	90

Finding the site	Search	Friend	Magazine	Other
%	45	30	5	20

Private investor: web use profile

From the following table we can see that the user is experienced on the web, is likely to use the site at least once a week, will be focussed on their purpose of use, and mostly hears about the site by word of mouth or searching using one of the standard search engines.

Design implications
The site will be reused regularly by users who find it useful, so they will become proficient with effective ways of using the site. They will therefore become annoyed if the site structure or navigation is changed. So, any further developments must be planned in as far as possible at the beginning. This puts a very high responsibility on designing the site correctly first time – any subsequent changes will be annoying unless there is a clear benefit to the user.

CONTEXT OF USE

Location	Work	Home	Educatn	Library	Other
%	14	80	3	3	

Distractions	Low	Medium	High		
%	65	25	10		

Machine	<=486	Pentium	>200Mhz	>400Mhz	>600Mhz
%	15	15	20	20	30

Screen resolution	640x480	800x600	1024x768	1280x1024	>1280x1024
%	7	55	30	5	3

Modem	<33,600	56,000	ISDN	T1	Don't know
%	21	52	2	1	24

Operating system	W95	W98	W2000	NT	Mac
%	35	45	5	10	5

Browser	Netscape	MSIE	Other		
%	25	65	10		

Private investor – context of use

This profile tells us that the user is accessing the site largely from home, generally without distractions, on medium to high-end machines with at least 800x600 screen resolution, on a fast modem and using Microsoft's Internet Explorer.

Design implications

The site must be designed for a baseline 800×600 screen resolution, and must work just as well on higher resolutions. Since it is targetted at the UK market and will primarily be accessed from home, the phone charges for connection will be an issue. Therefore the efficiency and effectiveness will be paramount to these users; thankfully they will support themselves in doing this by mainly operating in an environment which does not have too many distractions. A positive aspect for the design is that most users have higher end machines and modems, and tend to use the more recent versions of browsers. The newer versions of JavaScript, Java, Flash will most likely be supported but this must not be presumed.

PERSONALIZING A HYPOTHETICAL USER

For the investment information system, let's take a mature private investor who we will call William. Thinking of what we know about William, we might come up with something like the following.

> *"William, 46, lives in a detached and spacious house in the suburbs of a major city. He has a wife (43) and three children (19, 17, 13), and drives a Volvo which is paid for by his company. He works hard, often late, values his weekends and doesn't like to waste his spare time. He plays squash and enjoys riding motor bikes (Harley and Sports). He takes holidays abroad. He reads historical novels, takes the* Financial Times *at weekends, and pays his bills on time. His house is usually tidy and his social life is full."*

We could also make this more personal, more identifiable, next to this summary, and photos of some of our characters like William, clustered together on the shared wall workspace along with a generic description we will write shortly.

Design implications
This profile suggests that the site must be designed for someone who wants clean, efficient effectiveness. He leads an active life with many other interests. To keep him satisfied, we will need to find out what he needs to know to make his decisions as quickly as possible. Investments are important, but not his life.

A GENERIC DESCRIPTION

We can now describe in characterization form, each class of user, and get a sense of who they are and what they are like.

For our private investor user, we might write the following generic description.

> *"The site should appeal mainly to well educated 35–54 year old men in full-time employment. They are financially aware and stable, web-aware people who have a need for investment information, are focussed and purposeful about their actions. They want to use the site at least once a week. They like to be effective with their finances, and want to improve their financial position. They want to improve their knowledge about financial investments. They will use the site during evenings and at weekends at home at their own expense."*

From the work we have done, it is clear there are also secondary groups of private investor which, as an exercise, you may wish to think about. The site will need to cater for their needs also.

Methods to obtain information

Invention

We can use *visioning* to get the team to create hypothetical users and much more. (For more detail see "Visioning" later in this chapter.)

This is powerful way of getting some real insights into what the users are like and what they do. You should involve a representative sample of real users and also team members.

Asking them

If you already have an earlier version of the site, you can use this to ask them while *Testing with users* (see Chapter 6, Use), of both the enthusiastic and the negatively biased, to see how people really are. You can also discuss their needs with them, what they like, what they dislike, what they expect and what they dream of. We find out more about them and their use.

We can interview using open questioning as well as a structured questionnaire. This can give us more insight than the more constrained form of questionnaires which are limited by our preconceptions and prejudices.

Questionnaire

We use the questionnaires to classify our knowledge. Question-naires can be sent out by mail, or they can be administered face to face. Face-to-face administration can generate much more useful insight, especially immediately after observation, since what a person says is sometimes different from what the reality was (see Chapter 6, Use).

Market research could also be conducted by an external consultancy.

THE USE — ACTIONS

A year or so ago, I ran a design workshop at an international conference. I facilitated the 45 delegates who came to my session and led them through the activities described in this chapter. I got them focussed on what they might want to achieve on a banking and savings website. Afterwards, I invited volunteer delegates to use any of about 80 banking sites to do what they wanted. I asked them to use the site they thought was most likely to provide what they needed. In one hour, and with different people trying eight different sites, not one could do what they wanted, let alone do it in a satisfying way.

It's pretty obvious really, but unless you are really clear about what the user wants to do, you cannot design to support the user. Yet so many websites fail to support the users' needs.

We must know what our users want to achieve, we need to know the users':

- purpose for visiting the site

- ideal process for achieving that purpose

- ideal outcome – their satisfaction.

This information will help us to understand the actions the user carries out and the information the users will need. One sensible way of obtaining this information is to obtain a representative sample of users to be involved from the start of the project. Involve them in the design process and run participatory workshops with them throughout, since they are useful at many stages of the development.

On projects I am involved with, I run workshops like this with perhaps 30–40 representative users to obtain definitions for this in the users' own words, and then analyze and generalize the results. Clearly, the budgetary and time constraints will influence the size of the representative user group, and useful results can be obtained from smaller groups. What we need now is a *use scenario*.

Use scenarios

A use scenario describes the user, their context of use, their use situation, their purpose, their ideal process of reaching their objectives, their ideal outcome and the criteria of use.

It's best to ask real people (who are candidate users of the system), face to face, to describe their own use scenarios. The facilitation of this needs some care, or you will only get what you want to hear, not necessarily the truth.

Each user will come up with a number of scenarios, and a collection of scenarios can be collated to create a profile of use scenarios for all the classes of user. Let's take a scenario written by our mature private investor, William.

Use scenario – example

ABOUT YOU
Male, 46, married, in full-time professional work, degree educated, financial awareness is medium, regularly use the web.

YOUR CONTEXT OF USE
I use the web mainly from home in the UK on a 400 Mhz Pentium running Windows 98, Internet Explorer 5.0 and use a 56K modem.

YOUR SITUATION
I have £3000 that I want to invest in equities for, say, the next three months. I don't mind some risk on the down side, but I would like to feel there is a good upside probability.

My investment criteria are based on the fundamentals, current equity price and the timing of purchase.

I am looking for a stock with long-term consistent growth over five years of the share price, turnover, earnings and currently within 15 percent of its all-time high. I want to be able to check various moving averages to test which way the price is moving. I want a consistent quality over five years of turnover, profit margin, EPS, dividend yield, dividend cover, total assets, current assets, current liabilities, stock, ROCE. SOCE from which I will create some ratio indicators noted below. I am looking for a current PE within 30 percent of the sector average.

My ratio indicators are:

> Profit margin %(TP/TO) Target>15%
> ROCE% (TP/TA-CL) Target>20
> SalesCE% (TO/TA-CL) Target>100
> Quick Ratio ((CA-Inv)/CL) Target>1
> PE within 30% of sector avg.

YOUR PURPOSE
I want to check out an equity, specifically Cable & Wireless to see if it may be worthwhile investing £3000 at present, for say the next three months.

My purpose is to obtain five years of share price data and the sector data in order to examine it, and if I like the share price data, I want to obtain the fundamental data to test it out against my metrics.

If I can also obtain any news information, that would be a bonus. (I would really like to be able to specify stock search criteria based on my investment strategy, but I do not really expect that to be supported.)

YOUR IDEAL PROCESS

- Enter the equity name or ticker symbol and search for the current price and the five-year graph history, applying 10, 40 and 105 day moving averages to the graph. Zoom in on the graph for various lengths of time and periods.
- Compare the graphs with the equivalent graphs for the industry sector, and compare the industry sector graphs with the equivalent graphs for FTSE and the DJIA.
- Obtain the fundamental data for the equity and test the various ratios I feel are important.
- Get any recent news that might affect my decision making.

If I can't do these processes quickly and efficiently online (which seems likely), I would like to do them off-line in a quick and efficient manner, so downloading the data in a suitable format to import into a local software system which supports the above.

YOUR IDEAL OUTCOME — SATISFACTION

All the above information on the chosen equity examined against my criteria within 5–10 minutes.

YOUR CRITERIA, CONSTRAINTS, COST BENEFITS

I would be willing to pay a small monthly fee for the more static data, providing I had a free or nominal cost software system to store it in, since I would only need that information periodically.

I would expect the price data free of charge; since I would be accessing it very often and a charge would be prohibitive, I'd find some other way which was more cost-effective for me.

Visioning – another way of getting use scenarios

A use scenario can also be done in the abstract by imagining what it should be. This technique is a little unusual, and should be used with care, but it can be very effective. I have used it very successfully running design workshops for a number of organizations, including Accenture (formerly known as Andersen Consulting), Hewlett Packard Research Laboratories and the Nationwide Building Society.

With a group of people (preferably representative users, but it can be members of the design team) introduce the concept of a use scenario and what information we are aiming to record. (If you don't have any users, this can be a very effective way for the design team to obtain use scenarios, and is much better than not having any at all.)

Ask the group if they recall times when they imagined things in their minds, about the future of whole aspects of their lives or replaying events from the past, making up mental or verbal pictures. Then invite them to do a *visioning*, a way of forming a strong mental picture about their ideal way of carrying out the actions.

Invite them to close their eyes and visualize a cinema screen. On this cinema screen, make a film of everything about their actions. Ask them to create the scene where they visualize themselves and get a full, real and complete picture of themselves on the screen, to picture what characterizes them, in a way they feel happy and satisfied with themselves (this is the "about you" part of the use scenario).

Suggest they make it as real as possible and bringing an image of all the colors, sights, sounds and feelings of them involved in the place they carry out their action ("context of use").

Ask them to think about and visualize what the background is to what they are doing, their action ("situation") and what their objective is in carrying out the activity or job, or action ("purpose").

Then invite them to achieve their purpose in this film about them, to achieve it in the way that is most satisfying and effective for them, to imagine and visualize each individual step, each individual shot in the film that tells the whole story in a most satisfying way for them, making it real in color, sounds, sights, feelings and smells even ("ideal process").

When they have visualized the whole film, ask them to imagine themselves totally satisfied by the outcome, to imagine and visualize what that is made up of, what they have as a result of their actions in physical or other terms and what the sights, sounds, feelings are associated with this ("ideal outcome"). Next ask them to recall what issues seemed to be core to them, what were the benefits and what were the costs, what were the constraints and what were the things that freed them up ("criteria," "constraints" and "cost benefits").

When they are finished visioning, ask them to spend time in silence, writing down everything they envisioned, taking as long as they need and keeping the silence until everyone is finished. This usually takes between 20 and 45 minutes.

When everyone has finished writing, ask them to share with someone else everything they have, and for them to listen to someone else about everything they have, updating their notes based on the feedback. Fully record and document the use scenarios, asking the participants to feel free to remove things of a highly personal nature, but to keep in as much as they can.

Understanding user actions

An effective way of understanding user actions is to examine the use scenario and extract all the verb phrases from it that are candidate actions the user will want to perform. This idea comes from object oriented technology. Initially, we can simply make a list. Let's look at our scenario again.

From the user's situation statement we have:

- invest capital in an equity
- examine equity fundamentals
- examine equity prices
- examine equity sector details
- calculate ratio indicators.

From the user's purpose statement we have:

- examine equity details
- obtain and examine five-year equity data
- examine equity sector data
- examine equity fundamental data
- calculate ratio indicators
- obtain equity news information
- search for equities meeting investment criteria.

From the user's ideal process we have:

- enter the equity name
- obtain current share price
- obtain five-year share price history
- graph share price history
- apply various moving averages

CASE
STUDY

- select various date ranges for graphs
- compare equity graphs with other graphs (industry sector, FTSE sector)
- obtain the fundamental data for the equity
- calculate and test my investment ratios
- get any recent news that might affect my decision making
- import data into local software system.

This was just one example scenario. As you get more information, you will be able to improve your knowledge of what the system should deliver to keep your customer satisfied. Not only are these use scenarios essential to the design creation process, but they can also be used later in the design validation process.

The next job is to bring all these elements together, structuring them and eliminating duplicates. This is best achieved using card sorting.

Card sorting

You should collect all the verb phrases from all of the scenarios with the same high level purpose (e.g. examine an equity to determine if I want to invest in it). Then eliminate only the exact duplicates; keeping any that are phrased differently. They may seem the same to you, but may have a subtly different meaning to users and therein is learning.

Write each verb phrase onto a small card about 3" × 2".

Now is another time to involve the users who helped create the use scenarios. Spread all the cards out on a table.

Invite the users to organize them in some way that makes sense to them in terms of actions. Ask them to put on one side any they don't need or don't understand. Ask them to say why they are putting them on one side. If they don't understand, ask them to explain what they think it means, is it still not needed, should we phrase it differently?

Spare cards should be provided so the user can add new cards should they feel they wish to, or need to so as to describe the actions better.

Any new cards should be added to the pack for subsequent exercises. Any discarded cards should be noted, and the reasons why, but they should be reintroduced to the pack for subsequent exercises and you can see if they get discarded again and if the reason for the discard is the same as on other occasions.

They will tend to cluster and arrange the cards based on their ideal process to carry out this action. So an action will be made up of "sub actions." It is helpful, even in the early stages of design to unpack at least one further level down so new details of the design are uncovered. Go down as far as you can without overloading yourself. Inevitably, at some point in the design process, the action hierarchy must be developed to the most specific and precise level.

This should be done with a variety of the users and you will record the end results and any comments made, so building up a generic action hierarchy. You can also ask them which of the activities are most important to them.

The big advantage of getting users to do this is that they will pick you up on verb phrases that don't mean much to them and will give you better phrases. These phrases are important, because they will be needed to get a user-centered language into the design of the interface. Not having a user-centered language is one of the biggest problems in unuseable designs.

You will also get an excellent understanding of what is most important for your representative users.

Getting more formal

In a large project, it is useful to get formal about what we have discovered, and this document will become the basis for the design stage, and will be continually updated during the design stage so that it is always up to date.

On a small project, the view may be taken that the code is the spec, but on anything of any reasonable size this should not be an option.

What we aim to record is the facts actually decided on. It is not worthwhile to have a formal specification of anything that is entirely speculative and changing rapidly. In those cases, the prototype is the spec until the prototype becomes stable. Of course, if you have tools that take code and create formal documentation which is program language independent, that is fine.

Studying an action in more detail
In most cases, there are three kinds of action structure.

B *followed by* C
B *or* C
B *repeats o to n times until Y is true*

any of which may form part of another Action A.
So we have the following:

Action A (*comprises of*
Action B *followed by*
Action C
)
Action A (*comprises of*
Action B
or
Action C
)
Action A (*comprises of*
Action B * *repeats o..n times, until Y is true*
)

Documenting an action

Now, we develop on the triad – user role, use action, information object – and document what we know about it.

To decide which is the first action to study, a good strategy is to just choose the most interesting one; at least that way it will be fun. Another is to choose the hardest one; that way it will be challenging. Another way is to develop something akin to a personal constructs grid as described by Kelly.

In this example, I chose one which, for me, came out top on all three of those strategies. From the private investor role, consider the action "examine an equity." With the above verb phrases, for the "examine an equity to determine if I want to invest in it" action, we came out with the following description and *action structure* from the collective card layouts from the card sorting.

- **Action** Examine an equity.
- **Purpose** To examine an equity in order to assess the quality of the equity for my investment portfolio, and to determine the price at which I would choose to invest in it.

CASE STUDY

- **Used by roles**:
  - private investor
  - marketing to market company
  - business development in private investor role
  - customer support in private investor role.
- **Affected roles**. System developers.
- **Action structure**

> Examine an equity (
> > (
> > Select an individual equity from a candidate
> > > equity list
> > *or*
> > Enter an equity name
> >)
>
> Examine equity price
>
> Examine equity price graphs (
> > Select various date ranges for graphs
> > Graph share price history
> > Apply various moving averages
> > Compare equity price graphs with other
> > > equities
> > Compare equity price graphs with standard
> > > sectors
> > Create personal sector
> > Compare equity price graphs with personal
> > > sectors
> > Obtain and examine five-year equity data
> >)
>
> Examine equity details
> > Obtain equity details
> Examine equity fundamentals
> > Obtain equity fundamentals
>
> Examine standard ratios
> > Calculate standard ratios

```
Examine personal ratios (
        Enter personal ratios definition
        Calculate personal ratios
        View personal ratios
        )


Examine equity news information
        Obtain equity news information


Examine sector information (
        Examine equity sector prices
        Examine equity sector details
        )


Download equity information (
        Download historic equity prices
        Download equity news
        )


Download sector information


Import data into local software system
        )
```

The technique of card sorting and the process of detailing the
objectives and actions of the private investor role has improved our
understanding of the design problem. Now let's look at what users use
in their activities.

THE INFORMATION — OBJECTS

The role of information

Information is fundamental. Actions are intended to fulfill our goals,
our purpose. Without information, in a virtual world, action cannot
occur. Information is represented as objects in software systems, such
as websites.

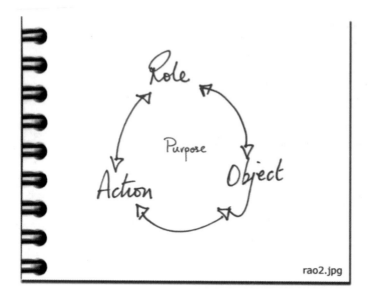

rao2.jpg

Information is the third crucial component of our role, action, object triad. (In this book I use information and object interchangeably. I use the word object, because it is a more generic abstract term and will later include all the things the user sees on the screen. It is also a useful term for the software developers to relate to in their object-oriented modelling of the user-centered design work we are doing here.)

In order to take any action, the user must first make a decision, whether to do it or not. That decision is based on information, and it must be appropriate and sufficient for the decision. As a result of any action, more information is revealed, and so we can determine whether our action has given us what we want, has met our goals.

When we get to designing the interaction, we will want to make sure the users have all the information they need, at the time they need it, in a way they can understand it in order to make decisions about what action to take. So, we must know what information we need to provide, and we must model the information in a way that fits with the way the users think.

Gathering all the pieces of information

From the initial work on "discover the system" we already have the following information components:

CASE
STUDY

- equity
- equity price
- equity price graph
- equity news information
- equity analyst reports
- equity dividend information
- equity results information
- equity corporate information
- dealing phone number
- other financial information
- portfolio.

But we can learn a great deal more. A highly effective way is to examine each use scenario and extract all the nouns or noun phrases from them in the same way we did in "discover the system." These become candidate objects in an object-oriented design. Initially we can simply make a list as shown in the following three tables.

£3000 – money	Equities	Three months
Risk	Upside probability	Investment criteria
Fundamentals	Equity price	Timing
Stock	Long-term consistent growth	Five years (data)
Share price	Turnover	Earnings
15% (share price)	All time high	Moving averages
Price	Consistent quality	Five years (data)
Turnover	Profit margin	EPS
Dividend yield	Dividend cover	Total assets
Current assets	Current liabilities	Stock
ROCE	SOCE	Ratio indicators
PE	30% (Sector PE)	Sector average

The user's situation statement

Equity	Cable & Wireless	£3000
Three months	Five years	Share price data
Sector data	Fundamental data	Metrics
News information	Stock search criteria	Investment strategy

Information from the user's purpose statement

Equity name	Ticker symbol	Current price
Five-year graph	10, 40 and 105 day moving averages	Time
Time periods	Industry sector	FTSE sector
Fundamental data	Equity	Ratios
Recent news	Data	Software system

Information from the user's ideal process

Collating it all

Remove duplicates

As with the verb phrases, in "discover the use," collect all the noun phrases from all the scenarios, eliminating only *exact* duplicates. Those that seem to mean the same to you may not mean the same thing to users.

Taking our original list and removing duplicates, we obtain the information shown opposite.

CASE
STUDY

£3000 – money	10, 40 and 105 day moving averages	15% (share price)
30% (Sector PE)	All time high	Cable & Wireless
Consistent quality	Current assets	Current liabilities
Current equity price	Dividend cover	Dividend yield
Earnings	EPS	Equity name
Five-year equity graph	Five-year equity price (data)	Five-year equity financials (data)
FTSE industry sector	Fundamental data (Fundamentals)	Investment criteria
Investment strategy – risk	News information	PE
Profit margin	Ratio indicators – ratios – metrics	Recent news
ROCE	Sector average	Sector data
Sector PE	SOCE	Stock search criteria
Ticker symbol	Time periods	Total assets
Turnover		

Information component structure

Create a structure of the information based on how information items are grouped to each other. This can be a time-consuming process. It is iterative. You need to devise a structure and then work at improving it.

Just as we used card sorting with representative users to get our action structure, we can also carry out a card sorting exercise with a number of representative users to get a good understanding of the users' conceptual models and the language they use to describe them.

With the above noun phrases, one user, male, 50–55 with medium knowledge of investments structured as below. The remaining cards were put to one side.

IMPORTANT TO ME	FEEL I SHOULD KNOW MORE ABOUT THESE	CONVEY NOTHING TO ME
Industry sector	Current assets	ROCE
PE	Current liabilities	Metrics
Timing	Dividend cover	Stock search criteria
Price	EPS	Ratio indicators
Equity name	10, 40 and 105 day moving averages	30% (Sector PE)
Fundamental data	Moving averages	Ratios
FTSE sector	Fundamentals	SOCE
Risk	Total assets	Ticker symbol
Investment strategy	Turnover	15% (share price)
News information		
Upside probability		
Current price		
Dividend yield		
Sector average		
Long-term consistent growth		
Recent news		
Consistent quality		

His priority was what is most readily understood by him and are most important to him. The terms which the user would like to find out more about present an education opportunity and the terms that mean nothing, an "advanced education" opportunity.

If we found this was a common way of users providing it, we can safely use the words in the left column, important to me, and provide valuable information on the second column.

Another user came up with a structure that was based on the structural logical relationship of the information. From this, I came to realize that the dynamic equity price information might be useful to investors when they were looking at the company results, so I included it in the structure associated with the results, and then tested the idea out on a sample of representative users.

Now we should analyze the data items to understand the logical structures. There are two primary concepts in what the users have said:

- how the information is related together

- how useful the information is to them.

This often happens, so you could use these conceptual categories as a basic structure for analysis.

Information relationships

Information can be thought of as having a structure and a relationship with other components of information. This is often formalized in entity relationship diagrams (ERDs) or object models. For further information, see *UML Distilled* by Martin Fowler.

Steve Cook and John Daniels suggested three perspectives on an object model: the conceptual (essential) perspective; the specification perspective; and the implementation perspective.

This book does not describe the important but orthogonal technical aspects of discovery, such as understanding the technology, exploring and understanding software tools and the like. I leave that to other authors.

Modelling the information

We should look at the conceptual perspective, and here I will not be over purist but look at what we might glean from modelling the information in this way. The basic relationships are *associations* and *subtypes*. For associations we define the multiplicity of the association relationship. The most common are:

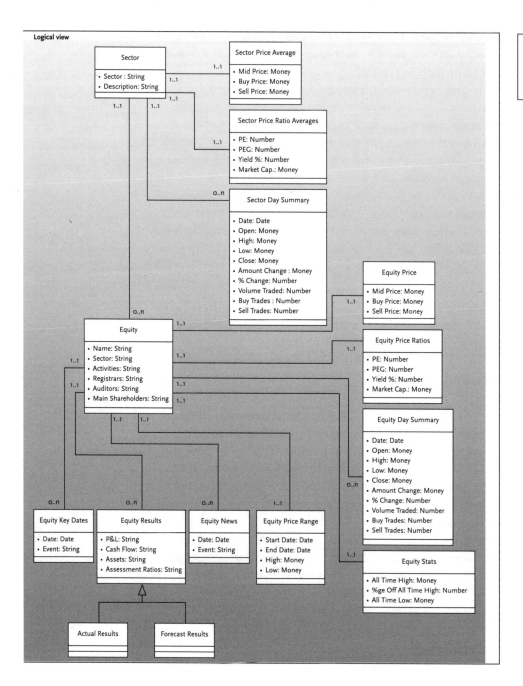

CAS
STU

- one to one – represented by 1 or 1..1

- one to 0 or 1 – represented by 0..1

- one to many – many (0..infinity) represented by an asterix (*).

The multiplicity defines the lower and upper constraints on the number of objects that may be in the relationship. Notice the strong similarities with action structures.

Objects might be thought of as a type. Types may also have subtypes. A subtype is a "specialization" of a type. For example, a Dodge is a specialization of "car."

Now, let's take our information from the discovery stage and see how it might look in a UML object model. These details combined with the card sorting lead to the object structure shown opposite.

Why model like this?

Modelling in this way can be a great deal of work. However, it can pay off handsomely in your understanding of the problem and the opportunities for design improvements based on new insights. The benefit, I trust you will see later in the chapter. The models can also be used as a starting point for the software developer's work, and can help in communication with them. If you are doing it all yourself, of course this is not a problem.

Once again, it is an *iterative* process, as you start with one structure and it then develops as you see how other parts of information logically fit into place.

How this helps us

First, let's look at the relationship between sector and equity. This is an association which says that a sector is associated with (comprises of) 0 to infinity equities. It also says that an equity is associated with one and only one sector, and never exists outside of a sector.

We can question with our users (the domain experts), whether this is true. If it is, we have established and confirmed a fact, and if it isn't, we have established a new understanding of how the users understand or model the information. For example, we may come to the realization that an equity can belong to more than one sector.

CASE
STUDY

We can also see how similar a sector is to an equity, in fact we might think of them as being almost identical, in that everything we might want to know or do with an equity, we may wish to do with a sector.

This leads us, by implication, to the thought that a sector may have sector stats, sector price range and sector news, all of which may be based on the same design ideas. Now we are getting leverage in our design thinking.

Even more, a sector is a collection of equities, and with very little abstraction we can see clearly that a portfolio (one of the users' needs) is perhaps just the same, a user-defined "sector." Later design can recognize the potential for design reuse by this generalization.

Now consider the relationship between equity and equity price. This tells us that there is a one-to-one relationship between them and if one exists the other must also. In this sense, equity price is an attribute of equity. Equity price comprises of mid price, buy price and sell price, and all these attributes are of type "money."

Again, we can question, is this true? We find this is true, *but* the values for these attributes change from second to second. So we should consider renaming this object to current equity price to make this clear. We may also find that some users are interested in how these prices change during the day, in which case we would have lots of them, and want to define them with a multiplicity of o..n and add an attribute called "time" to identify it. At discovery time we may represent this in our model, and at some point come to a decision on whether or not we wish to take on the added complexity of this in our requirement for action, interaction, presentation and implementation design.

Further, let's look at the relationship between equity and equity day summary. This says an equity has o to infinity equity day summaries. It also says that a particular equity day summary is associated with one and only one equity, and never exists outside of this association.

Because equity day summary has a multiplicity of o..n, it indicates a list of items. When we come to designing the user interface, we may wish to show it in a tabular form.

In addition, we see that we have two specializations of equity results, actual results and forecast results. Many of the facts and design ideas (and implementation) that are true for actual results will be true for forecast results.

Knowing this now will also give us leverage in all aspects of the development, discovery, design, implementation and use, and will reduce time and cost wastage. It also helps us greatly in the design of the user interface and the interaction. Since we can be consistent with the presentation and interaction, it will improve the learnability and use of the system.

All these relationships exist and many of them will need to be made visible to the user in their interactions with the system. These relationships will be in their subconscious mind even if not in their conscious mind. When we get to the detail of the interface design, this will help us clarify how we are going to communicate with the user, present the information and how we will define the navigation (because of the relationship between information structure and action design).

None of this details how to do it in a programming language; the design approach is deliberately implementation independent. It is like a jigsaw puzzle, built through logic, intuition and collaboration. Through regular involvement of real users, the design becomes refined.

The names of the information components are becoming important now. They should be meaningful to the design team, and as succinct as possible. They should also be as meaningful as possible to the users. In developing the design further, we will be referring to the information by these names – this will reduce ambiguity about what we mean when we are designing. This will become part of our *design language*.

Equally, we must remember that nothing is cast in stone at this stage. We may well want to use different names in the final visual interface design. We must not assume that the designer's terminology will ultimately be the same as the user's terminology. Later in the design process we can make sure we get this right.

We can also take this information into more detail discovery. As an example, and an indication of how much detail, and more, that will be needed by the programmers, see Appendix 1. This kind of activity will most likely be carried out by the programming team; however, make sure you – the designer – and the representative users are involved to make sure it is correct and meets the user-centered design needs.

We should expect to discover more during the creation/design stage. Despite our attention to getting all the understanding of the system during discovery stage, this is not unusual. Therefore, we will almost certainly be updating these documents as we proceed through from discovery to design.

Checking you have it all

How do we check that what we have is complete? Take all the roles, actions and objects and use the RAO model, and think of the system as an object to make sure everything is there. I did this as part of some consultancy work with a large multinational company, and found that their "complete" specification only covered around 40 percent of the actual system. It is worth doing, or you will find out along the way or close to the end that you haven't thought of everything, and then if left to this stage of the process, you could have a disaster on your hands.

The point

Designing is not just about fonts, colors, pretty pictures, animated gifts, it is much more about a thorough analysis and structuring of the action needs and the information needs of the user. The users must be involved from the very beginning. If the function (action) and information (object) needs of the user (role) are not fully supported, you will end up with a poor design.

Form follows function.

Scenarios of use and RAO analysis are essential techniques in Discovery.

4 | DESIGNING THE SYSTEM

> *"The design process is one which demands creative behavior from its participants. Solutions which merely 'work' and do no more, do not represent what we can refer to as being 'creative solutions.' Creative solutions are different... they are those which lead, inspire and provoke. They turn us on to their correctness, obviousness and simplicity. Creative designers are people who intend to go beyond mere function and stability."*

The Universal Traveller, Don Koberg and Jim Bagnall, 1973.

From discovery

We have been looking into the discovery stage of design and now have a pretty good understanding of:

- the organization *objectives* and the *scope* of the system

- the classes of user – the *roles*

- the use scenarios describing the goals, *actions* and the outcomes desired

- the information the user needs to support their use scenarios – the *objects*.

... to the mindsets of design

From the inside out – the corporate view

From a software developer's point of view, we think of the system as a technologically engineered product meeting a business need. From this point of view, we spend our time wondering what we can do technologically, how we can make all the pieces work in software, whether to use java, html, xml, xhtml, javascript, vb, c, and so on.

We think about the hardware constraints, how to make the software architecture work, how to manage reuse of software components, performance, what new tricks can we pull in from the state of the art, etc. We also think about how we integrate with existing corporate systems, what we can use from them and what the problems are. We think about function and the business needs and constraints.

Every aspect of design in this mode of thought comes from the organization, and the machine perspective. It brings a whole culture of thinking from "the inside out."

There is nothing wrong about dealing with these considerations, but thinking only in these terms subconsciously drives us to create systems which people *must* use rather than those which people *want* to use. The business systems of old were like this, and many still are. Many corporate websites and intranets come from this place.

Thinking from the inside out supports the functional objectives. However, it often misses the other, most important, half of the relationship.

From the outside in – the user's view

As users, we want supporting, involving, satisfying and delighting. From our point of view, the system is an immersive experience. What we do should be our choice, having control over what we do and how we do it. We arrive, engage, immerse, feel emotions and leave with both physical and emotional outcomes. Our feelings of satisfaction and a desire to return is determined by how much attention the designers have given to thinking about our needs and us.

All users on the web and new media are *discretionary* users. We can choose what we will do, what we like and dislike, and how much dissatisfaction we will put up with. As designers, we should think of the designed site as an experience for people. We should think of it in more human terms, for enjoyment and useful benefit, for improving the quality of the day.

When we engage with the user, and use their language, we subconsciously relate to thinking of the users as people like us, who want involvement and satisfaction.

"You employ stone, wood, and concrete, and with these materials you   Le Corbusier
build houses and palaces. That is construction. Ingenuity is at work.

"But suddenly, you touch my heart, you do me good, I am happy and I
say: 'This is beautiful.' That is architecture. Art enters in.

"My house is practical. I thank you, as I might thank Railway
engineers, or the Telephone service. You have not touched my heart.

"But suppose that walls rise toward heaven in such a way that I am
moved. I perceive your intentions. Your mood has been gentle, brutal,
charming, or noble. The stones you have erected tell me so. You fix me
to the place and my eyes regard it. They behold something which
expresses a thought. A thought which reveals itself without word or
sound, but solely by means of shapes which stand in a certain

relationship to one another. These shapes are such that they are clearly
revealed in light. The relationships between them have not necessarily
any reference to what is practical or descriptive. They are a
mathematical creation of your mind. They are the language of
Architecture. By use of raw materials and starting from conditions
more or less utilitarian, you have established certain relationships
which have aroused my emotions. This is Architecture."

The Medusa–sun image and the quote are taken from Ching's
Architecture: Form, Space and Order. Take this quote, put it on your
project wall, get your people to read it and discuss it.

The holistic view

We must bring both of these viewpoints to a meeting point. We must
instill the creative spirit of design for use, and map it even-handedly
onto the developer's mindset.

We must use the skills of technology and the skills of creative design
to produce a design which meets the business needs and creates a
satisfying experience for the user.

The user experience

We create the user experience in whatever way we choose. We choose
whether we think primarily from the inside out or from the outside in.
It's not a given, we don't have to follow the normal corporate control
mold, we can choose to follow the way of meeting the user's needs and
maintaining sensible reality with the organizational needs.

Let's think from the outside in. The question is, how do we design
the user experience, the way the user will move through the site, what
happens and when, the things they can see and use, the presentation,
interaction, emotion, satisfaction of use?

The right user experience is one that satisfies the "target" users at
the levels of function, form and emotion. This is why we must involve
the users from very early on, during discovery, so we can fully
understand their needs, desires, language, ways of relating to things
and what makes them satisfied and happy. How we do it is something
else. We can choose how we are going to make the experience a totally
satisfying one. We know from work carried out in understanding users
and developing use scenarios the kind of experience they want.

Now we need a framework for thinking so we can manage the
complexity of the issues and develop a satisfying user experience.

A framework for design thinking

As I have said many times, any method is better than no method. This method develops step by step through the layers of design thinking. The discovery stage is done for now. Now we bring that knowledge and understanding forward to crafting our design.

The steps, which are to a large extent an ordered sequence, in practice interleave with one another. Follow the steps, but recognize that you will go back to previous steps as the design develops.

- **Areas.** Deciding on how to group together areas of information and activity, understanding the basic building blocks of the system. Understanding mood and feel, and deciding what kind of user experience we want.

- **What are the pages?** Creating a design storyboard to represent when and how users want to obtain information and carry out processes and actions.

- **What is on a page?** Detailing what are the contents of each page in an area.

- **Interaction design.** Deciding on what can be done and designing the way the user will interact on each page and carry out useful activity.

- **Visual design.** Designing the details of what it all looks like and how the presentation should be to reach out to the user and satisfy the business.

AREAS

Begin by breaking down the design into primary areas. These will generally be predominantly "areas of activity" or "areas of information."

We know the areas from our card sorting exercises with users when we were discovering the actions and objects. These were derived from the use scenarios, a core part of the design process.

The high level objectives of the user gives us the insights about how we should structure the broadest level of information and action and how the pieces fit together. We identify all the key processes and how they work as structural groupings.

During discovery, we made a list and spatially organized them.

Amazon use scenario

The following is a use scenario developed at a design workshop I ran at a recent conference recently, as written by the person.

ABOUT YOU
I am female, 24, single, in full-time professional work, degree educated, financial awareness is medium. I regularly use the web and am fascinated by design and graphic design.

YOUR CONTEXT OF USE
I use the web mainly from work [I use] Windows 98, Internet Explorer 5.0.

YOUR SITUATION
I heard from a friend that Tufte's book *Envisioning Information* is a "must have." I want to add it to my library.

YOUR PURPOSE
I want to find out if I can get hold of the book, and I want it sometime during the next week or two.

YOUR IDEAL PROCESS
Enter Tufte's name and get a list of his books. While I want *Envisioning Information*, I would be interested in whatever else he has written.
   I want to buy it whatever, and then check out his other works. Since I will be doing this as part of my work, I don't mind being online for a while, so long as I am getting useful information. However, I don't want to waste my time.

YOUR IDEAL OUTCOME – SATISFACTION
Satisfied I have the book ordered, and a clear idea when it will arrive.

YOUR CRITERIA, CONSTRAINTS, COST BENEFITS
I want to buy it online if I feel it will be quicker than buying it in a bookshop. I want to be sure that I am satisfied with the feel of it.

Amazon

Amazon.com has chunked their areas as follows:

- **Information – primary:**
  - welcome
  - books
  - music
  - DVD and video
  - electronics
  - software
  - toys and video games
  - health and beauty
  - home living.

- **Information – secondary:**
  - auctions
  - art and collectables
  - shops
  - kitchen
  - lawn and patio
  - tools and hardware.

- **Information finding:** search.

- **Action:**
  - your account
  - help
  - checkout.

We can see that these match on to the use scenario pretty well. The primary areas of information are broken down as home, music, books and so on. These are areas where users can find what they are looking for and "register interest" by adding the items to a shopping cart. These provide the interest and the hook.

The areas of activity are "your account" and "checkout," where the user carries out the primary positive actions of purchasing. This satisfies the user objective and the business one also.

Home is maintained simply, with little other detail; the decision here was to have a standard welcoming screen which has much navigation and some information. Amazon is known for books, and the decision has been made to reinforce the books area on the home screen, though we can see many other information areas available from here. All the information areas are distinguishable from the action areas.

The user experience, mood and feel

We should now go back to thinking about the user experience. What kind of experience do we want them to have, that will meet their needs, expectations and enjoyment? What mood and feel do we want to create that will work for them? Understanding the mood and feel will help us design the structure, and the dynamics.

Users of an entertainment site will want a different experience to those on a financial site. Entertainment is concerned with leisure, visual stimulation, wandering and exploring, locating and discovering. Finance is concerned with precision and correctness, accuracy and timeliness, speed and clear communication.

Both are purposeful, but they are very different from each other. Their differences need to be reflected throughout the design, all the way from the structural and user process detail, through the details of interaction, down to the presentational detail.

USER EXPERIENCE AT AMAZON

Amazon is a well-known brand name. It has a reputation to keep up. It must deliver its promise quickly and efficiently. It must look after its customers superlatively. It must entice people to use the site and to enjoy the books and music on offer. It must add value to the experience, so the customer has an added extra over going down to the local bookstore. It must save the customer time. It must develop a long-term relationship with customers.

We can make a list of attributes:

- professional
- businesslike
- approachable
- visually simple
- enticing
- efficient
- supporting and helpful.

The mood must be a balance between calm efficiency and relaxed browsing. The paths through the site must show up new areas of interest, especially those that appeal to me particularly, and when the user wants to buy, it must be very effective and secure.

Now we have the areas, let's start understanding how it all fits together.

| WHAT ARE THE PAGES? — THE ACTION PROCESS |

The structure

For each primary area of activity or information, you need to get a structure that models and defines how the user's ideal process works. Again, the use scenarios point the way forward. These are the basis for the design of the structure and shape; the navigation.

Our objective is to design a useful, effective, efficient and satisfying experience for the user.

The storyboard

The use scenarios drive the design. The way to make it real is by using storyboards. The idea of a storyboard comes from filmcraft. The storyboard describes all the script in a linear and graphic style, describing in sketch form the scenes, camera angles, dialog and so on.

In film, an engaging story is perhaps the most important part. A poor story with excellent production values is still an unsatisfying film. A good story with a good script can often succeed even with poor production values.

The same is true of a software interface. The best images and sound in the world are useless without a good story. The "story" in a software interface is the way the functionality develops. A good story develops the way the user wants and needs it to, immersing them in the environment so they hardly notice it. Like a good tool, such as a well-balanced hammer, hitting the nail on the head comes naturally; the hammer doing the work, the handle comfortable and sure, the head just the right weight and distance from the handle to drive home squarely and with little "user" effort. It feels right, comfortable, natural. It fits our mood.

The software system must also have a well-balanced feel to it, the handle being comfortable and sure, the functionality providing just the right amount of weight to do the job easily, the user just controlling it effortlessly.

So, the story must develop progressively in just the right way with just the right tempo. The controls and handles provided must be sure, clean, obvious and comfortable. The functionality coming at just the right time and with just the right weight. This all needs designing, prototyping and testing until it feels just right – a storyboard is the basic starting point.

What do we want from the storyboard? Unlike a film storyboard, which is linear, we want it to show all the different ways the "story" might develop, and in that it is like a flow chart. We want it to give us a framework, what is in the system and what is not, and in this it is like a visual scoping document. Its advantage is that it gives us an easily understandable overview of the whole system, the total possible set of user experiences, the mood and development of the performance.

A paper-based storyboard should show:

- the *structure* – providing action points at the right time for the user's action needs

- the *navigation* and *action* controls available to the user

- the *information* provided by the computer to assist the user's *decisions* concerning action

- the information provided by the user to *control* the action

- the information or transition provided by the computer as a *result* of a user action.

At a later stage, making it visual will help make it real, but we don't want to get bogged down in the fine details of the visual presentation too early. It starts with a series of sketches with little embellishment, describing the primary components of flow, tempo, control and functionality.

If you think of the experience as being a play or piece of theater (see Brenda Laurel, *Computers as Theatre*), there are two actors in this play – the user and the computer. Each actor (performing a role) takes it in turns with their script, the user controlling and the computer serving. They work together, as one, to perform an action.

As with a tool of any kind, we need to keep in mind the type of person (role) who will be using the system, before we create our storyboard.

Consider objectives and sub-objectives for each screen. Provide efficient routes for navigation of your map. Provide appropriate actions to meet the objectives. Later work on the visual image (see Chapter 5, Visual design) makes your system objects visible.

When we have the basic storyboard, this becomes a major basis of our design work and our project plans. The degree of effort we put into it is tempered at all times by our question "What's the Use?" This depends upon the size of the project, how high profile it is, how the team dynamics work, how much you feel the need to have a measure of how far you have got in the development.

This first storyboard should make clear what is where in the story; the navigation, the action and the information. It should not yet detail the graphic design – that comes later.

Each primary action sequence has to be designed, so that it stands alone as a coherent piece and also fits in with all other possible action sequences. Since any action sequence can be initiated in any order the user wants, each action sequence must behave coherently within the overall system, in whatever way the user wants it.

A film is a linear experience, in the sense that the observer cannot influence the outcome. A website is a much more complex production and so perhaps in greater need of careful design.

FINANCIAL INFORMATION SITE

Let's return to our investment website first discussed in Chapter 3, *Discovery*. For the private investor role, we want to end up with something that is effective, efficient and satisfying to 35–50-year-olds who value their time, are focussed and purposeful, want quality information fast, and want additional information on demand – when thoughts cross their mind.

We develop the storyboard from the use scenarios and sketch out what we have. There are three key parts, or acts, for this kind of user's action:

- finding the names of equities which they will consider investing in
- examining an equity to decide whether it is worth investing at this time
- making the investment – dealing.

These activities are interlinked, yet they could be carried out independently by the user. For this example, I will treat the first and last of the above actions as "black boxes." I will describe what they should do at the highest level only, and describe the storyboard in more depth for the second action.

Begin by sketching out the primary action structure for the combined three actions, and then in more detail for the second action. From the work on use scenarios, we have details of the actions the user will want to carry out, and we have an understanding of how the information is structured. We can now create the following storyboard:

CASE STUDY

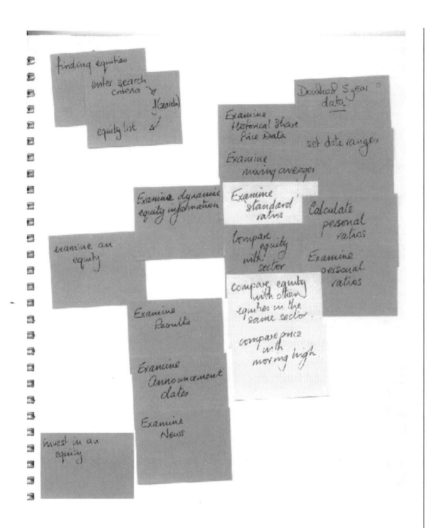

Now we have the basic structure illustrating our basic storyboard. Sometimes when we design, we might want to put more effort into our map. It all comes down to the fundamental question "What's the use?" This is a cost benefit question.

Amazon as a storyboard

For the Amazon site (see page 75), I have used a word processor, an equally good tool, especially when you are working after the first pass of storyboard design or outline documenting an existing structure, but not as fast and flexible as PostIts and paper or printouts for team working and communication.

Welcome
    How to order
    Gift ideas
    Top sellers
    Friends and favourites
    Free E-Cards
Books
    Search books
        Search results
            Specific book detail
                Shopping cart –
                checkout process
    Browse subjects
    Best sellers
    Featured in the media
    Award winners
    Computers and Internet
    Children's books
    Business and investing
Music
    Search music
    Browse styles
    Classical
    Top sellers
    New and future releases
    Free downloads
    Recommendation center
    Bargain music
Shopping cart – checkout process
    Sign in
        Select addresses
            Select shipping
                Payment
                    Confirm
                    your order.

Each part of the storyboard is a page in our website design. There will be many more pages than are represented here. We will find them as we develop the design further.

WHAT'S ON A PAGE? — THE INFORMATION OBJECTS

We now have the structure and shape of the design. We know what all the areas of the site are going to be, what the user process is going to be, and we know what all the pages are. What we have to do now is begin detailing everything that will be on a page. We are not so interested at this stage how it will look, though some visual sketches and ideas may come to mind and they should be recorded since they infer ideas about what else might need to be here.

The objective is to have a complete understanding of everything we need for a detailed design. We will need a detailed:

- understanding of all the information needed on each page, and why it is there.

- understanding of all the action and interaction on each page.

- navigation plan; so far we have a rough navigation plan based on the action process.

If we do an excellent job of designing for the user, we should never need to provide any user support or help systems; all the support and help should be designed-in as a natural product of the design. (See Norman's *Psychology of Everyday Things*, in the chapter on *"Design for Use."*) However, time or budget constraints may dictate that you have to resort to help and support systems and it is important to bear this in mind.

How to develop page content

Use cards, pieces of paper or PostIts to draft up your storyboard. This helps you move the design around more quickly and change it more quickly.

A good size for this is about A6 or 6"×4" (or even smaller, such as 4"×3") because you should be able to get enough on it to be useful. If you can't fit everything on a 6"×4" piece of paper, it is likely that you are putting too much in one place.

Those of you more accustomed to working in a formal way may feel it is strange to be using PostIts or tearing up pieces of paper to use on a professional project. However, it is probably the most effective way of reaching the desired result. Software packages can produce nice drawings, but are generally much slower than pen and paper. Also, most authors on creativity would suggest that this more "feely" stuff helps to some small degree get you in touch with your right brain, the intuitive side. Try it and see which method works best for you.

Use spatial layout or color of paper to indicate domain. The domains should become self-evident as we start laying out everything. On each card, use spatial layout or color of ink (or both) to indicate *information*, *action* and *navigation*. We are not interested in the visuals yet; we are getting a detail plan, adding more detail to the storyboard.

Examples of "what's on a page"

An Amazon.com process

Here is what part of the Amazon site would look like at this stage. It provides an outline of "What's on a page" for the Amazon.com process to find a book.

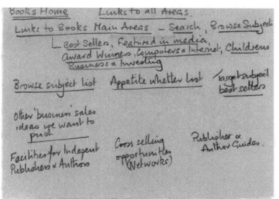

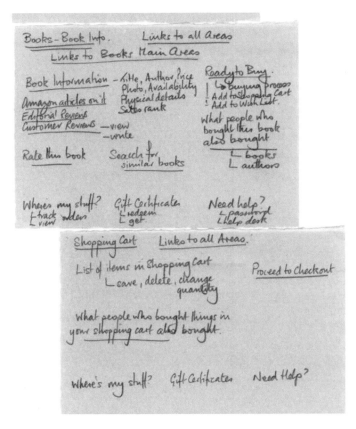

The following shows the outline "What's on a page" for the Amazon.com process to "checkout" a book or any other item, assuming that you don't select gift wrapping and have only one address to ship to.

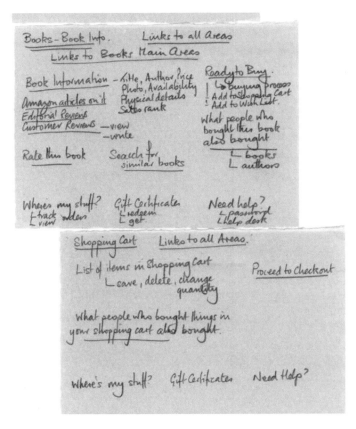

Checkout Select Address   Pointer to where you are in
                           the checkout process
one address or multiple addresses

edit address   enter new address

        use this address

Checkout Shipping   Pointer to where you are in
                     the checkout process

Shipping address

Select shipping method   continue
    - standard
    - worldmail
    - international priority
How long will it take?

Order summary
    - item, price, availability, quantity, packaging

                        change   change
                                    (edit)

Checkout Payment   Pointer to where you are in the
                    checkout process

Select Payment Method

    - visa
    - enter a new credit card
    - pay by cheque or money order

Do you have a gift certificate?
    enter certificate ▭   continue

Getting deeper, the following illustrates a detail of "What's on a page" for part of the Amazon process to "checkout" a book or any other item.

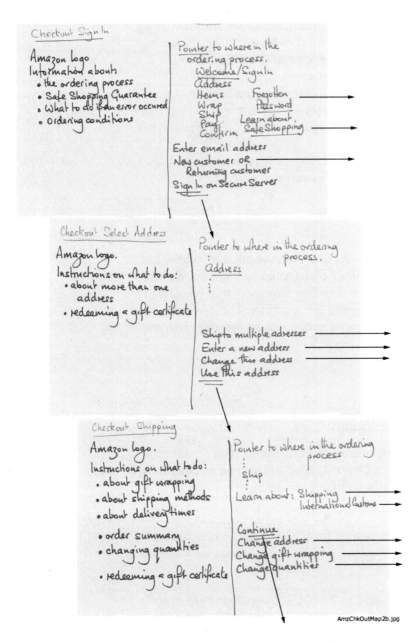

Checkout Sign In

Amazon logo
Information abouts
• the ordering process
• Safe Shopping Guarantee
• What to do if an error occured
• Ordering conditions

Pointer to where in the
ordering process.
Welcome/Sign In
Address
Items   Forgotten
Wrap   Password
Ship
Pay   Learn about
Confirm   Safe Shopping

Enter email address
New customer OR
  Returning customer
Sign In on Secure Server

Checkout Select Address

Amazon logo.
Instructions on what to do:
• about more than one
  address
• redeeming a gift certificate

Pointer to where in the ordering
                  process.

Address

Ship to multiple adresses
Enter a new address
Change this address
Use this address

Checkout Shipping

Amazon logo.
Instructions on what to do:
• about gift wrapping
• about shipping methods
• about delivery times

• order summary
• changing quantities

• redeeming a gift certificate

Pointer to where in the ordering
                  process
:
Ship
:
Learn about: Shipping
             International Customs

Continue
Change address
Change gift wrapping
Change quantities

AmzChkOutMap2b.jpg

I have used blue ink to represent information, green ink to represent navigation and red ink to represent action. You can see that sometimes, the distinction between action and navigation blurs – this is not a cause for concern.

What we have may not seem very much, but we are already at a stage where we could carry out a useability test with users – even before any visuals are added, and it could be very cost effective. (See also in Chapter 6, Use, *Useability testing a paper prototype*.)

Planning on multiple iterations of design with evaluations along the way (known as *formative evaluation*), you should test now and test again later when sketch visuals are added and again as interactive prototypes are built and refined.

Now, let's look deeper still at checkout select address, the middle page of the three pages represented on cards on page 87.

Amazon.com checkout select address

INFORMATION

It is important to reaffirm that the user is on the Amazon website and this is achieved by consistent reuse of the Amazon.com logo. We also want to inform the user what to do if they have more than one delivery address and how they can redeem a gift certificate. The idea behind the gift certificate is to provide a way of encouraging more users on to the site and to develop loyalty and repeat business.

Amazon logo
Information on what to do:
- about more than one address
- redeeming a gift certificate.

We will provide a small amount of useful information on this page about these options, and put more detailed information on other linked pages specifically to describe them in more detail.

ACTION AND INTERACTION

We want to make sure the support for all the user actions regarding addresses is supported. From the work on use scenarios, we found the user may want to:

- ship to multiple addresses

- enter a new address

- change this address.

If they have used our services before, we will already have their last used address, so we need to offer them "use this address."

We will make the activities (ship to multiple addresses; enter a new address; change this address) links to other pages so the design of those can be stand alone components. (**Note**: this is the design decision Amazon have settled on in this version – decide for yourself if it is the right decision from a user-centered design point of view.) These activities therefore become navigation links.

NAVIGATION
We want an indication as to where we are in the ordering process. Its purpose is to show the user where they are and how much more there is to do. It is intended to reassure the user that there is a final confirmation stage and to inform them.

The pointer must show:

- welcome – sign in
- address – identified as this is where the user is
- items
- wrap
- ship
- pay
- confirm.

This will work strictly as a pointer to where they are in the process, since we do not want the user to miss any steps out. It will not work as an active navigation device.

Navigation to further information on what to do:

- about more than one address
- redeeming a gift certificate

(from the information needs).

Navigation to further action:

- ship to multiple addresses
- enter a new address
- change this address

(from the action needs).

How Amazon have presented and implemented this is discussed later.

FINANCIAL INFORMATION SITE — EXAMINE AN EQUITY

First I sketched what I might want on the pages, based on the information structures and the action structures. This gives me a feel for the kind of things I want on a page.

CASE
STUDY

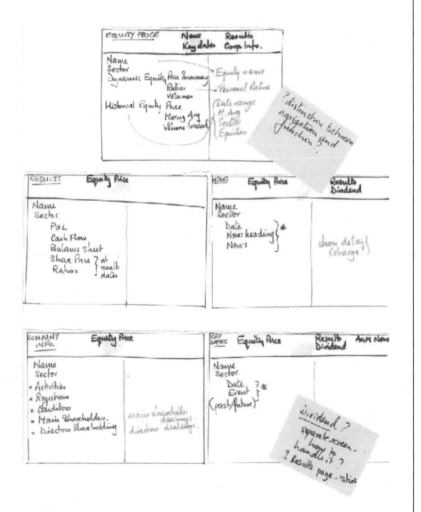

I then decided that the core action was "examine an equity" and it could be the focus of the private investor activity. I made this decision as a result of studying all the discovery information, including the object modelling, and the other steps we have been through in design.

So I went into more detail for "What's on a page" for the user action "examine an equity."

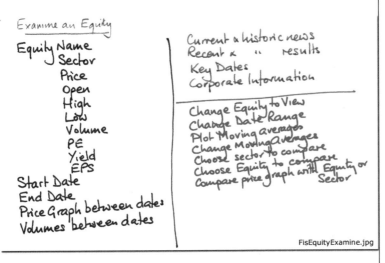

Examine an Equity

Equity Name
      Sector
      Price
      Open
      High
      Low
      Volume
      PE
      Yield
      EPS
Start Date
End Date
Price Graph between dates
Volumes between dates

Current & historic news
Recent & "   results
Key Dates
Corporate Information

Change Equity to View
Change Date Range
Plot Moving averages
Change MovingAverages
Choose sector to compare
Choose Equity to compare
Compare price graph with Equity or Sector

FisEquityExamine.jpg

We already know from our work in discovery (discover the use, discover the information) what each of these components is, how it is calculated or derived, and where it fits into the overall scheme of things. Now let's look a little deeper.

Information
We want as much information as possible available to the user without having to leave this page. We know what actions the user wants to carry out, and we are making this page the focus of most of them. With careful design thinking, this will work out to be one of the most user-centered ways of doing this design.

For our first iteration, we will have:

- equity name
- equity sector
- equity price
- equity open
- equity high
- equity low
- equity volume
- equity PE

- equity yield
- equity EPS
- start date
- end date
- price graph between start date and end date
- volumes between start date and end date.

This covers most of the key information the private investor wants all in one place.

The following information is needed from the discovery on the use scenarios, but it will not be shown on this page because it is of a sufficiently different class of information:

- news
- results
- key dates
- corporate information.

The user also wants to be able to define their own ratio calculations and filters. As a design decision, we believe we can plug this into this screen later, so will not consider further the page design issues on this here.

Action and interaction
We want to make sure the support for all the key user actions we discovered when getting the use scenarios. We found the user may want to:

- change the equity they are examining
- change the date range for the price graph
- plot moving averages
- change moving averages
- choose sector to compare
- choose equity to compare
- compare the equity price graph with the sector or another equity
- get current and historic news
- get most recent and historic results
- examine key dates
- study the corporate information.

Navigation
We want this to be the primary focus of all activity. So this will be like a "dashboard" and everything will be displayed from this information console. If the user moves off the "equity dashboard," other pages will have navigation systems to support the user in coming back to this point.

We will make the activities of:

- get current and historic news
- get most recent and historic results
- examine key dates
- study the corporate information

links to other pages so the design of those can be stand alone components. Therefore, these become navigation links.
    Later, at the end of Chapter 5, we will look at how we might present this.

INTERACTION DESIGN — THE AUA MODEL

Now we need to look at the detail of how the interaction design should work. This is before we look at the detail visual design of the interaction, though I will use a visual example to discuss it.

Principles of interaction

In Chapter 1, Design for use, I introduced the awareness, understanding, action (AUA) model. let's take a look at that again.

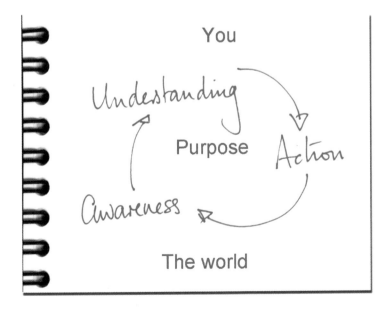

The awareness, understanding, action cycle is continually repeating, causing changes to the world and the things in it. This is going on for a multitude of different living and physical objects all the time, and we see it happening through our own point of view.

In a website, and any software system, we are largely limited to what is going on for us and in the world of the computer system. The model can be further developed as illustrated.

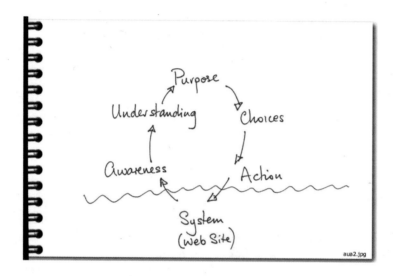

In any interaction we carry out, we look at the website, become *aware* of what is happening on the screen, *understand* what that means to us, relate that to our *purpose* and intentions, make some decision based on the *choices* we perceive to be presented to us and take some *action* based on those choices to cause the website to change and, we hope, match our goals. We then become aware of what is happening... and so on until we have met our purpose.[1]

The way the detail manifests itself is continually changing and dynamic.

The model is not yet complete, now let's look at it deeper still. The aim is to make the interaction consistent yet changing, powerful and supportive, enabling and enjoyable. We need to think about what information is needed by the user and what knowledge they have. We need to think about what information outcome is desired and what their idea of satisfaction is. So the model develops further to give:

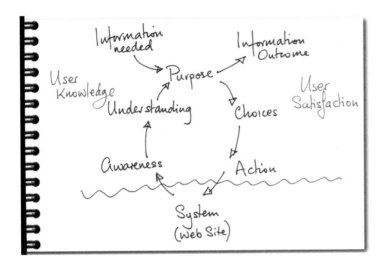

Using the detailed AUA model

Each action sequence and each specific interaction should be created by thinking about this model and drawing on all the work we have done in discovery understanding the user and what their use scenarios are.

Let's look at each part of the model in greater detail.

User knowledge   Each user brings their knowledge to the use of the website. We draw on our understanding of the users so we can create an environment in harmony with their mindset and knowledge.

User satisfaction   We want the user to complete their actions on the site with a feeling of satisfaction. Satisfaction will be determined by the degree to which the actions (specific and sequences) were useful, efficient and effective and how much the presentation and feedback was clear, unambiguous, easy and in tune with their mindset.

Information needed   We should provide a complete representation of all the information, in the appropriate state, that the user needs to support their decision making or understanding (this can also be thought of as "prerequisites").

Information outcome It is necessary to be clear about what constitutes success, when can it be said that the objective is satisfied, and what results from the actions taken here. Information outcome can be results on the screen, physical printed pieces of paper, a message telling the user they will be contacted shortly, a screen transition to another screen and so on. (Formally, this can also be thought of as "deliverables.")

Purpose You must be clear what the purpose is in terms of meeting the user's objective.

For example, a "screen" represents a decision point and feedback for a user objective. After a user action, the screen has changed, and the user's objectives may have been met or they may not. As a result of the change, the user's objectives may have changed. The new state of the website must enable the user to continue to meet their objectives in a manner that fits with the kind of person they are.

Choices Provide a complete representation of all the actions the user may wish to carry out to support meeting that objective.

It must be clear what action choices are available. It must be clear what will happen if the user chooses any of them. Here, nothing is worse than destroyed expectations. The language and communication in the presentation will make or break the ease of use (see *Awareness*, and *Understanding* below).

Chosen action It must be clear how the user starts an action, what thing the action is being done to, and it must enable them to do it.

System (website)   The HTML, Dynamic HTML, Java, Javascript, XML, C, C++, VBScript or whatever does its stuff. As designers, from a user-centered design perspective, the details of what the underlying technology are, is less relevant than what it can do for us. We need to understand the capability, not necessarily the coding (though it helps sometimes).

Awareness   Before any user action, the system must communicate all aspects of the information needs and action needs clearly.

After a user action, it must be clear what has changed and that change must be timely (feedback). This connects strongly with presentation design and visual image, as well as the technology providing the implementation of the feedback and display systems.

Understanding   It must be clear before any user action what everything on the screen means. After a user action, it must be clear what any changes mean to the user. This is not only about the presentation, but also language. The language (words and images) must be one the user can understand simply and quickly. This also will depend upon the kind of user who is using it – this is why we spent so much time on understanding the user.

Purpose   After a user action, something has changed, and the user's objectives may have been met or they may not. Also, as a result of the change, the user's objectives may have changed. The new state of the website must enable the user to continue to meet their objectives in a manner that fits with the kind of person they are.

The Point

The AUA model can be applied to the design at any level of the interaction. This means you should apply it to the whole action process of the user, or apply it to the smallest little thing the user interacts with.

The AUA model may be applied to analyze not only a screen, a button or any other widget, but also a system, subsystem or a business process.

The principle components of the AUA cycle are universally consistent and may be used as a formal template for useful, efficient, effective and satisfying user-centered interaction design. This model can also be used as a formal template for interaction design and useability evaluation. You should ensure that the user has appropriate and satisfactory support for each part of the AUA process cycle, for each goal (purpose) and sub-goal.

What a page should show

Every page should show all the choices of what the user may wish to do, at the time they may want to do it. It should show all the information they need to do the action, and signpost what will happen as a result of the action. It should provide all the design for feedback information. All of this should be couched in the user's language to avoid confusion, and the visual design should support immediate recognition of all the components of the screen. If any part of the detailed AUA model is not attended to, there could be a useability problem.

The Amazon example

On the checkout address page, Amazon have done nothing particularly inventive, preferring to keep it very simple. Every action point and every navigation point is simply a link, with the one exception of a check box which asks the user to click on it if there are any gifts in this order.

Let's see how they have designed this, in terms of what happened before and what happens next. So, I am ordering a copy of *Envisioning Information* by Edward R. Tufte and placing it in my "shopping cart."

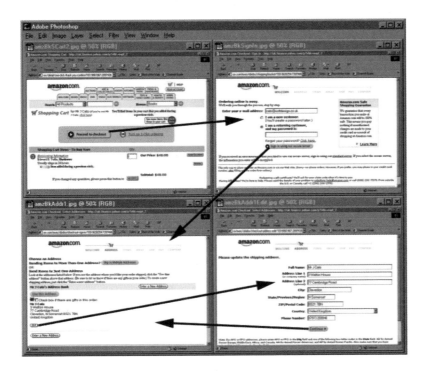

Taking the AUA model and looking at just this part of the process, the following information is revealed.

- **Purpose.** The purpose of this sequence is to order one book and ensure it is sent to the correct address. A later part of the sequence requires that the correct person is billed.

- **User knowledge.** The user brings knowledge of books, book descriptions, the notion of quantity and price, who they are, their e-mail address and password, and their desired delivery address.

- **Information needed.** The user needs to know that the book they have selected earlier is indeed the one they will be ordering and having mailed to the address of their choice.

- **Information outcome.** The user needs to have confirmation the book they are ordering will be sent to the correct address, the address of their choice.

- **User satisfaction.** The user will be satisfied if they can carry out the process with least effort in terms of their actions and their understanding of what is going on. (*This design does not really do that as well as it could because of the extra effort to change address.*)

- **Choices.** The choices are whether or not to order this book, how many of this book they want, and saying where they want them to be delivered.

- **Chosen actions.** The user has chosen to order one copy of this book, they have had to sign in to identify themselves, and they want to change the delivery address. (*Changing delivery address takes the user forward to another screen containing essentially the same information as the first address screen, and then returns them to the first address screen when they press continue. It is hardly continue – it's more of a "back."*)

- **System (website).** The system responds by making the screen transitions as shown above. We are not concerned with how the system works internally, only what the external evidence is.

- **Awareness.** The user can see clearly they are in different parts of the process.

- **Understanding.** The understanding is reasonably clear, but what can we find out by analyzing the address page?

Evaluation and design of "choose address" page

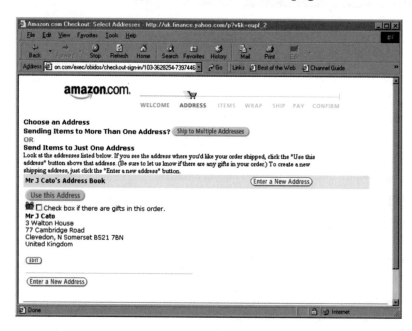

Considering Amazon's "choose address" page in the context of the user's process just described, we have the following.

- **Purpose.** The purpose of this page is to ensure the order of one copy of *Envisioning Information* is sent to the correct address. *So far as this goes, the objective is met.*

- **User knowledge.** The user brings knowledge about which books they are trying to order and how many of them. They also bring the notion of quantity and price, who they are and their desired delivery address. *User knowledge is correctly assumed.*

- **Information needed.** The user needs reassurance that the books they have selected earlier are indeed the ones that will be mailed to the address of their choice. (*We can see there is no carrying forward of information reassuring them about the books they are ordering.*)

- **Information outcome.** The user needs to have confirmation that the books they are ordering will be sent to the correct address, the address of their choice. This is not shown here since this will be the next screen after dealing with the address.

- **User satisfaction.** The user will be satisfied if they can carry out the process with least effort in terms of their actions and their understanding of what is going on. (*As we have seen earlier, if the user wants to change the delivery address, they have to go to another screen and then they will be returned to this one. This makes more transitions and user actions than necessary. These users will exhibit less satisfaction with the efficiency of the process.*)

- **Choices.** The choice is simply whether to use this address or to change the address. (*Since there is only one book, "Shipping to Multiple Addresses" is not a choice, and should not be presented to the user. This only adds to things the user has to think about and is confusing because it is meaningless.*)

- **Chosen actions.** The user has choosen to change the address, so they have to click on "edit." (*The language "edit" is oriented towards a computer user; it makes assumptions that everyone buying on the site is computer literate. Why not "Change this address." Additionally, the user could find it easier just to change the address on this screen and carry on. So, this screen and the next could be combined.*)

● **Awareness.** There is a lot of text on the screen so the user has to use effort to scan and understand what is there. The action buttons are hard to find and relate to. (*The location of the buttons is not easy to find in the context of the information and user actions related to that information. Place actions near to the information to which it is related.*)

● **Understanding.** The understanding is reasonably clear, but it is clouded by the overload of the text and the use of "techy" language on the "edit" button.
  - *Less is more, especially in screen design of an interactive system, reduce, reduce, reduce all unnecessary text and imagery. The amount of text needs to be reduced so everything can be assimilated quickly.*
  - *Use a language you know the users will always and quickly understand.*

What Amazon could have done

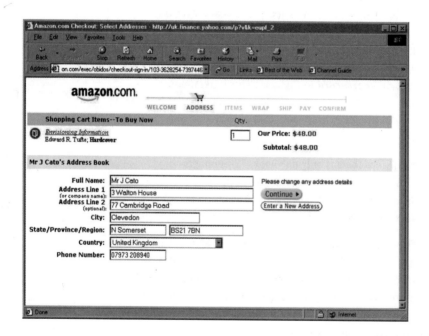

I have taken the original screens and edited up a screen to illustrate what Amazon could have done to solve all the issues discussed above. For example, it reduces the number of screen transitions, improves clarity, brings forward information from before, enables immediate "editing" of changeable information, and reduces description and guidance support text.

Note that if we looked at the multiple book scenario, we may have to reconsider some of the details, but the principle holds true.

The point

The attention to interaction design using the detailed AUA model gives us a logical formal framework for designing, questioning and extending the design and for carrying out evaluation. It draws the threads together from discovery.

It can be applied instead of, or in conjunction with, heuristic evaluation; which you should also refer to, and use the heuristics described there as a set of interaction design guidelines and principles. (See *Useability evaluation* in Chapter 6, *Use*.)

User support design

It is my basic philosophy that you should not need a help system. Help systems, by definition, are there to help the user when they get stuck. When someone is stuck, it means something is unuseable. When did you ever need help on how to hold and swing a hammer (and would they put the help text on the handle, perhaps with a phone number to call?) or how to push a child on a swing? The only thing you needed was practice and possible hints from the affordances, natural mappings and your culturally based natural understanding. See Norman's *Psychology of Everyday Things*.[2]

> **If the user needs a help system, or warnings of any kind, you
> have probably got it wrong.**

However, there are times when a help system is needed. Work on the basis that the above rule is true. Then, only put in a user support system if you can prove the rule wrong.

Footnotes

1. John Teire, a remarkable and truly good man at enabling thinking and awareness through doing. He runs courses and offers

consultancy on "People Management" which is mostly about enabling the individual and the organization. It is through him, in 1987 or so, that I was introduced to and really *understood* the awareness, understanding, action cycle and developed the detailed AUA model. At the time, it was introduced only as a way of thinking about people and management, but its potential for interaction design is enormous.

2. See also Don Norman, *The Psychology of Everyday Things*, Basic Books, 1988. His framework of action is a little different from this model in that it is a seven-stage model and doesn't include the notions of prerequisites (information needed) and deliverables (information outcome) in the cycle. I developed these into the AUA model based on software Engineering Formal Methods such as VDM, Z and Fusion.

5 | VISUAL DESIGN

Style is something we recognize but is not always easy to create or classify. Style makes us think of clothes, cars, architecture or graphic design. It pervades the world we live in; it is a distinctive, consistent and coherent form. Creating a style is to draw all the individual pieces of the design together in a coherency of design.

What style will you choose? What is your corporate style? What is your personal style? Think how you can make your web "story" – your virtual world – fit with your physical reality. The style communicates a message subliminally and touches the emotion and experience the user has of you.

Make sure the style you use is consistent with all the other organization, user, supplier and customer style. Bring the style through from your marketing and corporate communication material. If you use blue clean lines and all wear suits, bring that image through to your website. The style must be in keeping with your mission, your vision for the future and the intended user experience.

Exploration of your visions and dreams will help you to focus on which style you will go for and what experience you will try to give your visitor. The audience is a key aspect here, and reiterates the question "What's the use?"

Make sure that the whole website holds together as a consonant and consistent whole. Keep all the elements of the design in harmony with one another. Don't mix styles unless you consciously want to create a disjoint to say, shake the user into a new mode of thinking.

When you have chosen a style, make it as clear and distinctive as you can. Be bold about it. Make it stand out.

If you can employ an excellent graphic designer, do so; otherwise you will have to do your best with the material that lies all around you.

Stylistic forms

The style of websites varies enormously, but underlying it there is a common set of themes or styles. In theory, there is a wide range of possible website styles. However, of the 100 top sites identified in the January 2000 Yahoo magazine and January 2000 Internet magazine, I found only a limited number of standard forms emerging. I found it surprising how many of the "top" sites look very similar. Perhaps this is because style is so hard to create.

I guess some of the "new" standard forms will pass away and others will develop a longer life in the history of website style.

I was also very surprised to find the *newsprint style* seems to have gained predominance. Just behind that is what I call the *magazine style*, which is very similar to the newspaper style. Then there is the *arty style*, often used by modern art museums. Finally, there is the *graphic designer style* used by people who are going for communication of both image and text.

Some sites mix styles, mostly in the same genre, others cross genres. The styles are discussed below.

The newsprint style

The *Washington Post* web page has a four-column style, navigation left and right, with content in two columns down the middle. It looks like a color newpaper, which of course it is.

It is littered with navigation and has a search facility to help you locate news or stories of interest. The site has a vast number of pages, and navigation and location is paramount.

The white background is typical of many sites, emulating the world of paper. This also is in keeping for a newspaper.

It is fascinating that around half the top 100 sites followed superficially this general design style. There is hardly any difference in layout between this site and, say, the *San Francisco Examiner*, or ostensibly, the *Internet Bookshop*.

The magazine style

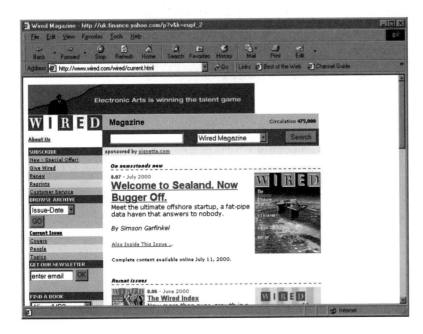

Wired Magazine repeats the fluorescent colors of the printed version on its website and makes sure you know you are here. It follows the conceptual form of the newsprint sites, keeping fundamentally the same strategy though losing the right-hand navigation column that typifies the normal newsprint grid layout.

It provides clear visual signposts to the current and previous editions of the magazine.

The arty style

Don't you just love the visual impact of this home page for London's Tate Gallery? It has a strong, clean and wonderful arty yet graphic design. The use of color is minimal, and the white-gray eggs set in just the right place on the black background just draws you right in. The style is ultra modern, and yet one can see the graphic design roots going back to the 1930s.

It has a very small number of small images, no clever animation and it loads quickly. It is an excellent design from both the visual and the technical perspectives.

It meets the Tate's needs and the customer's needs. The gallery visitor is drawn right in.

The graphic designer style

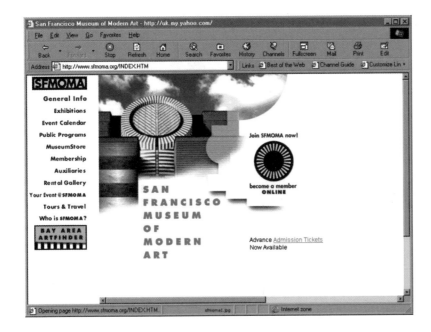

The style of the website of the San Francisco Museum of Modern Art is slightly old modern, and one can see the graphic design roots going back to the 1930s.

The use of a strong architectural image, set and faded into the graphic design, using the left of the page for navigation works cleanly and well. The load times are slower than the Tate, which can work well if leisurely browsing and slow development of interest is what they were after.

This works for some people, but not for others, and probably owes its design roots to the graphics designers more than the user-centered designers.

Mixed styles

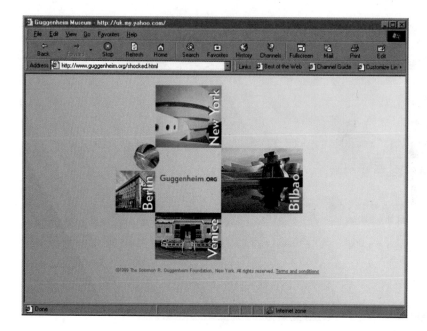

The Guggenheim opening page has some animation that results in the first image. The animation generated interest and curiosity and the design appeared out of it and became stable. I would call the first image a mixture of arty and graphic design styles, with the predominance of arty.

The page is clean and excellently arranged. Everything is clear and the use of the colors is subtle and in quiet keeping with the notion of a modern museum. The new design is different, and to me, less appealing, but not by much.

Further in the site, this subsequent page is very much more strongly graphic design modern and classic, with a rich and imaginative use of color and tone, font and layout.

The colors are vibrant and yet not overloaded; the background is black, the white text standing out strongly.

The Guggenheim text is colored the same as the art object, while all the other colors show off well and clearly.

The page has impact and great presence. It shouts modern design, and retains a professional accomplished and classic feel to it.

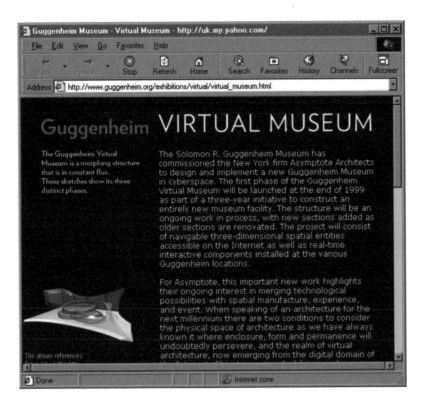

Purpose and style

VISITOR'S PURPOSE	BUSINESS PURPOSE
• to purchase – air tickets, books, toys, CDs	• selling – e-commerce
• to look at – leisure, reflection, visual entertainment	• obtain involvement
• to live in – regular daily business, transactional	• reduce daily overhead costs
• to communicate – group space	• relationship, marketing, communication
• to visit occasionally – examining bank balances, stock prices	• provide more cost-effective financial services
• to explore – information, education	• sell information

Remember this? We should consider which of the styles discussed earlier fits best with both the visitor's purpose and the business purpose. For example, if the purpose is to provide a site for users to look at, we might choose to go for any of a wide range of arty or graphic designer styles, depending on the deeper purpose and mood and feel we want to convey.

Let's see what others have done.

Entertainment

The entertainment websites (eonline.com, howletts.net, culturefinder.com and disney.com) each have different ways of making their impact, though one might argue there is little impact with the culturefinder site.

Culturefinder goes for the simple full screen menu approach, based on a tabular grid layout, inviting their users to go for what they see as labels or carrying out a search.

Eonline has chosen the newpaper format, aiming at creating a magazine "look and feel" effect – quite trendy and stylish in the current vogue.

Howletts.net is a grid-based and highly uncool image format, which is going for the functional approach, which doesn't work for me.

Disney.com is a rule unto themselves; appealing to the Disney cartoon market audience and is highly inefficient in page load terms.

TV and film

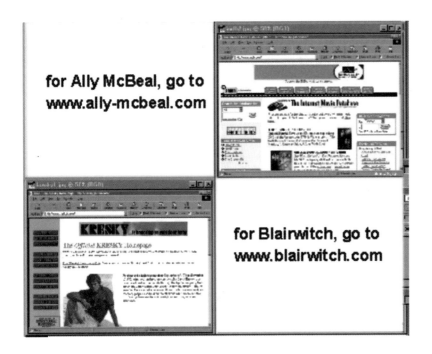

These sites (Ally McBeal, Blairwitch, Kresky and IMDb), which are all to do with TV and film, mix two current styles. The Ally McBeal and Blairwitch sites both go for dark backgrounds and a small amount of white or light yellow contrasting text, providing an airy feel to them, while Kresky and IMDb both use the old favorite newspaper/magazine style.

The IMDb site, providing a wealth of detail about movies for movie buffs, has chosen a style which is not too dissimilar to the successful book sites, and this is a wise choice for their material, lots of content needs an effective navigation and information location system.

Dear John,

Thank you for your interest in Fox Online. Unfortunately, we do not license our content to other Web sites or individuals. If you find an item of interest on our site, feel free to create a text link to it. However, we cannot grant you permission to use, in any way or any form, the articles, photographs, video or any other material found on any Fox website. Thanks for visiting and we hope you continue to return to find the most engaging information available on the Web at Fox Online.

Elizabeth Guilamo
News Digital Media
15 November 2000

Fox has gone for involvement and movement. Theme parks and film producers know the benefits of total experience and dynamic involvement. They look at the approach, the experience and the satisfaction.

Fox has created an approach sequence which is intended to lead the user into the involvement in the experience. A highly dynamic and visually involving sequence is used to grab the interest of the user.

When in the experience, the visual style settles down into a three-column approach which is used to advertise their TV shows. Many of the shows are also introduced by highly professional dynamic flash "advertising" sequences which lead into providing a wealth of material about the shows, the characters, show memorabilia and souvenirs, and also prizes which can be won. The content is maintained up to date so the forthcoming show is advertised.

Choose your style

When choosing the style for your website, consider whether you want it cluttered or airy. Do you want arty, the form most "design" based interfaces use, or do you want it newsprint? Think of your choices;

think of the experience you want the user to have. Reflect on what I have shown here, and the implications for you.

| SCREEN |

How big is your screen?

In my browser, Microsoft's Internet Explorer and setting a screen resolution of 800×600 resolution (still a very common resolution), approximately 115 pixels of depth are used by the browser, or approximately 19 percent of the available screen space. If we account for the lower information bar and the scroll bar as well it reduces the available screen space to about 74 percent of the total display. It gets worse if you use the browser with its default settings – Macromedia suggest an available space of 760×420 for a maximized browser.

Space is a precious commodity on a web page, so it makes good sense to use every bit of it. But this does not mean you have to fill it all up with visual and functional paraphernalia. You could also take a minimalist approach. However, most of the bookshop sites in the examples below do not.

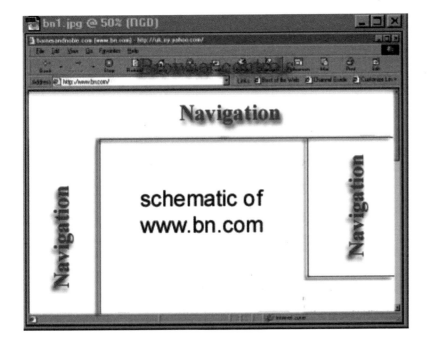

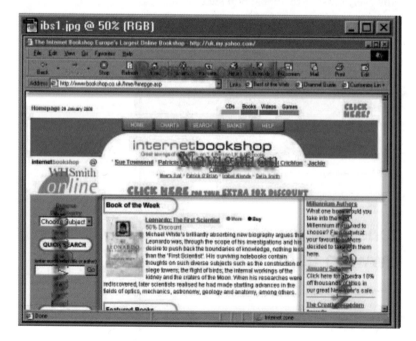

Use of space

The sites above are all remarkably similar. They all use considerable amounts of space for the navigation, along the top and down each side; perhaps reflecting the highly navigational nature of these selling sites.

The space utilized for navigation and content varies, as shown in the table.

SITE	TOP NAVIGATION	OTHER NAVIGATION	"CONTENT" SPACE
Barnes & Noble	23%	30%	47%
Blackwells	25%	30%	45%
Internet Bookshop	49%	23%	28%
Amazon	61%	21%	18%

Interestingly, Amazon is the most used internet book site and has the least immediately obvious content. The lesson here is that with a large number of items available for the user's interest, you must give a high degree of space for finding those items, but still retain some hook in terms of content. Amazon provides the hook by a dominating image placed in the lower center of the screen, to lead the user's eye down and encourage scrolling down by attracting the interest.

Consider how much space you will use for information, how much for action and interaction, and how much for navigation.

You know, from your work on designing the system, the details of each of these components. You also know how the pages connect together, what the actions and interactions need to be and what information is needed to support the user's needs. So, you can decide how to lay out the space for each of these components.

The grid

Most – if not all – styles are based on *grids*. We sometimes do this subconsciously. Let's take a few moments to look at grids consciously.

The Ken

A unit of measure – the Ken – was introduced in the latter half of Japan's Middle Ages. It was an absolute unit of measurement for the design and construction of buildings, of approximately six feet (six shaku). It was used to determine center-to-center spacing between columns. The Ken measured vertically was the right height for doorways. It enabled designers to ensure everything was in proportion and had good aesthetics.

It then became the basis of measurement for the Tatami floor mats, which were 1 × ½ Ken in size. The size of the Tatami suited two people sitting or one person lying down. Since rooms were multiples of the Ken, a set of floor mats could be organized to fit, and the Japanese even had a formula to calculate the height of the room based on the number of Tatami mats. The floor mats could be laid out in a number of ways, each of aesthetically pleasing arrangements.

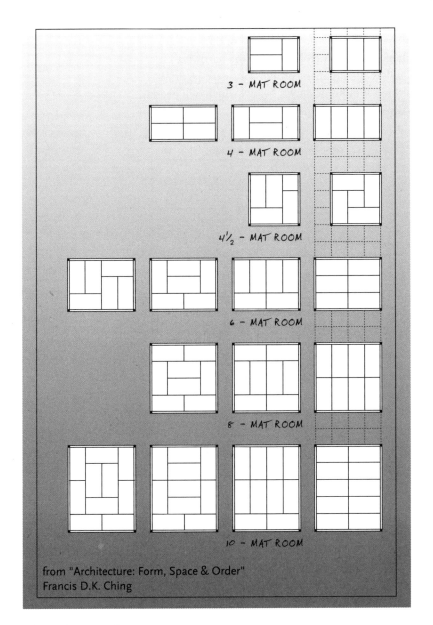

3 – MAT ROOM

4 – MAT ROOM

4½ – MAT ROOM

6 – MAT ROOM

8 – MAT ROOM

10 – MAT ROOM

from "Architecture: Form, Space & Order"
Francis D.K. Ching

The WebKen grid

We can take this idea through to web design and create a "WebKen," loosely based on the idea of the Ken and the Tatami floor mats.

So I experimented. I took the current baseline screen size of 800×600 pixels. Taking off the common browser controls (which accounts for approximately 132 pixels of height) and allowing 32 pixels for the right-hand scroll bar and some slack. Because of the proportions of the available space, which is fixed by the hardware technology, we cannot follow the Japanese proportions exactly. So, I experimented with the three WebKens shown below, which will overlap to make up other structures on the web page.

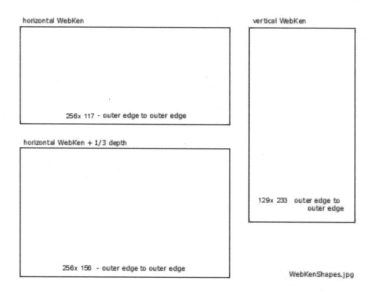

horizontal WebKen

256x 117 - outer edge to outer edge

horizontal WebKen + 1/3 depth

256x 156 - outer edge to outer edge

vertical WebKen

129x 233 outer edge to outer edge

WebKenShapes.jpg

Designing with grids

There are four basic grid patterns available to you:

- 3×3
- 3×4
- 4×3
- 4×4.

Additionally, you can make up more varied arrangements as indicated by Ching.

Think how you might lay out your page components on each of these basic grid patterns, or experiment with other aesthetics.

Taking the idea of a WebKen-based grid pattern, I then overlaid them on to existing sites to see how they might look, given the thought that grids are used subconsciously, and a pattern may appear.

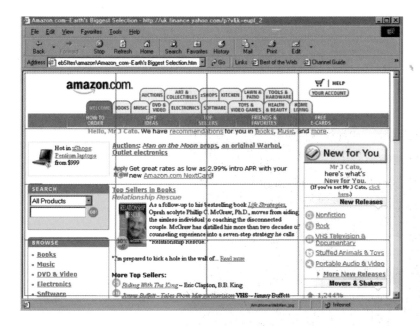

I have applied a 4×4 horizontal WebKen to the Amazon page, and we find a remarkable match with the WebKen grid, consciously or not. Amazon has ostensibly adopted a newsprint style, but replaced the newspaper heading with a more simple logo and navigation area.

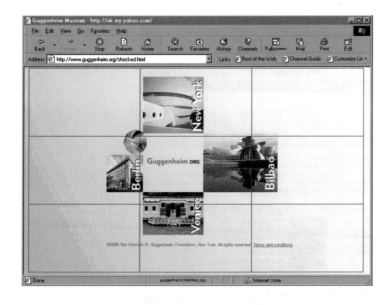

As shown here, the Guggenheim has chosen a 3×3 grid. In jazz, blue notes are introduced to provide a little discord and interest; the same is true of the visual display of the Guggenheim page.

The Tate has taken the same route as the Guggenheim, and used a 3×3 grid with added blue notes. This version was live in January 2000; it has since changed, much for the worse in my opinion.

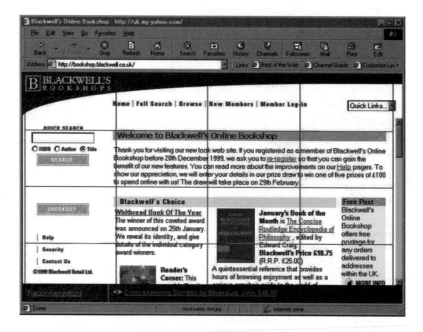

Blackwell's bookshop have followed the 4×4 WebKen grid layout and then broken the rules to get more communication space and less navigation space. It is worth noticing they have taken the opposite strategy to Amazon, and they are less successful in business terms.

Choose your grid

Use a grid, try out different grid styles that may work for you and your organization. Consider what mood and feel you want the site to have, do you want it light and airy, or do you want it tight and full and information rich?

Consider what you want to show in the way of information, what action and navigation you will have. You already know much of this from the designing the system stage.

Recognize that you must use your current best judgment, and also recognize that as the design becomes more refined with each successive iteration, any decision you make on the first iteration can change – don't feel it is cast in stone.

> **Whatever you do with your design, aim to keep a sense of order and consistency with it.**

AREAS

Area design

We discussed areas earlier, in Chapter 4. Now we look at how we might communicate those areas to the user.

> **The primary question is:**
> **What is the essence?**

What characterizes this piece, this area? What colors, images, feel and sounds come to mind?

For the private investor, finding out about an equity, the essence of the area must be one of professional efficiency (from the work we did in *The Users* in Chapter 3). For me, what springs to mind is the color of money, the presentation of annual results, the clean professionalism, the sound of business, and effectiveness of action. So the area design for this action process needs to embody all of these characteristics.

I am a great believer in standing on the shoulders of others, and of course, we all do that whether we own up to it or not. We came into this world with no knowledge, so whatever skills we have, ideas or thoughts we have, we have gained from others, directly attributable or not.

We can study company brochures and look for those that embody every aspect we like, and look to how we might learn from what others have done to make our set absolutely excellent. (You must of course be careful with copyright issues.)

Opposite are some examples of contents of annual reports. For the private investor, this is familiar territory, and familiar is intuitive, and intuitive is what we are after.

We can use the look of these styles to design the background, layout and feel of the area. Each area must be distinctive in its own right and also be designed to be consonant with the whole site.

What Amazon did

Amazon has used a simple and subtle approach of color clues to indicate different areas. This works well. They use blue for the entry (welcome) page, and change to green for their books home page. This is continued through into their search and browse headers. It means they can retain the overall presentation structure while communicating "area."

When we were considering the mood and feel of Amazon, we said it must be:

- professional
- businesslike
- approachable
- visually simple
- enticing
- efficient
- supporting and helpful.

The mood must be a balance between calm efficiency and relaxed browsing. The paths through the site must show up new areas of

A Future of Opportunity

interest, especially those that appeal to me particularly, and when the user wants to buy, it must be very effective and secure. This version of the site gives off much of that feel.

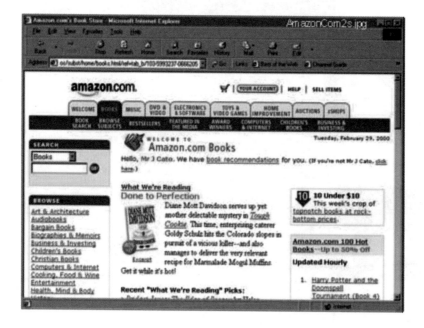

A newer version of their site (below) is more cluttered and visually overloaded. As they develop a wider range of their business, maintaining this interface may become a problem.

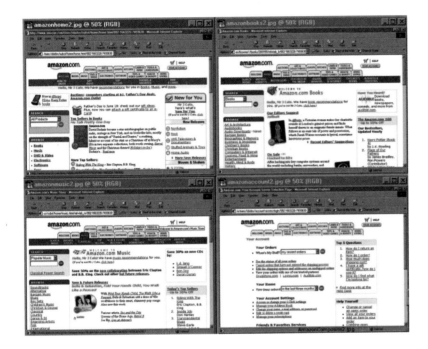

Home is maintained as a standard welcoming screen which has much navigation and some information. Amazon is known for books, and the decision has been made to reinforce the books area on the home screen, though we can see many other information areas available from here.

All the information areas are distinguishable from the action areas. Each area is color-coded, and the color code, combined with the obvious nature of the content, is sufficient to define the areas.

What Farmaervas did

This site is overloaded with cleverness, using shockwave. If you have the time, it is a very interesting lead-in sequence which sets the mood and brings you into the "home" page where you can see all the areas at a glance.

While this is loading, your cursor has a butterfly as a cursor trace. After the load sequence is completed "100%", and you click on the "Entrar" (to enter) button, you are presented with an extraordinarily

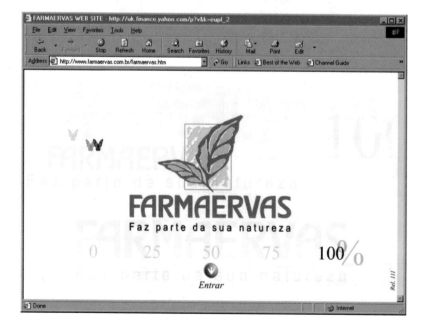

presented video animation bringing through the concept of the butterfly (the leaf image is also a butterfly image) combined with sound of the jungle of the Amazon basin and local music.

The site is concerned with supply of natural remedies, and the introduction supports that feel – it comes over like a movie introduction sequence.

You are then left settled on the "home" page which is totally different from the approach sequence.

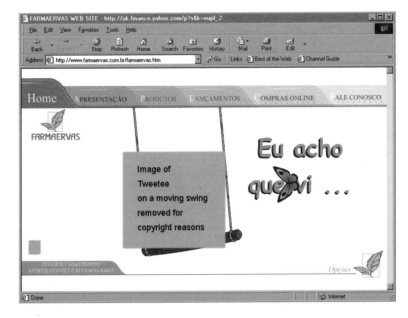

How areas help

Areas help to give the user a sense of location. It keeps them comfortable and well oriented with what they are doing. Just as when you walk around a city or town, you know what kind of area you are in by the visual image and other senses, and those clues give you reassurance and support, so also on a website.

See the side trip on *City image, narrative and interaction design* for further thoughts on communicating a sense of understanding and comfort.

WHAT ARE THE PAGES? — THE ACTION PROCESS

Navigation

It is of paramount importance that the users understand how to find their way around the site, that they know where they are and how to get anywhere. The work on discovery, the users, the use and the information all comes together here.

Navigation is about maps in the head, conceptual models in the user's mind. It is about visual signposts that are easily understandable to the user. It is about language, the user's language. Navigation must therefore support the user's action processes in a language the user understands, make it clear where the user is, and how they can do what they want to achieve. We learned a great deal about this in the card sorting exercise in Chapter 3.

In principle, navigation should be provided in a consistent place on the screen, somewhere the user can rely on, know and feel confident about. Typically, these locations will be along the top, perhaps in the top third or quarter of the display, or down the left-hand side. Sometimes they work well in other locations, such as along the bottom of the screen if the page size can reliably be fixed. Of course, this can be impossible when we don't know what screen resolutions will be used or what browsers, though on a corporate intranet, these things may be controlled.

What Amazon did

Navigation on the Amazon website is primarily achieved by the tabs along the top of the display area. The graphics are simple and the text is clear. The labels are short and obvious. This tab structure gives 9 domains and up to 9 sub-domains; 81 separate and easily accessible areas, as well as access to the shopping cart, your account, help, and sell items.

They also provide hyperlinks (on the left) into subsections by topic such as architecture, cooking and children's books. This is like being able to walk into the bookshop and go to those specific sections to find what is new or what is currently being promoted.

On the right, they provide links into the special offers and special sales areas, to meet the needs of those buying popular books at low prices, perhaps for gifts.

Navigation is one of the big problem areas in website design, and Amazon have done a good job of it. The trick is to match the users' needs (action needs) with the navigation support provided on the site. To achieve this, they will have given much hard and concentrated work on understanding their customers' needs and how they naturally want to browse and buy.

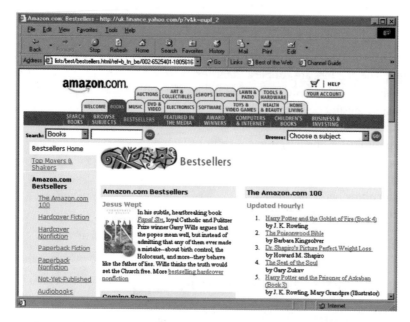

Then, in the last few months, Amazon added more to their site. They followed the same tab-based arrangement. Curiously, I think it still works perfectly well.

Recall the Amazon use scenario in Chapter 4, Designing the system.

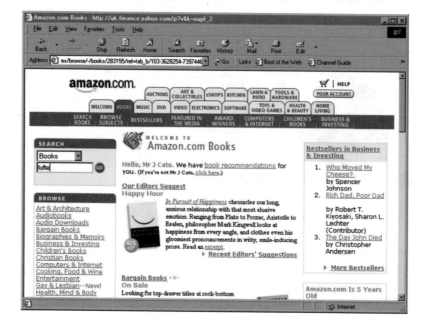

The action here is to locate and buy a book. I searched using a keyword – Tufte – and was given back the screen below which was exactly what I wanted.

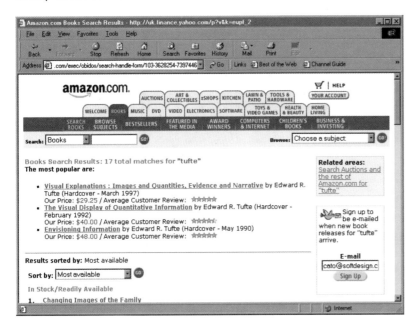

My action process is well supported, the next obvious thing to do is click on the title of interest, *Envisioning Information*. This leads naturally to the screen showing details of the book.

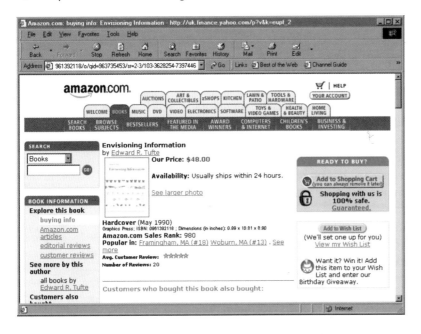

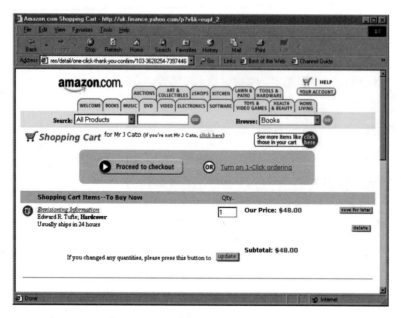

We then naturally move into adding the book into our shopping cart and here the visual clues change again to show the neutral color which indicates we have moved out of an interest specific domain (such as books or music) into the checkout domain. This is just like moving through a large store to a checkout where all your items are collected together and paid for, with delivery details organized at that point.

Amazon's action design is kept very simple, either by providing process support as already described, or by providing a simple search system that works very effectively.

What PriceWaterhouseCoopers did

PriceWaterhouseCoopers used a tab-based high level design, and kept it down to three simple headings. The buttons are very buttony, which is good. They have used roughly a 3×3 grid based on a 640×480 screen resolution, the lowest common denominator at present. The design is clear and clean, and the picture image is very clear and inviting, but does not navigate anywhere and has no purpose other than enhancing the visual image. It changes each time you refresh and comes from a corporate image bank.

The primary navigation is maintained at the top of the screen, good from the point of view of consistency, and they have stayed away from using frames, a good idea.

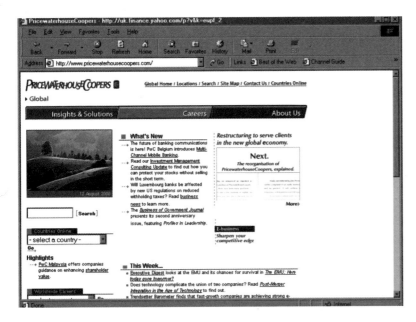

Let's say we click on "Insights and Solutions." This develops into the next layer down of navigation, representing sub-categories of information. Here they are clearly designing based on *information* structure rather than *action* structure.

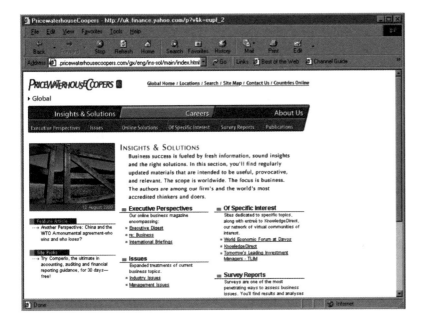

They repeat the sub-categories of information on the page, showing what is in each category using text, and allowing the user to go a further two levels deeper straight from this page without using the navigation buttons. This suggests that their top level menu design cannot support the depth and breadth of their information content, and so the second level is there more for show than for use.

But what happens if we go from their home page into "What's new – Multi Channel Mobile Banking"? We end up on the Belgium information page, maintained in the same way and with the same tab structure, though with a different column design.

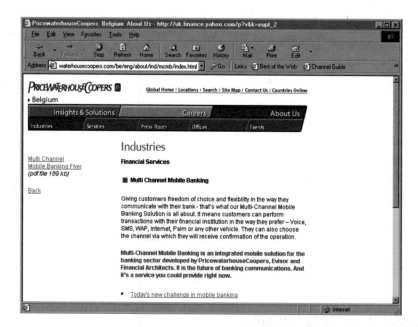

And we end up on the "About Us" tab, though the lack of contrast in the colors does not make that immediately obvious. Also, you would think that What's New would be structured under Insights and Solutions. They have a good idea to include a link (middle left) to download a .pdf file summarizing the whole piece. The only problem is, on 12 August 2000, it did not work and could not load anything. So I tried clicking on Insights and Solutions.

I arrived at a page which looked very similar to the worldwide home page (they have maintained the consistency). However, bearing in mind how I reached this point, and the fact that I had just come from "What's New – Multi-Channel Mobile Banking" (which had been on the home page of the worldwide "site"), and that the button "About Us" was not really obviously depressed, I experienced a feeling of "how do I get to 'What's New – Multi-Channel Mobile Banking' from here?" The only thing I could do was go back on the browser.

It seems there may be different development teams and the co-ordination of those teams is not quite as good as we were led to believe by the superficial consistency. The consistency is maintained, largely, at the presentation level, but not at the content level. A useability evaluation (see Chapter 6, Use) would have found this out. Now let's see a non-tab design.

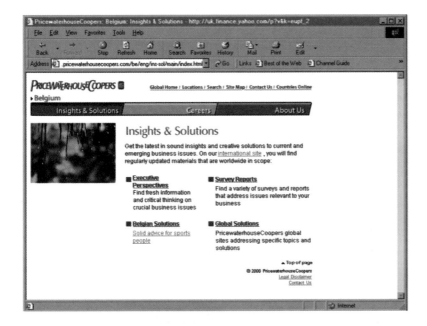

What the San Francisco Museum of Modern Art did

Since the last time I visited the site, it has changed again and now has a completely new style. The navigation is supported by the white strip through the middle; they are clearly trying to break the mold. How well does it work?

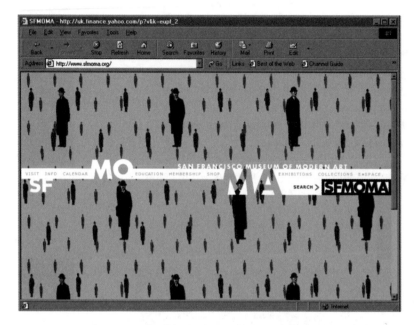

The San Francisco Museum of Modern Art site

They have tried to keep the color range small, so they have reused the same blue of the background for the text across the middle. These are actually buttons, but they do not stand out as such. It is not easy to

read the text on the buttons; the light blue on the white is relatively illegible. The text is also very small, so difficult for any visually impaired people, with glasses say.

If you mouse over the text "MEMBERSHIP," you can see it, but you have to keep moving over from left to right, or how ever you choose, to see what the text says. They hit the memory problem, as most people on an interactive display like this will have trouble remembering more than five of these headings, and there are nine here. Membership is placed more or less center screen, implying that is what they want people to do.

So, what happens next? (See the next page.)

They have now moved the navigation to nearly the top of the screen, changed the visibility of the names, but kept the font and layout consistent. The color of the background is different, and it feels very different from the entry page. They are back on their "graphic design" style here.

The biggest apparent problems now are the smallness of the font, the lack of contrast between the text and the background and the lack of clarity about what is a link and what isn't. This causes excessive user effort (recall the AUA model with regard to the effort required to reach an objective). So, what did I discover?

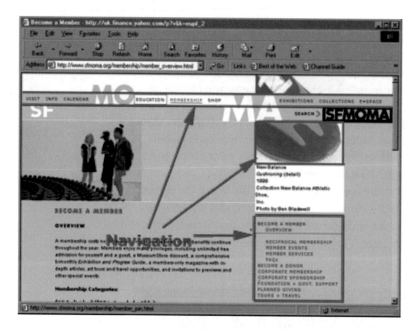

The navigation areas are in three locations; two I guessed reasonably quickly, one I didn't, and I had to "mouse over" the whole screen to identify what was and what wasn't navigation. Not all the images indicated "navigation." Additionally, when I mouse over the image on "menu" on the lower right, the text describing where it links to disappears. Not so good.

The point

To recap, navigation is about maps in the head, conceptual models in the user's mind. These models, as we saw during discovery, may be based on *information* structures or *action* structures, and often they are tightly interconnected.

It is also about visual signposts that are easily understandable to the user. These signposts must give sufficient information about where the user will get to, where they are, and where they have come from.

In addition, it is about language – the user's language. If the language is not clear, the signposts, even if graphically clearly visible, will not serve their purpose.

Navigation must support the user's action processes in a language the user understands, make it clear where the user is, and how they can do what they want to achieve.

WHAT'S ON A PAGE? — THE INFORMATION OBJECTS

Content is king. After all, that is really the main reason why the user is there. Content informs decision making and forms a result. All action by the user is based on content. So, what information is provided, when it is provided, and the way it is provided are crucial. We have already dealt with what and when, based on our use scenarios, let's now look at the way it is provided.

The use of space

Aim to use space as effectively as possible, reducing anything that is unnecessary. Maintain a consistency of form and position across the pages and throughout the site so as to reduce any additional mental effort.

What Schwab did

For its website, Schwab has designed the screen for a 640×480 base minimum screen resolution, but it looks better on 800×600. Even on 640×480, users can clearly see that they must scroll down to see the graph.

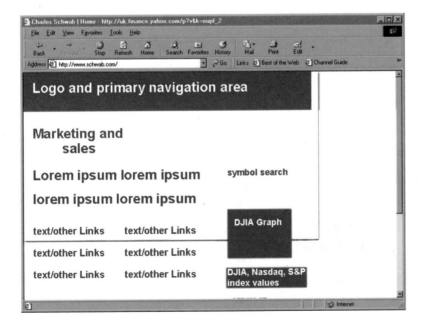

A graph is a natural way of displaying information a "smarter investor" would want. This is good. The layout chosen is a three-column layout with variations in presentation, and this works fairly well. However, the graph is the primary focal point, and they have put it off on one side, and below the crease for their screen design size.

They have chosen to show very little information on the home page. At 640×480 they force the user to scroll (user action = user effort) to see useful information. At 800×600, with no scrolling they use about 5.9 percent of the available screen or 7.9 percent of the available browser display area for useful information, the rest is white space, navigation, adverts, etc.

The information the user – a "smarter investor" – may want is relegated way behind the information marketing and the business wants to display. Whenever there is an imbalance like this, the user will notice very quickly that it is not so useful for them, and make their choices – usually to go to another site.

What BigCharts did

BigCharts designed the screen for somewhere between a 640×480 and an 800×600 screen resolution. This seems very odd, and seems even odder when you see the transition display, which uses the full 800×600.

Again the information is shown by a graph, and they have studied the user base to determine the typical user will want the DJIA and the NASDAQ. This is good, and better than the Schwab site. BigCharts have recognized that the graphs are of key primary interest and have placed them in good positions as a focal point. They use 18.6 percent of the available browser display area for useful information. Not brilliant, but 2.35 times as much as Schwab, and it is in a better position on the screen. They also provide one click to get to a detailed graph (below), although the user must scroll down a little to get it.

For this, they use 46 percent of the available browser display area for useful information, and also, not much "ChartJunk" or "non-data" ink on the graph.

ChartJunk

ChartJunk is Tufte's term (in *The Visual Display of Quantitative Information*) for overloading images with graphics that do not inform the user anything new. Tufte's concept of *maximizing data ink* is also an important principle, the idea of reducing everything which is not data to the barest minimum.

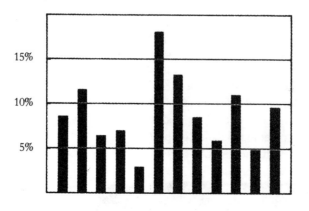

ChartJunk –
redesign of a
histogram

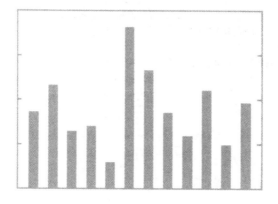

Lighten the
darkness

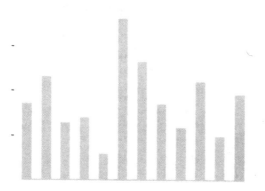

Eliminate the box

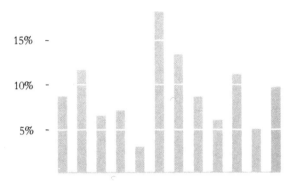

Make a white grid line, and add the y values back in. The result is a chart where everything is useful information.

The language of communication

Use "industry standards" and cultural norms in the way you present and communicate, this will reduce user effort in understanding what is being said.

Make sure all the information displayed is correct and up to date. If users notice any mistakes, they will begin to doubt the quality and correctness of the other information.

What Blackwell's did

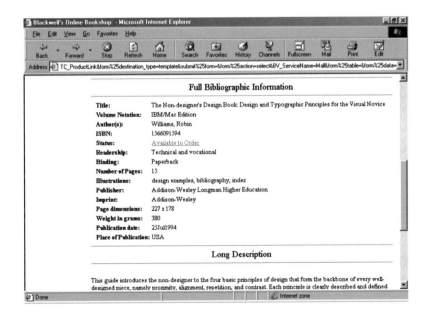

The Blackwell's site is good and uses a clear language of communication based on industry and cultural norms. However, they have got the number of pages wrong and this stands out as an indicator they may have other things wrong.

Get anything wrong, and the user will assume other things may be wrong also.

On the Blackwell's page, when you enter your name, you have to delete the other text in the box.

Lesson: make it easy for the user.

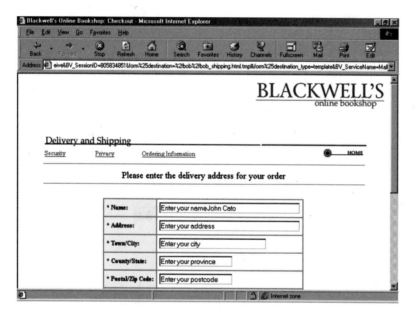

Although it looks like a very clean design, the waste of available space, and forcing the user to scroll is counterproductive.

It is possible the content of all three of these screens could be combined in a clear and understandable way, so reducing the user's actions and making the whole process much more satisfying. Perhaps you might like to try it yourself as an exercise.

Lesson: Tighten the presentation and reduce user action.

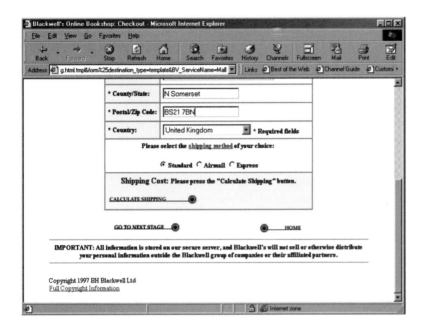

Information clarity

Think about how you can present information clearly. There are a number of important points to bear in mind.

- *use color judiciously*; don't use more than are necessary. When using color, think about the symbology of the color, the obvious ones being red (negative, anger, vibrancy) and green (positive, country values, ethical), black (dark character, sexy) and so on.

- *ensure that everything is clearly identified* and of appropriate sizes and layout for the information and the user.

- *make headings clear*, put headings at the top of what they head, make them related to the content, and use a language which is the user's language.

- *provide all other text in the user's language* – you will know this from your card sorting exercises with your users (see Chapter 3, Discovery).

- *cluster information in an appropriate manner*, making sure that similar user concepts (again from the card sorting) are presented together both visually and in the user's action process. Don't create discord in their thinking, unless you are consciously trying to do that.

- *make graphs easy to read* and understand (see Tufte's books on presenting information).

What Market-Eye did

This is an example of how to do it badly. Market-Eye designed their web page screen for 800×600 resolution.

They use only 3.3 percent of the available browser display area for useful market information. The information is not shown by a graph at all, they show the information as numeric values. They show the numeric values in unfathomable colors, and it is hard to understand quickly what it means. I do not understand what the time is for (presuming it is a time – it does not have any correlation with my understanding of the world. I assumed it was the time of the last update of the values, but since the market closed for the weekend over 15 hours ago, why is it showing a time of before market close?)

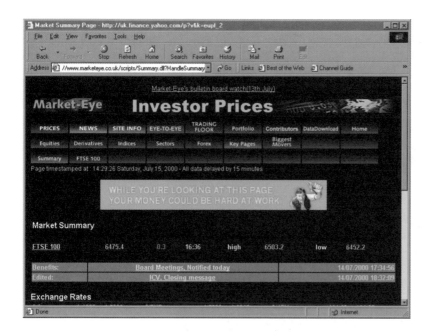

One click to get more information on the FTSE 100 brings up the next screen.

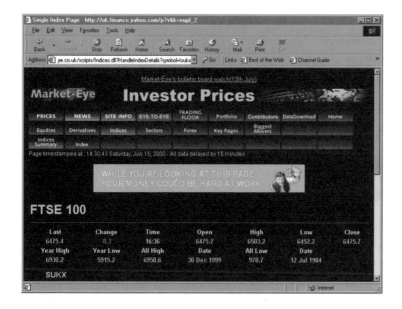

Now, they have provided 15.5 percent of the available browser display area for useful market information. This is still less than BigCharts did on their first screen, and we still don't have a graph.

Now, the user must guess to scroll down, and finally, a graph can be viewed which is what the user wanted in the first place.

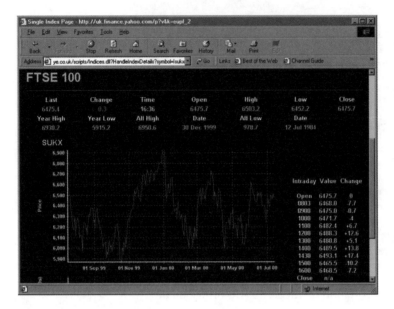

Marke-Eye redesign

Based on the above ideas and concepts, I came up with a variation (for the first page) in 15 minutes on Photoshop – compare the two. Even if they made only this change, it would stand out more, contains more information, is clearer and actually uses less space than they do, so leaving more space to communicate other information such as percentage change and even a miniature graph of the day's trading.

With 20 minutes' work on the graph, I lightened everything up, reduced the non-data ink, and added extra information with a moving average. I used only three colors on a white background, very light gray for the gridlines, a dark blue (businesslike, conservative) for the labelling and moving average, black for the data – the graph itself.

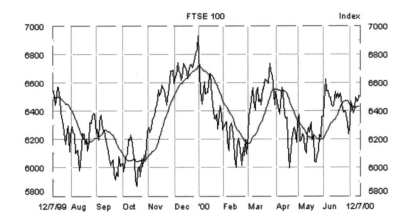

Think what a difference you can make to your site if you gave it a little time. Both of these could obviously be improved further; consider how you would do it.

Specials

A train timetable

Consider other graphical ways of presenting information, for example, a way of presenting a train timetable (from Tufte's *The Visual Display of Quantitative Information*).

The stations are listed along the side, and the times along the bottom. Tufte recommends removing or lightening the grid lines to enhance the information lines, representing the time at any given location.

The stations are placed on the y axis relative to their distance apart, so you can see from the slope of the graph, how quick a train is and you can see clearly which trains connect with any other train.

The whole graph could be made interactive, so the user could zoom in on any part of the graph. The interactive nature could be employed to purchase tickets by clicking on the from and to stations at the appropriate times on the graph.

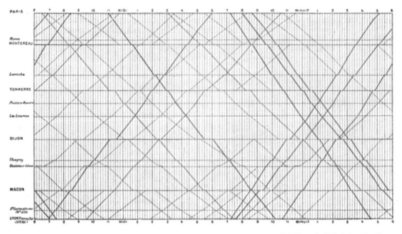

GRAPHICAL EXCELLENCE   31

E. J. Marey, *La Méthode Graphique* (Paris, 1885), p. 20. The method is attributed to the French engineer, Ibry.

Visual information

Tufte, in *Visual Explanations*, provides another excellent example by illustrating the development of storm clouds, which could also be made interactive.

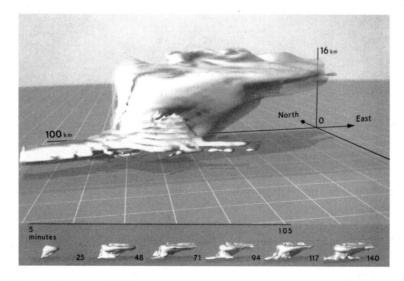

This works wonderfully.

Small can be big

In Amsterdam's Schiphol airport, they have used a small black outline of a fly, etched into the porcelain. It is noticed because of its position and clarity in a pristine background.

"It improves the aim," says Aad Kieboom, an economist who directs Schiphol's building expansion. "If a man sees a fly, he aims at it."

Kieboom's staff conducted fly-in-urinal trials and found that etchings reduce spillage by 80 percent, and the attendant cleaning costs.

"We will put flies in the urinal, yes. It gives a guy something to think about. That's the perfect example of process control. Fine, laugh at me; it works."

So, look around and read widely. Do look at Tufte's work, and notice other everyday things. Think about how you might apply the underlying principles in your designs.

ACTION AND INTERACTION

Action is what keeps the user involved and engaged in the site, providing it is easy and efficient. Action overlaps with navigation, but is more process or functional in nature.

There are a number of different aspects to action and interaction:

- navigation and transitions

- controlling the display of information

- computational functions.

All of these must be designed using the principles of the AUA model, and must be taken in context of the organization, the users in their role, their situation, their context of use, their objectives, their overall ideal process, and their overall definition of satisfaction.

To recap on the AUA model:

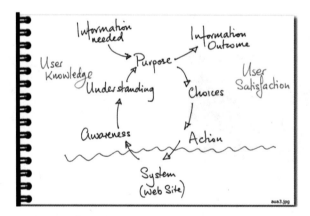

The model tells you what to think about and to consider how the display might indicate "state," action and change of state, at any level of "granularity," particularly:

- *user knowledge* – ensuring we recognize the user knowledge

- *awareness* – making sure the user is quickly aware of what is there

- *understanding* – making sure the "language" is easily understandable to the user

- *information needed* – providing all the information the user needs before an action

- *purpose* – ensuring that it supports the action or sub-action of the user

- *choices* – providing all the action choices the user may need clearly

- *chosen action* – making it clear the user has chosen an action and what is happening

- *awareness* – making sure the user is quickly aware of what the change is and what is there

- *understanding* – making sure it is clear when an action is complete the "language" is easily understandable

- *information outcome* – providing all the information the user needs after an action

- *satisfaction* – ensuring the outcome constitutes success of the action or sub-action in the user's terms and supports the next user action.

You can use the model formally, or, as you get to understand it better, you will find you do it quite quickly informally. With this as a backdrop, let's begin with navigation and navigation transitions. I will do it formally with the first example.

Navigation and transitions

What Farmaervas did

THE ORGANIZATION AND THE USERS

Farmaervas.com.br is a Brazilian site designed primarily for Spanish speakers in Brazil, but the site does have an English option also. It is concerned with selling natural health and beauty products. So, visitors to the site may well have time to spend and they will probably also have money to spend. They are likely to be using the site from home, or they may be using it from one of the many internet cafes in Latin America. They are likely to be reasonably familiar with the web. In parts of Latin America, the communication systems are slow.

OVERALL USER PURPOSE

The user wants to find and purchase a beauty cream.

USING THE AUA MODEL

Let's see how well it fits with the AUA model.

- **User knowledge.** The user brings knowledge of what they want and a background understanding of web interfaces.

- **Awareness.** It is clear this is a navigation only screen. There are some options available bottom right, which will probably be ignored at this stage. There is an animated encouragement to go to the children's products, which is quite a nice idea, but the sound effects are most distracting for the older clients.

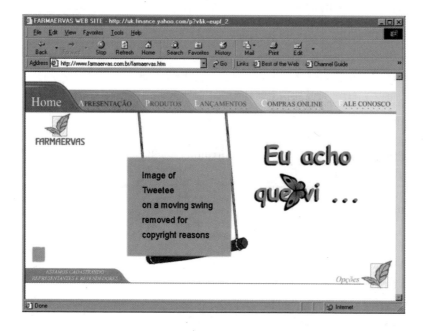

- **Understanding.** The language is clear, concise and understandable. The noises are less clearly understandable, which is a pity after such an interesting opening sequence.

- **Information needed.** Yes, that's all there, the user only needs to know what is available and what they can do.

- **Page purpose.** The user wants to find beauty products, and the page matches the purpose.

- **Choices.** Yes, it is clear the user must now choose one of the categories, and the one the user wants is presented here, in the right place and the right time, the tab metaphor is universally understood and each tab is clearly identifiable. The range of choices seems appropriate. It is clear how to choose an action; the metaphor draws and invites the user to mouse over the tabs. As you mouse over the tabs, you get visual and aural feedback. The visual feedback is good (see image), but the aural feedback is a poor rendition of what I assume is paper being pulled forward but actually sounds like an old cash register.

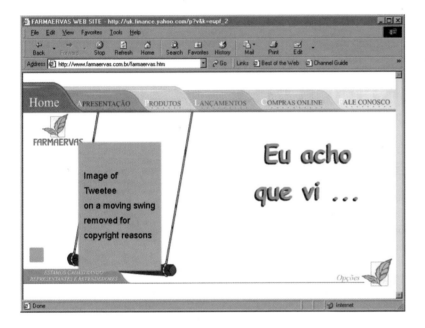

- **Chosen action.** It is clear something is happening – when you click on the tab, the page reverts rapidly to the "normal" screen and then rolls the page across with sound effects. It is disconcerting that the display changes so radically and quickly; it should be a smoother transition if it is going to be so dramatic.

- **Awareness.** The resultant screen is easy to recognize. The tab layout is curious. I would have expected the "Home" tab to be before the "Produtos" tab, since it is structurally "before" it. This way round it separates the "Produtos" from the "Produtos" categories.

- **Understanding.** It is clear this is a new navigation area, and that it is navigation only.

- **Information outcome.** The result is nearly what the user would
  expect after choosing "Produtos." It is clear the user must now
  choose a sub-category of product (from Hair, Body, Children, Make
  Up, Face or Medicaments) or we can go "Home."

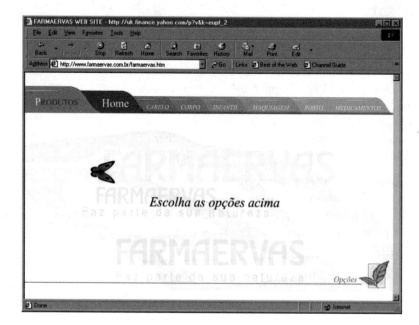

- **Satisfaction.** Partially, in that the user is one step closer to their objective. However, the user still has more work to do. If statistics were maintained about the product categories which were most popular, the outcome of this could be to make a transition to the most popular category. It would not cause the user any more "work" than not doing that. It might be the right location for them, and if it wasn't, it would advertise other products of Farmaervas.

OVERALL IMPRESSIONS OF THIS SITE

Good try, following interaction design principles quite well; but overloaded with gratuitous aural feedback, and actually the detail of the mood and feel (especially the overlaid sound) and user action processes is poorly thought out.

Controlling the display of information

What iii did

iii.co.uk is a website which shows financial information and news stories.

I have chosen a page that displays an equity index, and we'll see what we can do on that page. Our user purpose on this page is to examine what is happening on the FTSE 100 (it could just as easily be the NASDAQ or DJIA, etc).

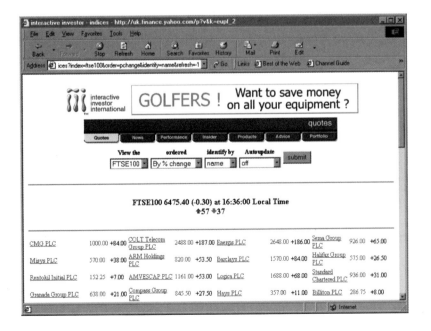

We are presented with this screen view. In essence, it is a good design. However, even on a good design there are many lessons to be learned.

We examine the page to become aware of what we can see on it. From our awareness, we understand that we have a number of areas of the screen.

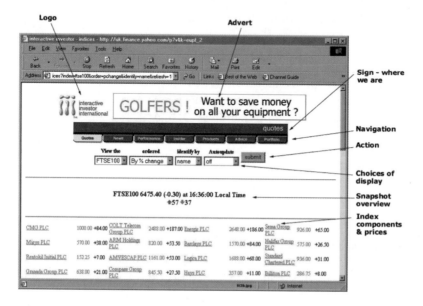

Nearly everything is easy to understand. This is a very clear presentation, with a couple of exceptions.

- The "Sign – where we are" which rather hides until we study the page in detail. On the other hand, it is appropriately close to the navigation bar and is actually irrelevant since we know this already by the light-blue tab button.

- The display layout of the index components and prices is not as clear as it could be because of the proximity of the columns.

We have a number of choices of how we control the display of information, indicated by "drop down" boxes.

- View the [FTSE 100]

- ordered [By % change]

- identify by [name]

- Auto update [off].

As we can see, the headings of the choices are mixed leading letter upper case or lower case.

> **Lesson: be consistent, unless you are trying to draw attention to something – then create a discord.**

Some questions raised in interaction design

Let's take the choices the user has of:

- ordered [By % change]

- identify by [name]

The first has the "By" in the box and it has a leading capital letter, the second has the "by" as the heading and is all lower case. This is another inconsistency perhaps?

We might question why this is; perhaps the "ordered" box has some option in it which is not "By" something? However, the user cannot tell without clicking on the drop down, so to find out they must use an extra mouse click. It might not sound like much, but it is when taken in conjunction with other things.

> **Lesson: Don't raise questions for no reason, unless there is absolutely no way to design it any other way.**

> **Lesson: Don't put a question in the user's mind, without making it easy to answer. Any "question" on the screen must provide an easy way for the user to find an answer.**

> **Lesson: Aim to reduce user effort to the minimum.**

Clicking on the "ordered" drop down produces the following figure:

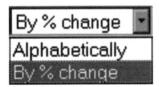

We find there is a reason for the "By," and we note the options all have a leading capital. Also the default option is second in the list. And, since there are only two choices, why has this been presented in a drop down box? This could have been presented as a radio button group.

ordered
◉ by % change
○ alphabetically

This would solve all the problems. It would reduce the awareness, understanding, action cycles the user would have to do! (You could do an AUA analysis yourself as an exercise.)

Using radios would:

- eliminate an uncertainty, not raise any questions – both choices would be immediately obvious.

- place the default option first, and that could be pre-selected.

- reduce the user effort from "see, wonder what is under it, move mouse, click, move mouse, click" to "see, move mouse, click." Since any user action is normally preceded by a "see, move mouse" we have reduced the subsequent actions from 3 to 1.

- remove the possibility of the user performing a wasted action.

> **Lesson: Reduce user effort – physical and mental – whenever you can.**

> **Lesson: If there are fewer than four to six items in the list, consider using radio buttons.**

Now, what are the choices under the headings of "View the," "identify by" and "Auto update"? First, "View the." Clicking on the drop down produces the following options (see top of page 163). The same issues discussed above are raised. Perhaps we could use radio buttons for this also, or we may have plans to add other indexes to the list, which may prevent us from doing this. On the other hand we may not be planning to extend it – it rather depends upon the scope and the brief.

Lesson: If the designers are not clear about the organization's future visions, they may be forced to design poor interactions.

It also depends upon the target audience and their use scenarios. If the target audience will be interested in finding out what is going on in the USA with high tech stocks, they will want to view the NASDAQ easily.

Lesson: If you don't know who your users are, and you don't know what they want, you can't create a highly useable design.

Next, "identify by." Clicking on the drop down produces the options shown below. Once again the same issues are raised, this doesn't seem likely to be extended. It would be much better to have two radio buttons. Also, they have been inconsistent, in that this time, the options are not preceded by a capital.

Then, "Auto update." Clicking on the drop down produces the options shown on page 164. Once again the same issues are raised, we are offering five choices, and this may not be well handled by radio buttons – it's a close call.

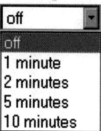

Also, other questions (among others) for the design team include the following.

- Why are we providing these options – what is the use?

- Why have we chosen these time delays?

- What is the target audience's natural preferences?

- What kind of internet connections do they have?

If most of the users are connected online for extensive periods of time, the auto update facility is potentially useful. If they are, what other activities will they be carrying out? How will the auto update be useful to them? Will they want the information in a separate window? Would they prefer a ticker tape continually scrolling updated prices for the index? Would they want to be able to select a subset of the index to view? Would they like to see the index value changing? How often do they typically want updates? Do they want alarms when an index or an equity moves up beyond a value or down below a value?

> **Lesson (repeat): If you don't know who your users are, and you don't know what they want, you can't create a highly useable design.**

> **Lesson: If you don't know where your users access the site from, you can't decide what facilities to provide them.**

Computational functions

What E-Loan did on a prototype

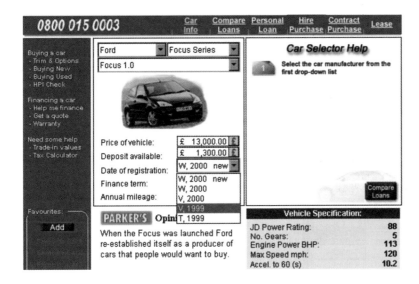

On an early version of its website, E-Loan used a pull-down list for the user to select the "date of registration." In this context it works well, and radios are not an option. On selecting the registration date, the user is presented with the following screen.

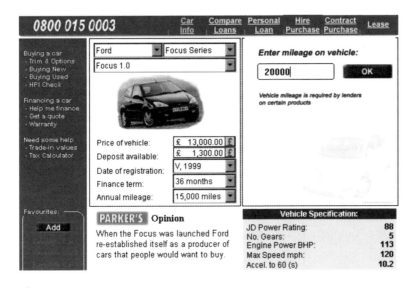

This allows you to enter the mileage of this older car, which while the entry box is a long way away from the last action, it is clearly noticed, and the cursor is sitting in the entry text field so the user does not have to move the mouse. On OK, or the enter key the user is then presented with the following screen. All the users I evaluated then pressed on the button "compare loans" and none noticed that the price of the vehicle had changed.

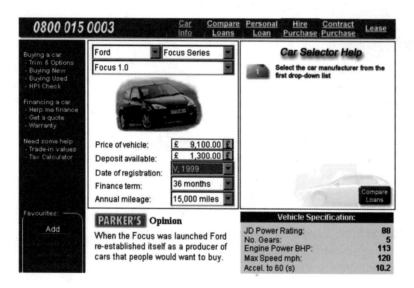

Here is a real cause and effect problem. No one noticed the change to the value. When one user noticed the price was "wrong," some 5–10 minutes later, he began to doubt the correctness of the system. "I know it was a £13,000 car, and it's changed..., perhaps it's not right, maybe I should call to check." The saving grace is that a phone number had been very prominently placed so the user felt comfortable about doing that.

This summarizes what happened. The user changes the date of registration (the age of the car), enters the mileage of the vehicle they are buying, presses OK. The system responds by looking up a database of prices of this model for this mileage and age and puts the book value price in the "Price of Vehicle" box and changes the bigger part of the display so the "Compare Loans" button is prominent. The user doesn't notice the price change (and there is no signposting that would happen) and does notice the "Compare Loans" button. They are forced

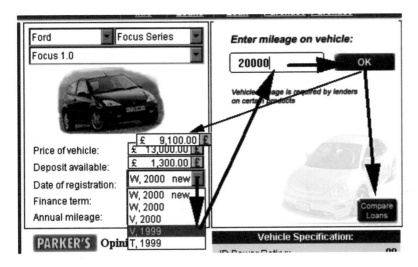

by the dynamic to press this button (which is what they should do next) but they have totally missed a small but very important part of the interaction.

How would you solve the problem?

Specials – buttons, mouseovers and animation

Think about the many different ways of providing "special" devices, - such as buttons, a date entry system, etc.

What PriceWaterhouseCoopers did

PriceWaterhouseCoopers have clear and obvious buttons, with a good, three-dimensional look to them. This is the way to do buttons.

But, then they are let down, because the depressed state on the "About Us" button color tone is not distinct enough, as we saw in the section on navigation earlier in this chapter.

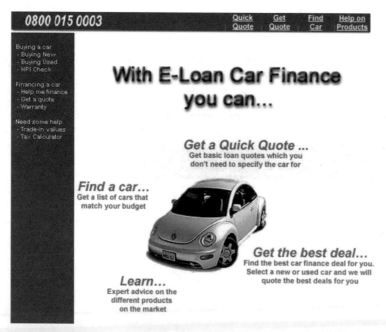

And again, while they put mouseovers on the buttons to flash up the text below, which in itself is good, it is a little distance from the action.

Try and make the cause and effect relate as closely as possible. So, while in this case it works, if the distances are larger and the effect is smaller, the relationship is not obvious. It's like pushing the handle on a coffee cup and have the spoon on the kitchen worktop move. As a down side to these embellished graphics, the download time was very slow on their site.

Another example of this follows, but here, even though the cause and effect are some distance apart, in fact it still works.

What E-Loan did on a prototype

When you mouseover "get quote," (previous page) the car's headlights light up and the little silver "turn over" appears next to the text.

This is very tidily done, but again there are lessons to learn. First, the distance between cause and effect is a long way away, and it still works. Why? Because the headlights on the car light up, and adds to the draw of the user's eyes away from the action. But the intention is that the blue text on the main part of the screen gives extra description about the moused over heading – and the text heading is completely different from the menu button, so it is hard for the user to reconcile the difference.

Lesson: Be consistent.

Also, the moused over menu item has not changed sufficiently (can you tell the difference?). If you are going to do it, make it obvious – but also remain sensible about it.

The other problem is the buttons themselves, not so much the ones at the top of the screen – which are not very buttony, but a good enough metaphor that they work for all this – but the ones all over the main display that you cannot see. All the blue text areas are in fact buttons, but no user under useability trials ever used them.

Other buttons

This is the magic text.

Here's a button pair done on the webmonkey site, one up, the other down. It works as a mouse over, but the point is that there is a clear relationship between them, and they are very buttony, they work fast, and they add extra information when moused over.

> **Make it buttony, and employ mouseovers to give confirmatory feedback.**

> **Go for creative ways of grabbing attention, they do not have to be large things.**

Date entry

There are many ways of entering a date. Consider them, apply the AUA model to each one and figure out which is best for your users in your users' context of use.

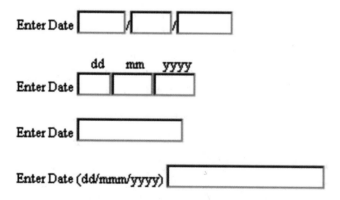

With dates on a white background, it is less clear where the visual focus should be. Format instructions are useful if the date is going to be validated, but check whether, in your use situation, it needs to be. Free text can be the fastest for the user to enter.

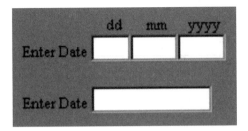

A colored background makes the entry fields more obvious, but consider making it more subtle than this, and consider the labelling, the font size and the need for labels – they could be much tidier – think Tufte. But bear in mind line speed if graphics are going to be used.

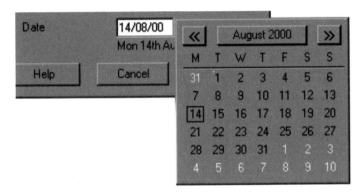

This is quite good, providing you don't want a date too far from the current date, otherwise the scrolling through the months is tedious.

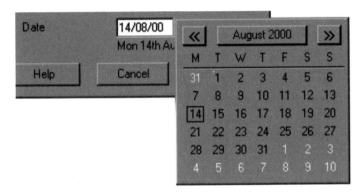

Palm™ Desktop Software

I also like the Palm™ Desktop Software.

Test out the various options on your representative users. Put them into prototypes, in the appropriate places in the action process and page layout, ensuring they are tested in the context of the user's activities. Then standardize on them throughout, so whenever the user needs to enter a date, they will have the same device to do it with.

The point

Use the AUA model. Make sure all aspects of user effort – physical, mental thought, visual searching, memory usage, process steps – are reduced to the minimum, unless you are trying to create a feeling of something that takes effort. Use your design thinking creatively on this, and ask about everything "how can I reduce the user effort?"

- *Physical* – mouse movement, scrolling, clicks – screen design, interaction design.

- *Mental thought* – clarity of understanding of language and computation, consistency across screens of images and words. Screen design and information for user action.

- *Memory usage* – bringing information forward – recall rather than memory, the goldfish user principle.

- *Visual searching* – don't say press "update" and have the   update button somewhere else on the display – think about screen design.

- *Screen transitioning and process* – process steps, i.e. 1,2,3 rather than 1,2,3,4,5,6.

Make sure that any action can be associated with the outcome of the action; make the cause and effect cycle clearly and identifiably visible.

Make sure areas of action, interaction and navigation are clearly and identifiably different from areas of "passive" information. Also, make sure action, interaction and navigation are clearly and identifiably different from each other. I saw on the Blackwell's site we were looking at earlier, that they used the same style of button to link to a new page as they used to jump to an anchor point within the page – very confusing.

Make sure the language – visual, textual and aural – is consistent across your site, and follows genre norms.

Make sure all areas where the user can enter information are clearly identified, appropriately labelled and easy to use.

REALIZATION — MAKING IT WORK

From what's on a page to the visual design

Now let's look at how the work we did on discovery and designing the system is brought forward into a visual interactive design.

What Amazon did

Here is what Amazon did for the small piece we looked at in What's on a Page – Check Out Sign In, Address and Shipping. Take some time to study them and consider what works and what doesn't.

First, the Sign In.

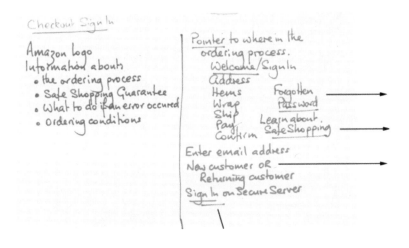

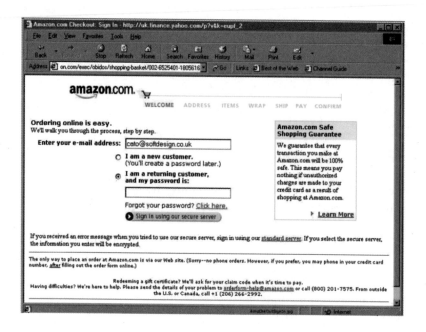

Now the address

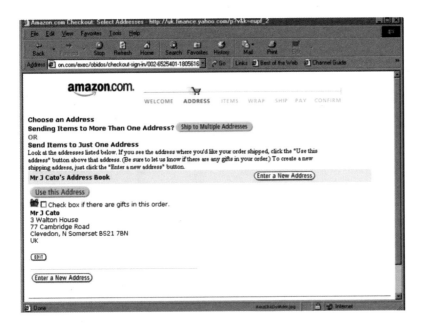

Then the
shipping

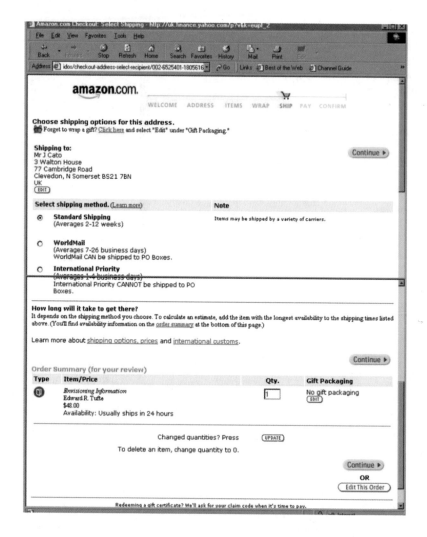

EXAMINE AN EQUITY

CASE
STUDY

The whole point of the design is to support the user's desired action in a way that is useful, effective, efficient and satisfying. It must respect their skills and abilities, be of sufficiently good presentation and be easily learnable.
   Let's revisit the user's ideal process.

- Enter the equity name or ticker symbol and search for the current price and the five-year graph history, applying 10, 40 and 105 day moving averages to the graph. Zoom in on the graph for various lengths of time and periods.

Logical view

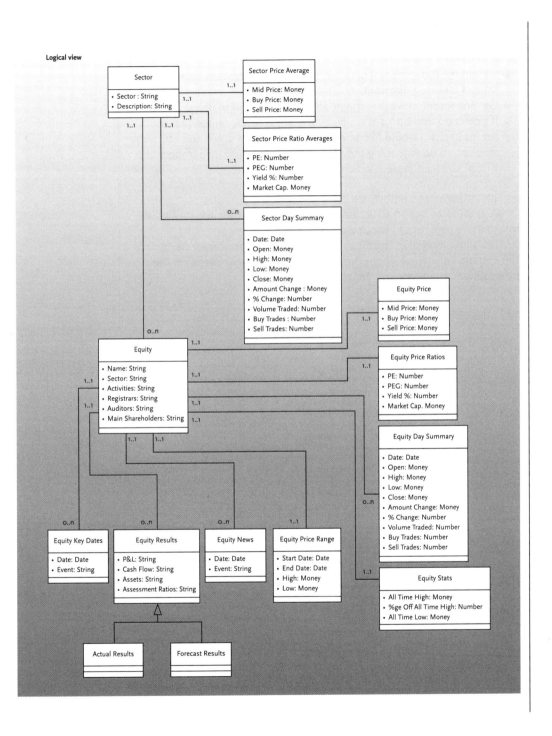

- Compare the graphs with the equivalent graphs for the industry sector, and compare the industry sector graphs with the equivalent graphs for FTSE and the DJIA.
- Obtain the fundamental data for the equity and test the various ratios I feel are important.
- Get any recent news that might affect my decision making.
- If I can't do these processes quickly and efficiently online (which seems likely), I would like to do them off-line in a quick and efficient manner, so downloading the data in a suitable format to import into a local software system which supports the above.

This is therefore what we are aiming to achieve.

We created an action structure based on this and then we studied the information objects and created a model.

This all took place in the discovery stage. After that, during designing the system, I sketched what I might want on the pages, based on the information structures and the action structures.

Then I decided the core action was "examine an equity" and it would be the focus of the private investor activity. So I went into more detail for "What's on a page" for this action.

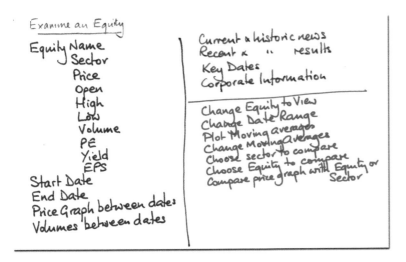

Now, we need the visuals to make it real.

We need draft screen designs for each action. In this case we are focussing on one action. The screens do not need to be particularly good at this stage, just good enough to get a feel for what we *might* do.

The most important starting point of "examine an equity" is the dynamic equity price because it is the focus of much user action. We consider what we want based on the "examine an equity" use scenario. I made a notebook sketch, which began to show all the components we need on this screen. It is only important at this stage that you, the designer, know what all the scribbles mean.

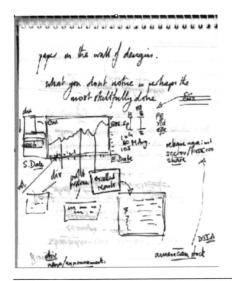

Now to develop other aspects of the action. We need to take account of how the user will interact with this focal point to examine the equity in more detail and make sure the appropriate handles are provided. We know from the discovery stage that the designs must be made to work for 800×600 resolution, and we know that most of our audience will be using Internet Explorer. To make it easier for me to explore the designs, I created a draft screen template.

I like to work with sketches, though you can work with text descriptors only for the first pass through. Some see sketching as premature, and adversely influences the design because if you show it to users, they tend to discuss the layout and position rather than the structure and navigation. Others feel that by the second iteration it helps to get a visual for how it may come out. I think it is helpful to start getting a visual at this time, but I will stay with low quality sketches.

Visual design scenarios

Don't assume your first design thoughts are right. Consider ways of getting more than one design in the first few passes. With a group of four people, you could split into two teams of two and develop two initial design scenarios, and then merge the good ideas from both. Or you could have four " teams." Or you could imagine you were coming at it from another discipline: "What if I was designing the system from a mind set of a film director, or a seamstress, or an architect, or a landscape gardener, or a racing driver?" It helps to do this before you become too fixed in your ways. For me, thinking of it from a racing driver perspective of information and control, reinforced my idea of a focal console.

EXAMINE AN EQUITY — SECOND SKETCH

Building on the action structure, I came out with the following sketch and some of other displays. I tested it out with users (iteration 1) to understand how they might see it. I then received their feedback and created a new design.

CASE
STUDY

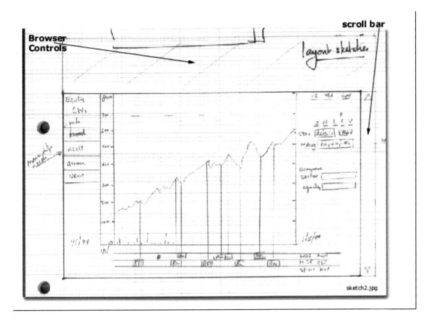

EXAMINE AN EQUITY — THIRD "SKETCH"

The new design, still not polished, but now implemented as a prototype in HTML.

Links to other pages were implemented, and the other pages had simple sketches on them to give the user an idea of what they would get. The detail interactivity was not implemented, after all this is still only the "second" version.

Discussion and assessment

Next, I carried out a testing with users trial on it and make summarizing comments based on the ideal process and the use.

CASE
STUDY

SUPPORTING THE USER'S ACTIONS
Enter the equity name or ticker symbol and search for the current price and the five-year graph history, applying 10-, 40- and 105-day moving averages to the graph. Zoom in on the graph for various lengths of time and periods.

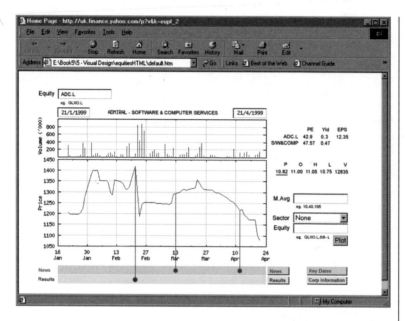

The user was able to enter the equity name or ticker symbol on the same screen, and can see and adjust the date ranges, as well as applying moving averages of his choice. However, the user was not always clear about how to enter the ticker symbol.

Compare the graphs with the equivalent graphs for industry sector, and compare the industry sector graphs with the equivalent graphs for FTSE index sector.

The user was able to specify and see other graphs, such as other companies in the sector, the sector graph and information, or the FTSE index overlaid on top of the equity graph for comparison purposes.

Obtain the fundamental data for the equity and test the various ratios I feel are important.

The user was able to obtain the fundamental data (Results), and apply or examine any financial ratios. He could do this by clicking on the button [Results] or the pointer to get a specific date's information.

> Get any recent news that might affect my decision making.

The user was able to obtain any recent news, and additionally see graphically when those events took place. As with the results, he could also do this by clicking on the pointer to the news event. He liked this a lot. He also liked being able to get the key dates quickly.

> If I can't do these processes quickly and efficiently online (which seems likely), I would like to do them off-line in a quick and efficient manner, so downloading the data in a suitable format to import into a local software system which supports the above.

The user found it was efficient to get the information, and did not need a way of downloading the information for off-line assessment, since it was easy to just print the screen.

> YOUR IDEAL OUTCOME — SATISFACTION
> All the above information on the chosen equity examined against my criteria within 5–10 minutes.

The user found the above system, easy and quick to use and met his needs.

> IDEAS ARISING
> Since the user could now see the information more fully, he asked if it might be possible to provide functionality for visualizing trends and applying stop-loss criteria.

There is still plenty of screen space to do this and the functionality could easily be added.

- *The values are clustered together.* The user wants to see similar information together. Here the PE, Yld and EPS are presented together and compared with the shares sector values. The price information is collected together and headed by commonly used single letters Price, Open, High, Low, Volume. If the market is closed the Price becomes the Close price.
- *The available screen space is more fully utilized.* By concentrating on what the user wants, and tightening the visual design, we are able to show more information (including adding the daily volumes data) without making the user scroll and provide a far greater range of investigative functionality without overloading the user's short-term memory. Quick understanding and appreciation is well supported.
- *Use of color.* The use of colors is subtle and clean. Both News dates and Results dates are identified on the graph and are color-coded appropriately – salmon (a reddish color) for unusual news or key dates, and blue for corporate information such as results and other information.
- *Use of data ink.* Everything on the display is useful and relevant for the user.

This works well because the graphic presentation is clear, and it recognizes the user's needs appropriately.

WHAT WAS WRONG WITH THIS DESIGN?
- The graphic design needs improving. While moderately good, it will need the polish a professional graphic designer can give it. Perhaps not the next iteration but towards the final iteration, say 5 or 6.
- The user cannot define or display their own financial assessment ratios. It would be good to provide facilities for the user to do this.
- The user cannot examine the sector details directly.
- It would be good to be able to see the day's variation and open and close figures on the graph if examining smaller periods of time.
- There was some difficulty for the user when entering other equities to graph against. We need to find more clear or easier ways for them to do this, it is not intuitive enough yet.

What next?

So far, the bulk of the time in developing this has been in the discovery stage and involving representative users to get design right.

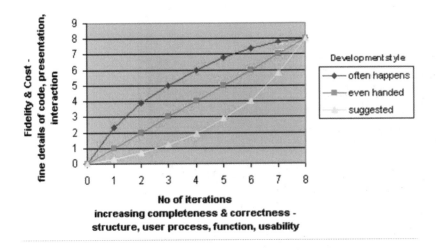

We are at the level of iteration 2 on the graph. The development costs are low so far, from here on we are gaining confidence we have a good design and are willing to put more of the budget against the work. Continue to apply the principles I have been describing in the book, deal with the issues and take on the user's ideas, and generate the third version.

A comparison example

Just to give you some idea of what is really out there, and this is not unusual – there are many sites in different business areas which are as bad. Opposite is a live site, which had been live, and like this, more or less, for at least a year. This screen shot was taken in August 2000. It should be noted the correctness and quality of the information on this site is excellent. However, it doesn't work well because it does not recognize the user's needs appropriately, and the graphic presentation is unclear.

SUPPORTING THE USER'S ACTIONS
Enter the equity name or ticker symbol and search for the current price and the five-year graph history, applying 10-, 40- and 105-day moving averages to the graph. Zoom in on the graph for various lengths of time and periods.

The user was able to enter the equity ticker symbol – though this cannot be seen on this screen, or even this page, and so cannot be used without scrolling and using the menu or the back button to examine other equities. The user cannot see or adjust the date ranges, nor can they apply or see moving averages though he thought it might be possible behind the interactive charting button.

Compare the graphs with the equivalent graphs for the industry sector, and compare the industry sector graphs with the equivalent graphs for FTSE sector.

The user was unable to specify or see other graphs, such as other companies in the sector, the sector graph and information, or the FTSE, though he thought it might be possible behind the interactive charting button. When he tried it, he found he had lost the volume data and the price, PE and so on only the graph was displayed. The display did not make it clear what sector this equity was in. When the user tried clicking on the sector button (of the top of the screen) they got a list of sectors, not details of the sector this equity was in.

> Obtain the fundamental data for the equity and test the various ratios I feel are important.

The user was unable to obtain the fundamental data, without scrolling back up, picking the fundamentals menu item from 18 choices, and going to another page. It was not possible to apply his own ratios.

> Get any recent news that might affect my decision making.

The user could get recent news, but could not find news related to events on the graph.

> If I can't do these processes quickly and efficiently online (which seems likely), I would like to do them off-line in a quick and efficient manner, so downloading the data in suitable format to import into a local software system which supports the above.

The user found it was not efficient to get the information, and could find no way of downloading the information for off-line assessment.

> YOUR IDEAL OUTCOME — SATISFACTION
> All the above information on the chosen equity examined against my criteria within 5–10 minutes.

The user found the above system, while in principle and practice holding all the information he needed, could not meet his needs.

Visual design issues

- *The values are spread all over the display.* The user wants to see similar information together; price information is spread along the top row under very dominant headings and also along the right-hand side. There appears to be little appreciation of modelling the user's information needs.

- *The available screen space is not fully utilized.* Approximately 60 percent of the screen is utilized to show 17 values in a shotgun display, while the user cannot see the graph date range, or any of the top of screen or bottom of screen information. Scrolling would lose this information and so cause the user to have to continually scroll up and down (or have an unusually excellent short-term memory). Quick understanding and appreciation is not well supported.

- *Use of color.* The use of colors is unsubtle and feels also rather shotgun in effect. The color keys for the data are inconsistent; volumes, time and trade type are all the same color, and are not semantically the same things.

- *Summary.* This is an excellent demonstration of what Edward Tufte would consider ChartJunk. (Sorry, Market-Eye.)

Tips on the process of design and realization

- Be clear what you want, and what you don't want.

- Think about what is the use, who, how, why, when, and when you have decided, stick to it, don't add new pieces willy nilly.

- Don't defer thinking about the whole thing, for example, pergola floor means more height, etc.

- Stay present and in the moment, in other words, when I eat I eat.

- Time to reflect, to incubate is absolutely necessary, even during the building.

- Check out what others have done and what works, what doesn't.

- Create a design spec that is sufficient for the purpose. Remember to bear in mind who will use it and how they will use it.

- Make sure you communicate well in writing, so it can be right, and maintained.

- It pays to know the procedure, so you don't have to think what to do next, and so you can get on with doing it. Practice the process.

- Don't believe you know what you are trying to do, make sure.

- Procrastination and delay are the root of all evil.

- Plan, plan, plan.

- Plan your materials and tools up front, so they don't cause delays on the critical path. Know your tools. Know your materials.

- Let the tool do the job, don't force it. Relax, with soaking in it and practice, you will get better and faster. You will get to know the tools and the medium and the task.

- If the tool won't do the job easily, you're either using it wrong (not enough practice), or it is the wrong tool.

- Be clear about consistency in your materials and tools.

- Practice your skills. If you haven't done it before, give yourself time to practice.

- Identify and deal with high risk things first – prove them out.

- Create the right working space.

- Organize your tools, equipment and materials so you can work efficiently.

- Know your craftsmen's skills and failings.

- Share work so things can go on in parallel.

- Watch the team management – a sense of success, contribution and being valued is vital. Work out what work each person should do to contribute best and feel valued most.

- Set yourself realistic "fit for purpose" quality constraints and review these from time to time.

- Get your measurements right. Measure before and during. Measure twice and cut once. Check things as you go along, make sure you are on target.

- Watch out for the interfaces with other things, think whether you want the join to show or not.

- Less is more, sometimes the simplicity pays off in more ways than you expect and will reduce complexity. As in a house less beams can result in a simpler roof.

- Know what items, if removed will make the whole system fall over, what keeps what in balance and what has to be done in what order – know the interdependencies. Get your structure right.

- Know the problems you might encounter and learn what they are from the experts and others who have gone before you. The foundations, structure and integrity are vital.

- Do things in the right order – you can't tell exactly what you need to do next until you've done something else. For example, if you are squaring the timber, then think through consequences.

- Make sure you have excellent foundations. Recognize it takes time, don't try and rush it, or you will slow the procedure. Get the plan and the foundations right; know the right order of doing things.

- Make sure it will stand the test of time.

- Be aware of the vogue and consciously choose to follow or not.

6 | USE

You can't be sure how well the design works until it is used and you get some measure of your success. So, we get to the third crucial part of the design process – the use.

Many companies fail to test with users, or do anything else to evaluate useability prior to system delivery. Instead they rely on negative feedback from customers after the event, after the launch. A customer on a website has so much choice. They are discretionary users who can hop just as easily to another website. Once lost, it is likely that they will not return. They won't take any of their time to comment on why they haven't used the site. The only sign you have is from the statistics of the number of people who visited the site and then did nothing on it. By then, it is too late.

The techniques that will help you most are as follows.

- Useability testing with users:
  - think aloud
  - co-participation
  - think aloud co-participation
  - remote use.

- Heuristic evaluation.

- AUA evaluation.

When to test

I strongly advocate testing from the very earliest stages of prototype delivery through to the end of development. The earliest prototypes may be paper based, subsequent ones may be implemented in quick HTML mockups, later ones may have the full functionality including database access and real time feeds. It is much much better for useability specialists to be involved with the project, to plan, guide and do user-centered design and useability testing, from the very beginning – from the earliest discovery stages.

The sanction trap

I have often been asked by team managers to carry out a useability evaluation of their product just before it is completed. This is "the sanction trap": *"Let's just run a useability trial to prove we have it right; our CEO wants to know it has passed useability, let's get a useability expert to sanction it."* Unfortunately, if useability testing hasn't been done before, the most likely outcome is all kinds of useability surprises which the team will not have time to fix and the politics can be horrendous to manage.

So, beware – if you test just before rollout, be sure the management team have planned in the time for the changes, or they are prepared to manage the consequences.

Information required for useability evaluation

Before you start a useability evaluation, you need to know:

- business purpose

- intended outcome of the system for the organization and for the user

- scope

- scope under trial

- development state of the system

- what stage of delivery, early/late

- what you want to gain from the trial

- target audience.

What to test

Test what you have, iteration by iteration. Early in the design, perhaps when you have little really built other than a low fidelity system (even a paper prototype), you may want to test out only that – concentrating on the scope, structure, user process, function and useability. You will gain a good understanding about whether it is sufficient to support the activities of the target audience and whether the language you are using to communicate is appropriate and understandable for them. If you have done your discovery work well, you should have few surprises by the time you get to this stage.

Later, you may want to concentrate on specific areas of user activity. Later still, as the site becomes more complete, you will want to test out the whole user experience – high fidelity with all the code, graphics and details highly refined – from start to end of a use scenario.

As I said earlier, a low fidelity prototype can even be better than high fidelity for initial user testing and has the added benefit of less resistance to making the changes indicated by the evaluation. However, if you are carring out user testing late, on an existing system which has been designed with little thought to user-centered design, the design and development team could get the shock of their lives.

Useability testing with users

Testing with representative users throughout the development is the only real way of finding out the real issues of useability before going live. Useability is a combination of the site's usefulness, effectiveness, efficiency, satisfaction, respect for the user, presentation and learnability. In testing with users, I have seen the obvious made obvious; except until it was tested with users, no one on the design team thought it was obvious. For example, for one web page, we created a multimedia touchscreen system and used miniature

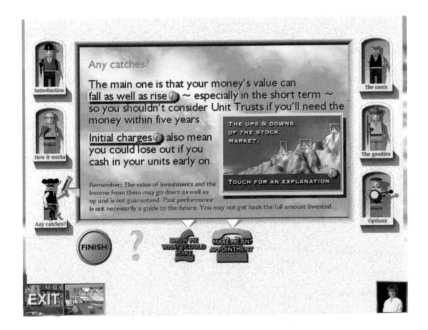

thumbnail images at the bottom left of the screen as a picture strip showing where the user had been, so they could touch on any miniature image to get to anywhere they had been before or to exit. If there was no interaction from the user for a period of time (20 seconds) a video playback assistant popped up from the bottom right to remind the user "if you have any difficulty in knowing what to do, just use the thumbnails."

One user was having trouble getting the system to respond. The touchscreen was not recognizing her finger touches on the screen, though in fact she knew clearly what she wanted to do and was doing. When this message came up, she reversed her hand and literally touched the screen with her thumbnail. Because the touchscreen responded to the electrostatics from the finger (none from a fingernail) this just made the situation worse.

This highlighted how much – despite our conscious efforts to use the user's language – the language of design made its way into the interface as a useability problem.

Cost benefit

While I am a practicing pragmatist, I can be grateful to people like Jakob Nielsen for producing results to support my intuition and experience, and also to give me pointers for further improvements in what I do. Nielsen and Landauer produced a model based on their studies and experience, the cost-benefit trade-off curve for a "typical" project, varying

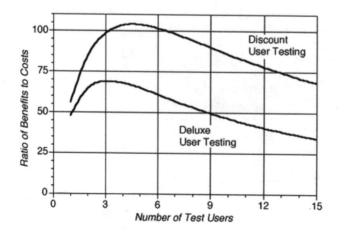

the number of test users, using the model and average parameters described by Nielsen and Landauer (1993). The curve shows the ratio of benefits to costs, that is, how many times the benefits are larger than the costs. For example, a benefit-to-cost ratio of 50 might correspond to costs of $10,000 and benefits of $500,000.

The techniques described below are what I do, those I find most useful and cost effective. They fit broadly into what Nielsen describes as Discount User Testing.

The think aloud technique

The first people I came across who were investigating and writing about this were Peter Wright and Andrew Monk at York University in the early 1990s. I spent some time talking to them about this and other areas of their research when at HCI conferences. They are not very well known outside of UK useability circles, but their work formed the foundation, for me, of the exploration and use of this cost-effective technique with users. I have been using these principles since about 1991 using small numbers for test sessions, and it has been a most insightful tool.

The breakthrough in doing this effectively came from Nielsen's research and observation that small numbers of users carrying out purposeful activities on a system gives high quality and cost-effective results. It bore out and reinforced my opinion, which I had no statistical evidence to support at the time.

The idea is for a representative sample of users to use the system and to collect information about their experience of use while they think aloud. You will need six users. The first four or five will give you most of what you need to know on any given iteration, and the sixth confirms. If you are really uncertain, or you expect some no shows, go for eight users.

The technique is effective to test early prototypes through to delivered systems.

RECRUITING USERS

First, you can't recruit just anybody – you must have a representative sample of users. If you have been working through the stages of this book, you will have a complete set of user profiles and user descriptions. If so, your representative sample will be easy to define. If you have an existing website which you are trying to improve, it may be this has not been done, and you will need to do all the discovery work concerned with users and user profiles before you can start.

Select which area of the site you are testing and recruit users from the target set that are expected to use these areas of activity. For

observed testing trials, you need to carry out about six individual test
sessions with users to obtain meaningful and useful results. Recruit six
users for think aloud tests, and twelve for co-participation.

For unobserved testing, more participants will be needed, since the
volume, quality and reliability of information from remotes is
considerably less. Aim for 20–30 for remote tests and hope for the
best. If you can't get that many, you will have to settle for less.

Remember, this is generally not a one-shot experience – you will be
iterating the design to the release quality. From the first trial sessions
to the last you may have to carry out up to eight or so iterations. These
sessions must be clearly focussed, objective, fast and cost-effective.

Users can be recruited by putting messages on appropriate bulletin
boards, or a recruitment agency could be appointed to do this for you.

SCREENING PARTICIPANT USERS
You will need to carry out careful screening to ensure the participants
come close enough to your user profiles to make it meaningful. So, you
need to have a good idea which of the attributes on your person profiles
are the most important and critical. The most important things to do
are as follows.

- Make sure the user's usage profile matches the target audience for
  the design.

- Make sure the user is representative of the kind of people who
  would use the system.

- Make sure the user is currently actively interested in the objective
  of the site and actively being tested.

When a person is an existing user, they already have a relationship
with the company and with the system. This may affect the way they
use the site and the prejudices they may have, both positive and
negative. When carrying out a trial, try to get a balance of existing
customers and new users. Base it on the percentages of existing and
new users you are targetting in your business objectives. Make sure the
expectations of existing users for the outcome of the trials are set
realistically. If you have a customer support or customer feedback
system in operation, that can be a source of recruitment. While some
argue that you should not use disgruntled users in a useability trial,
don't shy away from using unhappy customers, they can be a source of
much learning.

)CEDURE

. *Booking.* Make sure the users for the trials are booked in advance (perhaps a week or two). Make sure the user participants are clear about what they need to do beforehand (if anything). Tell them where they are coming to, what they might expect to be doing in general terms, what time they will need to arrive, and how much time they will need to put aside. Tell them what rewards they will get for helping out, and what is expected of them. You want to be open and honest so there are few surprises and you need to make reasonably sure they have willingly committed to being there.

2. *Pre-briefing the users.* Let them know beforehand what they can expect to happen during the trial. Make sure you advise them of the following.

   ● We are testing the design of the website, and we think you are the kind of person who would be interested in this site and can provide us with useful information by carrying out a test of the site.

   ● The purpose of the website is XXXX, and we understand you have a current active interest in XXXX. We would like you to come with the intention of using the site in some way that you feel will be useful to you. If you have a number of things you would find useful, please consider which are of primary importance to you and which you would like to be able to do but feel they are more for the future.

   ● We will be learning how the site is good and how it is bad and any other opinions you have. We are collecting information from a number of selected people. Everything you say is very important to us, but we cannot guarantee that everything you say will be acted on.

   ● Anything you say will be treated in strict confidence. Anything you see during the trial is strictly confidential to the company.

3. *The test location.* This is important both logistically and for usefulness. Logistically, if you want users who come from a particular part of the country, carry out the trial in their area. For example, people from one area may have a different propensity over those in another area towards entering personal information on the web. You may need to test this out with people from different geographic locations. If your system includes an interactive interview, you may have to structure it differently to make best use of the communication opportunity.

4. *The use context.* It is important that the test is carried out in a "use context" which is as close to the normal reality as possible.

You will learn far more if you can.

If the context is not recreated, some issues will not surface during the trials. For example, if the user is normally surrounded by reference material they do not have present at the trial, then they cannot carry out the trial in a similar way. So, entering information may not be carried out in a realistic manner, and that may fail to show up a useability problem. If they are usually surrounded by other people, then they need to be surrounded by a representative group of people; otherwise you will not get the interruption, interactions with people, distractions and support.

If their workspace is usually constrained, make it constrained, and make sure the computer system they use is set to be as good a match to theirs as you can.

5. *Who should be involved?* I generally find it is best to carry this out one on one. This reduces the imbalance of "power" – there is just the user and you. It makes for a more even, trusting and useful environment to get information.

If there are two of you running the test, make sure you both are very calm, supportive and sensitive to the user's needs. It can sometimes be helpful if the second person present is a designer, because they will see any problems first hand. But only do this if they know how to listen and accept criticism. Don't let the defensive type in the room – I have seen designers twitch with desire to explain to users what to do, and even jump in and do it.

Make sure the user is relaxed and at ease. If possible, avoid having a formal testing lab. Users cannot behave naturally in such artificial, film set environments. Make the session informal and as natural as possible. Make sure that the guiding principle in your mind is "the user is always right" – all their feelings, opinions and needs have just validity and should be respected.

6. *The start of the test.* Put participants at ease – welcome them in an open, friendly and professional way. Talk about things that may be on their minds, such as their journey, whether they would like refreshments, and find out if they have any concerns or needs before you start, such as children at home, work commitments, when they have to leave by, etc.

Assure them that everything they say and do is in confidence, and will not be identified to them unless they expressly want to be identified. You might be surprised, but some long-term customers of organizations, if they have experienced not being heard, want the CEO to know what they are thinking and who said it.

Tell them what you are going to be doing and outline how long it is likely to take. Tell them about the briefing, the use and the de-briefing.

Tell them about the equipment you are using (video, tape, etc.) and how and why you are using it. I generally point the video camera at the screen and keep the user out of direct shot, so I explain I am not filming them, I'm filming the screen. This helps to keep their stress levels down. You can tell a great deal from their body language, it's true, but you can see their body language manifest on the screen and the interaction they have with it, so this is generally not a problem.

It is important to recognize, in any participative evaluation method, the intrusive nature of observation and the artificial quality of evaluation. Aim to be sympathetic to this.

Remind participants about confidentiality and check that they feel comfortable with it. Assure them that they can stop at any time for any reason. Give them a permissions and confidentiality form to sign.

7. *Getting focussed*. In asking the user to carry out the activity, I say as little as possible about how to do it. Nor do I tell them what the designed activity structure is. Instead, I give them an objective that matches their own objective.

I choose one of two ways of doing this. The first is to invite users to discuss their needs and to direct them into creating a use scenario (see Chapter 3 Discovery) which relates in some way to the activity under trial before we begin using the system. This way, participants are focussed, before they begin, on the objective, what they think they want to do and what they think would be their definition of success or satisfaction. As a result, their use session is more sharply defined. It is clearer whether the site gives what they want, in the way they want it. Their positive comments are more substantial and their negative comments are clearer and more suggestive of what needs to be done. Additionally, it draws out more use scenarios we can use for design.

The second way is to give the user an activity to carry out described in terms of objectives – what to do, not how to do it. For example, to find out what the PE and EPS are for Cable and Wireless.

8. *Briefing for use*. I want to know everything that comes up in the user's mind. I remind them what it is like to be a child, how a child will just say whatever comes into their mind without any judgment, or inhibition. The detailed AUA model of interaction is always in my mind and points to asking what is the information they need, what

is their purpose, what would be a successful outcome, what are their choices, what is their action, what will the system do, what will the user be aware of, what will they understand from that, does it meet their purpose, are they satisfied. I ask participants to talk about what they think or feel about something.

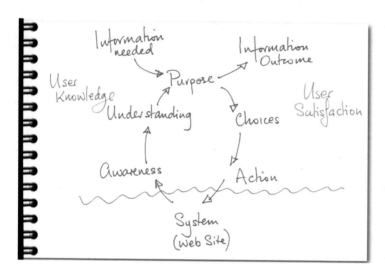

TO TALK ABOUT	MODEL OF INTERACTION
anything on the display, including the opening screen	awareness and understanding
what they understand by things they see	awareness, understanding and user knowledge
what they want to do	objectives and purpose
what they are curious or interested in	focus of interest – objectives and purpose
what they are going to do and what they expect to happen	choice, action, expectation and information outcome
anytime they feel stuck or awkward about what to do	choice, action, uncertainty and information outcome
what they think about the outcome of any action	awareness and understanding, user satisfaction

These points cover all the primary areas of interaction and increase the probability that the user will give you more useful information.

9. *The feeling dumb issue.* An issue to be aware of is the "looking or feeling dumb" issue. Nobody likes to think they are appearing to be dumb. This can usually be allayed by explaining, clearly and sensitively, that you are testing the system not them. I often ask users if they can remember a time when they used something and felt frustrated or even a little awkward about using it because they just couldn't figure out how it worked. I may say something like, "I remember feeling like that myself recently. The other day I came into the building and tried to open the door, you know the double doors downstairs. I pulled on the one on the left, and it wouldn't open. So, feeling awkward, I pushed on the one on the right and it wouldn't open, and now I felt even more awkward. Finally I pushed on the one on the left, and at last it opened. I used to think it was me being stupid. Now, I just remind myself it is just another example of bad design. It isn't me that made the mistake but the designers of the doors that got it wrong.

Well, that's what I am trying to find out here: all the things the designers thought were right, but are in fact not very easy to use. If you ever feel awkward about anything, I'd really like to know about it, because it's not anything you are doing wrong; it's a useful and helpful sign we have a bad design."

I also ask participants to behave as themselves, don't think the purpose of this is to please me and say nice things about the design. I say I had nothing to do with the design (even if I have), I'm just running the trials. That all comments about the design, either positive or negative, are equally valid and useful. They should be encouraged not to hold back.

10. *Carrying out the test – use.* Remind participants of their purpose and ask them to use the website to meet their objective. Tell them you are here to observe how well the system supports or hinders what they are doing, and so will not be offering help on how to use it.

Getting to the start screen should be achieved in as natural a way as possible, based on what the user has told you about how they find websites and their situation. Make it as real as possible.

Watch and pay attention all the time. There will be big signals and little signals. The little signals can be particularly fascinating. Sometimes they tell you more than the big signals. Try to watch where their eyes move, when they frown a little, whether they fidget, lean forward or back. Watch how the cursor

moves on the screen – whether it is smooth and directed and
confident or hesitant and uncertain. Watch where it goes and
whether the user uses it for action, just for pointing or just to do
something while they are thinking. Try and figure out what it
means; if they stop talking pick up on these cues somehow, for
example saying, "You're not saying anything at the moment, but
I got the feeling there was something on your mind just then".
This is an open question – it does not lead in any way. They are
bound to be thinking something, so you almost can't be wrong.
Do not say "I thought you were confused just then", which is
leading and does not get to the truth of the situation. It is far too
easy for them to answer "yes" and tell you what they think you
want to hear (they are intelligent too), or "no" because they feel
embarrassed about being confused. It is likely that they have
had a thought you could not guess at. You have to allow the
opportunity for them to say it.

Some people need reassurance that they are being heard, and
need a confirmation signal that they have been. So, if
participants are talking, and need reassurance, try not to use
words that confirm they are saying what you want to hear. For
example, if they say "I really don't like that," don't say "Right"
which is like saying "You got that right, that's what we think also,
good you are confirming my prejudices." Instead say, "I
understand" or "Hmmm, that's helpful"; something which
neither confirms nor denies your own opinions.

When real users actually sit down to use the system they will
be attempting their own tasks in their own work environment
without access to explanations from the designer or other helper.
So, if they get stuck and ask for help, try bouncing it back. Say
"I'm sorry, I can't help, please try and figure it for yourself
because in a real situation I wouldn't be here." Alternatively, you
could appear ignorant yourself, "Hmmm, that's a good question,
I'm not sure, what do you think *you* should do OR what do *you*
think that means?" What you say will depend upon the rapport
you have built with them and the type of character they are. Have
the patience to let them flounder if that is what is happening –
don't rescue them too soon. Make sure no designer jumps in and
starts explaining. If you have to have a designer present, give
them something to do, like hold the camcorder and tell them to
stay silent – both in verbal terms and in body language.

Only if participants are in a really black hole should you try to help them out. "Yes, it's a design problem some other people have found to be bad, what you need to do is...." or "I wonder if you tried xxxx would that work perhaps?" If they get really stuck and start becoming embarrassed or feel awkward, go back to the principle that the design is wrong. You may have to remind them the system is badly designed at this point (by definition). Help them out of the awkwardness. Say something like, "That is such a confusing part of the design, you've really helped us spot how bad that is, we really must get that looked at."

Try not to take too many notes by hand at the time because this can distract your attention, just jot the key points on PostIts (this makes them easier to organize later). Rely on the video/tape to collect and study the information in detail. If you need results for a very fast turnaround, you may have to make more notes at the use session. Recognize that you will miss or lose information, but you will get the material to the design team quickly.

Using the storyboard to stick the PostIt notes on during this session can be a very efficient way of recording information. However, it may also distract the user and get in the way of the flow of the dialog and the attention you can give to the use session.

11. *Winding up the test.* The test may have a natural conclusion, such as when the user's purpose is met. At other times, the user doesn't reach a satisfactory resolution of their use of the site. You have to make a judgment about how much longer to continue the test. Generally, if you sense they would normally give up at a certain point, get the user to admit it. Often, in a test situation, they will persevere longer than they would in reality because they know you want them to reach their purpose. Spot the body language that tells you they want to quit, but are persevering. Be aware also of what they said in the use scenario about what constitutes satisfaction for them and the timescale they would expect to get to it. Ask directly, if you are reasonably sure, "I have the feeling that you might have stopped using the site by now if I wasn't here, is that right?" If they say yes, then ask, "Well, what would you do now?" another open question, and find out what their next action would be.

AFTER THE USER TEST SESSION

Talk about the immediate feelings participants have. Use your listening skills and leave silent gaps so their thoughts and reflections

have a chance to come out. Keep recording this. When they have
finished talking openly about their feelings, move into the stage of the
open qualitative questionnaire. After the open questionnaire, move on
to the quantitative questionnaire (see *Useability Questionnaires* later
in this chapter).

Make sure you spend enough time at the end of the session for proper
closure of the trial. Thank participants for their time, and make sure they
are paid what they expected. Thank them for their ideas, thoughts and
contributions to the test of the website. No one likes to think their ideas
are being ignored – you must make sure they appreciate the way their
contributions are being examined and taken up.

Reiterate that everything will be given detailed consideration and
considered in the light of all the other trials you are carrying out.
Explain that it may be that not all their thoughts and opinions will
make their way into the final system. This is particularly important
when the users are existing customers, and also when you may want
their contributions again in the future.

MAKING A COLLECTIVE TAPE

There are two ways to make a collective tape. The first is to edit up a
tape which covers all the key issues from the collection of six tapes you
have. The second, and sometimes quicker way, is to act out all the
problems from the day, on to video. This is very quick. It is not the real
thing but a representation of it – you can always go back to the real
videos to support your cameo if you need to. This technique is
especially useful if you have particularly tight turnaround requirements
on useability evaluation and can be carried out satisfactorily if your
development team trust you.

I have worked on a project where I worked with a colleague on the
user trials on the Saturday, when the team of 25 developers were not
working. They wanted the results by first thing Monday morning so the
team did not get held up for even one day. The cameo approach was the
only realistic way of achieving the desired results. With two of us present
for each of the trials we could recall and act out the cameos. The only way
we could do this was to stay 100 percent present for the whole day, and
go into act out mode immediately the last participant left.

We then worked all of Sunday using the cameo as the basis for the
written report assessing and analyzing the results and producing a
summary of the issues and suggestions for solutions for the
development team.

Co-participation

A variation on think aloud, co-participation uses two users at a time working on the system as "buddies" or "partners." They are invited to carry out specific useful activities that we are interested in, such as "find and buy a book," and asked to use the system and talk with each other about what they are thinking as they are using it. The process is much the same as think aloud, but participants are not normally directed so much as to the areas to talk about. It is useful to tell them that whatever they do, they must make sure that both partners fully understand what is going on. Other than this, they are just left to get on with it. This tends to raise the level and quality of dialog between them. Observation is carried out in the same way as the think aloud method.

This can have the effect that the use of the system is much more natural than the more constrained single user in a think aloud test – the observer/moderator is much more in the background of the user's consciousness. As a result, it can produce greater quantity and diversity of comments than the think aloud technique. The fact there are two minds working on the use of the system can mean that issues in the interface are resolved faster than by one person, so it is important to understand and ensure this is a realistic use context.

Ensure that you have a realistic and representative choice of participants. Be mindful of unrealistic user pairings, for example, if assessing the use of a mortgage site, don't use father/son pairings if the interface is reasonably intended and designed for husband/wife.

In co-participation trials, you will obviously have to recruit more participants than for the think aloud method for the same number of test sessions. For further guidance, see also "Pros and Cons of Co-participation in Useability Studies" by Chauncey Wilson, *Useability Interface*, Vol 4, No. 4, April 1998.

Think aloud co-participation

Think aloud co-participation merges both techniques. Instead of having one user, we now have two, and follow the think aloud technique. It loses a little on the naturalness over the co-participation method but tends to generate more useful information on the interaction model. Participants should be prepared in the same way as in think aloud and co-participation.

Remote use

If you have a low budget or your typical users are spread far and wide, you may have to resort to remote testing. This is carried out in essentially the same way, except the users are remote and you cannot observe them. You will need more users, perhaps 25–30 if you are going to do it this way, and you will have to issue them with instructions in writing just as if you had done it face to face.

The main problem with remote users is that you cannot tell what they have done, so you cannot tell if the answers they put on the questionnaires reflect the "real" reality. Generally, people don't lie, but they do often miss out problems if, for example, they feel they solved the problem, and it was just something they were doing wrong. They can also score the quantitative questionnaire unduly highly or unduly low, i.e. not representing an objective view of what the reality was for them.

Useability testing a paper prototype

Useability testing a paper prototype works more or less the same as normal testing with users, except you don't have a computer system to run the design on.

Procedure

1. *Put the storyboard on the wall.* It is better to put the storyboard on a wall than on a table because you can see and work with it in front of you better. This also has other advantages. If it is left on the wall after the useability is done, it has all the comments still on it so the design team can refer to it easily. It can be the focus of design thinking and discussions in groups of between one and eight. It is a permanent, focussed reminder of what you are doing. It leaves a better mental image in the mind of how everything hangs together.
2. *Make a "screen window."* Using a big sheet of card, say about A1 or A0 (say a page of flipchart paper), cut a rectangular hole in the middle. Make the hole the same size as the paper or card you are using for the page representation.
3. *The evaluation team.* Run a useability trial, as in testing with users. Use real representative users, expert evaluators, or any person other than the designers, to act as users. It is useful to

have between three and five people involved. The essential three are the user, the user buddy/scribe and the designer. You could have a fourth – a designer buddy/scribe, and a fifth, an impartial observer. An observer is useful since their input can be most insightful – particularly with regard to the defensive actions of the designer.

The guidelines for the user are simple – it is just the same as in the normal testing, be themselves.

The rule for the user buddy/scribe is that they must encourage the user, ask clarifying questions, and write down everything that comes up on small PostIt notes, one point to a PostIt. The buddy should be chosen for his or her skills as a useability evaluator, unless the observer is doing that.

The rule for the designer is simple. They must act out being the computer and do whatever the design is capable of and must not speak. Note, all rules are just rules – if they are broken, this case, it means the design is wrong in some respect, and that is what we are here to learn.

The rule for the designer buddy/scribe is that, they must encourage the designer to do what they are asked to do, and write down everything that comes up on small PostIt notes, one point to a PostIt. The design scribe role could be omitted and carried out later by examination of a video recording.

4. *Evaluating.* Provide the user with a copy of your discovery notes to give them the background and a use scenario, or let them come up with their own use scenario. A designer should hold the big card, and act out being the computer. With the storyboard on the wall, the designer (computer) uses a cut-out mask to hide the other areas of the interface.

The mask gives the designer something to do and enables them to be involved. This seems to help keep them quiet, and more importantly make themselves more aware of when they have really got the design wrong. (When they speak, or can't do what the user wants, the design is probably inadequate.)

The designer starts the user at the chosen starting point. The user uses the paper model by talking through what actions they want to do, what they are actually doing and what they are thinking about. i.e. says to the "computer," "I am moving the cursor to the top left," "I am clicking on this icon." The computer (the designer) moves the cut-out mask to show the result of user actions.

The user buddy encourages the user to verbalize by asking both open and closed questions; it is important to be aware of the user's hesitation.

The design buddy, a member of the design team should be recording issues in the design, should focus on where the users needs are not being met.

The observer is best placed to observe when the players step outside of their roles; clues will be found here.

The PostIts are placed on the storyboard as you go along. If required, you can video the experience, but this is usually not justified at this stage, after all it is a low fidelity design and we are going for the main points. We are not looking at structure, process, tempo, convenience, usefulness, language, consistency, etc. We are generally not discussing the details of color, layout, or detail interaction design.

5. *Hints.* Recognize the importance of your feelings; perhaps uncertainty, frustration or pleasure. This is your subconscious telling you what is going on. Even if you cannot rationalize it, try to know it.

Buddy questions should be open and empathetic, for example:

- Do you know where you are in the system?
- What do you want to do now?
- How do you think you can do that?
- What do you think will happen if...?
- What are you doing now?
- Do you know what is happening?
- What is... for?
- Are you able to stop or undo that action?
- What do you think that means?
- How do you feel that should be?

Emotions are important indicators. As the design develops it will move from a very low fidelity representation of the design into increasingly high fidelity models, made up from real screen shots of the design. Keep the storyboard up there throughout – it will still be useful even when you have a real interactive system to test.

Useability questionnaires

I use two types of questionnaire, one open qualitative and the other quantitative. I have developed them over a few years and find they catch most of what I need to know. There are a number of other useability questionnaires in existence, such as SUMI, WAMMI, and so on.

Open qualitative questionnaires

It is important to do the open questionnaire before the quantitative questionnaire since that gives users a chance to review and relive the experience before they start to quantify it. This will probably give a more balanced, accurate and truthful result. However, there is the opposite view that this gives the user a chance to understand the problems they had, converse with you and make up subconscious excuses for the system and give a higher quantitative rating.

Ask users to complete the questionnaire. Remind them everything is confidential. Either get it in writing or record it on audio tape and get it typed up later. Don't be tempted to explain what went wrong – stay strictly in listening and reflecting back mode.

The open qualitative questionnaire

- What were your first impressions of the website?
- What were the most useful or attractive features of the website?
- What did you find surprising?
- How much were your needs, objectives or expectations met?
- What did you like?
- What did you dislike?
- What would have been better for you and in what way?
- Do you have any other comments?
- How do you feel about Company-X after using the website?
- What date(s) and time(s) did you use the website?
- How many minutes were you on the website?
- How many minutes did it take you to meet your objectives?

- How long would you expect it to take you?
- For the time you are interested in XXXXX, would you expect to use the website again?
  - No
  - Sporadically
  - Periodically
  - Regularly.
- Why?

Some people will not tell the complete truth, that is to say, their description of the experience will differ from your observation of the experience. Those who do will not believe themselves to be untruthful. I have seen user's experience to be evidently a very poor and unsatisfactory one. The site wasn't useful for them, and it didn't meet their objectives. Yet, when they completed the questionnaire or talked about it afterwards they described it as useful and satisfying. Try to understand why.

What are possible reasons for not telling the truth? Perhaps the user was left feeling incompetent or dumb. They did not want to admit it to you, or more importantly to themselves. Their subconscious defence came into play and they re-scripted it in the conscious as a successful and competent performance. They respond in like on the questionnaire. Or, perhaps they feel they don't want to be impolite to you and the designers, and are therefore more favorable in their comments.

It's your job to get them to express as much of the truth as possible by being present and available, while not encroaching on what they say, and by clarifying what they mean and reconciling that with your observations of their use of the site.

Quantitative questionnaires

It is also important also to carry out a quantitative questionaire to obtain a score of the user's perceptions; to measure improvements, or otherwise, of the succeeding iterations of the design. This questionnaire is devised and developed from all the principle areas of interaction design already discussed.

Please read the statements below and score each with a number between 1 and 7 to indicate how true the statement is for you. Please also add any comments you may have.	Totally Disagree				Totally Agree		
About the system	1	2	3	4	5	6	7
I never made any mistakes.							
I found it very useful.							
I always feel in control using it.							
I found it a very efficient way to get things done.							
It is very easy to understand straightaway.							
It was always clear what would happen when I clicked on something.							
The system provides everything I wanted.							
I never felt lost on this system.							
I found it a waste of my time.							
I found the use very pleasurable.							
I could always find what I wanted quickly.							
The calculations provided were everything I wanted.							
I found the visual presentation excellent.							
The information was excellent quality, concise, clear and understandable.							
I can always find out quickly if it doesn't have what I want.							
I never had to change or correct anything I entered.							
I found the performance too slow.							
The system was coherent and consistent.							
I feel it provides appropriate security and privacy.							
I can easily contact the right person when I want to on this system.							
I achieved what I wanted very effectively.							
I feel I want to use the company's services.							
I feel it enhances and enables my skills.							
I feel the language used is totally understandable.							
I could always get help quickly.							
Everything happened in the order I wanted it to.							
I felt the system always treated me with respect.							
I feel it greatly improves the quality of my task.							
I will tell my friends positive things about it.							

When users have completed the questionnaire, the collective scores can be summed and averaged for each statement. Then they can be collated under a number of useability headings and presented as a graph for a visual indicator of how well, or not, you are doing.

I use the headings below, based on my assessment of what is typically important, ISO 9241, and the newer developments in heuristic evaluation categories.

The graphs below (one in histogram form and the other as a spidergraph) represent the data from a job I consulted on recently. The data is for the first prototype and, after useability evaluation and redesign, the second prototype. We can clearly see measurable progress.

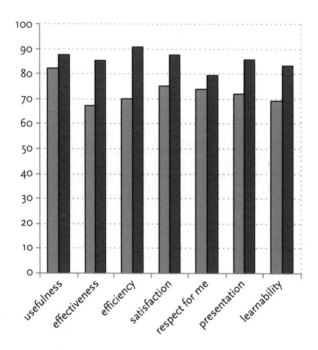

For a website, a discretionary use system, the target scores might be greater than 90 percent on each measure, average score between 6 and 7. For a non-discretionary used or regularly used system you can probably get away with 80 percent or so, average score between 5.5 and 6. We can use these indicators, in conjunction with the useability evaluation report and the open questionnaire results, to determine where our primary design focus on the next iteration should be.

After the first version, we applied our attention to effectiveness and efficiency, and they have improved markedly as well as improving the other measures.

In this example, it is evident we are not giving enough consideration to respect for the customer, either in security and privacy or "respect for them," perhaps in not recognizing their skills or culture or the using the wrong tone of language on the site. Since presentation, effectiveness and learnability are lower than the other metrics, perhaps that was the source of the problem?

These scores are pretty good for the first two iterations, and this came about largely because we adopted a user-centered design approach from the start.

Other measures

You can set and measure activity times, for example, you might say that a private investor should be able to locate an equity and determine the PE and EPS within 30 seconds. You can also set and measure user error rates. Set error rates for information entry, incorrect or wasted navigations, misunderstandings of results, language and meaning. These will provide a factual record of the success rate of the use of the system. The main problem with this is that it can take a great deal of time to go into this level of detail, unless suitable automated tools are used to capture the figures. Consider your tools, consider your budget, consider the benefit.

Heuristic evaluation

The first person to make heuristic evaluation into a popular useability technique was Jakob Nielsen. I first came across him in the late 1980s at human computer interaction conferences and have had the pleasure of meeting him a number of times at such events over the years. He has an irrepressible interest and passion in the subject and has contributed a great deal to the understanding, usefulness, effectiveness and popularity of useability techniques.

A *heuristic* (in this context) is a rule of thumb, a guideline or a principle. *Heuristic evaluation* is an evaluation based on a collection of these principles.

Nielsen was concerned with getting useability results as effectively as possible, something I aim to do also. He reduced a raft-load of rules and guidelines to a set of ten.

1. **Visibility of system status**. The system should always keep users informed about what is going on, through appropriate feedback within reasonable time.
2. **Match between system and the real world**. The system should speak the user's language, with words, phrases and concepts familiar to the user, rather than system-oriented terms. Follow real-world conventions, making information appear in a natural and logical order.
3. **User control and freedom**. Users often choose system functions by mistake and will need a clearly marked "emergency exit" to leave the unwanted state without having to go through an extended dialog. Support undo and redo.
4. **Consistency and standards**. Users should not have to wonder whether different words, situations, or actions mean the same thing. Follow platform conventions; be consistent.
5. **Error prevention**. Even better than good error messages is a careful design which prevents a problem from occurring in the first place.
6. **Recognition rather than recall**. Make objects, actions, and options visible. The user should not have to remember information from one part of the dialog to another. Instructions for use of the system should be visible or easily retrievable whenever appropriate.
7. **Flexibility and efficiency of use**. Accelerators – unseen by the novice user – may often speed up the interaction for the expert

user such that the system can cater to both inexperienced and experienced users. Allow users to tailor frequent actions.

8. **Aesthetic and minimalist design**. Dialogs should not contain information which is irrelevant or rarely needed. Every extra unit of information in a dialog competes with the relevant units of information and diminishes their relative visibility.

9. **Help users recognize, diagnose, and recover from errors**. Error messages should be expressed in plain language (no codes), precisely indicate the problem, and constructively suggest a solution.

10. **Help and documentation**. Even though it is better if the system can be used without documentation, it may be necessary to provide help and documentation. Any such information should be easy to search, focussed on the user's task, list concrete steps to be carried out, and not be too large.

Since Nielsen's paper, there have been suggestions that the Nielsen ten are product-oriented and they omit the user process-orientation. It has been suggested by Muller *et al.* to add other heuristics to cover this area of user process and work context.

1. **Task sequencing**. Users can select and sequence tasks (when appropriate) rather than the system taking control of the user's actions. Action support agents (wizards, etc.) are available but are optional and are under user control.

2. **Skills**. The system supports, extends, supplements or enhances the user's skills, background knowledge and expertise. The system does not replace them.

3. **Pleasurable and respectful interaction**. The user's interactions with the system enhance the quality of her or his experience. The user is treated with respect. The design reflects the user's professional role, personal identity or intention. The design is aesthetically pleasing – with an appropriate balance of artistic as well as functional values.

4. **Quality work**. The system supports the user in delivering quality work to her or his clients (if appropriate). Attitudes of quality work include timeliness, accuracy, aesthetic appeal, and appropriate levels of completeness.

5. **Privacy**. The system helps the user to protect personal or private information – belonging to the user or his or her clients.

Tying these heuristics into our design thinking

The principle areas of design, based on our discovery have been roles, actions, information (objects). Another foundation principle is the awareness, understanding action model. Another set of core aspects is structure (see *What are the pages? – the action process*), page (see *What's on a page? – the information objects*), action and interaction design.

I hope it goes without saying by now that any use of a website is based on the point of view of the user, and the role they are in. All the assessment of these heuristics should be based on the perspective of the user in the role they are playing and in their typical context of use.

The table below shows how Nielsen and Muller heuristics correspond to the language of discovery and design we have been using in this book.

NIELSEN AND MULLER	IN OUR LANGUAGE
Visibility of system status	Action, awareness, understanding interaction is effective
Task sequencing	Action, awareness, understanding interaction is effective
System equals the real world	Language and processes natural
User control and freedom	Action design timely, clear and complete
Consistency and standards	Consistency of presentation and action language Language (presentation/objects) and actions (buttons, fields and affordances)
Error prevention	Easyness to get it right (rather than an "error")
Recognition rather than recall	All information for action available
Flexibility and efficiency of use	Efficiency and efficiency improvement systems, the AUA model
Aesthetic and minimalist design	Simplicity, clarity and completeness of presentation and action
Error recognition, diagnosis and recovery	Action support and guidance
Help and documentation	Information and action Q&A documentation
Skills	Involve user knowledge

Pleasurable and respectful interaction	Satisfying outcome
Quality work	Satisfying outcome
Privacy	Support user values

WHAT YOU NEED TO DO

Get a number of people who know about useability and design, and are therefore familiar with these heuristics and the underlying thinking behind them. You need a number of people because one person's views will not catch everything. Nielsen suggests that between three and five evaluators is about the most cost-effective number, and certainly this is borne out by my own personal experience. The evaluators should be working as a useability expert, and also from the perspective of the user, their context of use and their objectives. It helps for the evaluators to be familiar with the use scenarios.

One reason to use heuristic evaluation in preference to think aloud or other user testing is to save the time and cost of recruiting real and representative users. In some circumstances, recruiting users represents a considerable difficulty, in others not so. If you have set up a process by which you involve users from the beginning, this should prove to be relatively easy. In this case, ask the users to join in the evaluation as experts. Give them basic training on the heuristics and proceed as below (this is a suggestion from Muller *et al.*).

Each person then assesses the part of the system under evaluation and applies their own subjective score to each category and makes notes and comments about how parts of the interface meet or fail under each heuristic. Scoring should be done on a scale of 1–7, where 1 is awful and 7 is excellent. They should work alone at this stage, since they retain their independence and are unbiased by others points of view.

It is sometimes difficult to get people who are familiar with useability and the domain in hand. If the evaluator is not a domain expert, they may need someone on hand to ask domain-based questions, but beware this can too easily become leading the evaluator, biasing them by the domain expert. Websites are "walk up and use" systems and should need no user support other than that which is designed in. So, I try to avoid this situation if possible, or at least make sure the domain expert is practiced at holding back until the design problems have been explored sufficiently.

An extensive study can take a great deal of time, so go for 80/20, work fast and light. Even if you or your client have extensive financial resources, it is doubtful whether it will be cost effective to take too long over it.

Recording your results by hand at the actual time of "using the system" can be time consuming and get in the way of the flow of the use and your attention to what is going on. Two techniques I have found useful are video recording and tape recording. They are used to enable you to go back to study the detail and so that you have material to show to the design and development team. Video gives much more information, but even a tape recording can be very useful, since listening to it makes the mental connections to recall the visual and kinaesthetic memories. Another technique is to use variations of the user/buddy/scribe team (see *Useability – testing a paper prototype*).

By sharing your findings afterwards, you can compare and discuss common themes and unique themes. This can be done remotely, but is better if the evaluators are physically present in the same room and facilitated to ensure that all viewpoints are openly and equitably discussed.

As well as drawing up a collective agreement of the primary issues, you can also revise your scores at this stage to reach a group consensus score. You should then compare the group consensus score with the amalgamation of the collected averaged individual scores – they should be roughly the same – if they are not, it gives you an idea whether the present consensus is likely to be right. If not, continue to debate and discuss until there is some resolution of the discrepancies.

The outcome will be a prioritized list of the useability issues (based on severity ratings) and suggestions on the nature of the solution. The detail of the solution should not be attempted at this stage; instead it should be worked on with the designer or the design team. The design team are steeped in knowledge from discovery and the technological possibilities. They must retain emotional ownership of the design. However, the evaluators or evaluators' representative must work with the design team until the design of the solution is arrived at. If not, there is a high probability that the subtleties of the design failings will be missed, and the next iteration may be a waste of time and money.

Heuristic evaluation with users

This is a combination of heuristic evaluation with think aloud, and can be successfully carried out with a small number of users. The users complement the process by helping the expert evaluators thinking from a more realistic, user-centered perspective.

AUA evaluation

The detailed AUA model gives us a logical formal framework for carrying out evaluation, as well as for its use in design. Some considerable progress can be made prior to user evaluation by applying this formal framework. It can be considered a kind of expert evaluation. It is inexpensive to conduct and forces a detailed assessment. It is better when carried out by those familiar with user-centered design and useability issues since they will have the skill and experience to spot the problems. However, anyone can benefit from it.

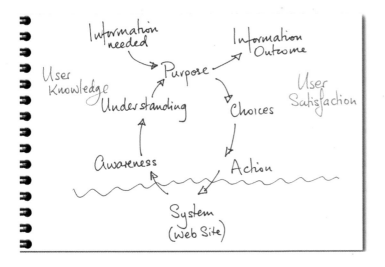

For an example of its application, see *Interaction Design* in Chapter 4. It can also be carried out in participation with representative users.

Analyzing and preparing the results

What to do

Review all the notes, comments, videos and questionnaires to determine the areas which exhibited problems. Structure your issues in the same way I structured the design process.

Deal with the site as a whole – scope and structure. Then deal with areas of activity – the action processes, then deal with individual pages

– the information presentation and understanding, then details of interaction on each page. Under each heading, detail any other issues and ideas arising, and record system faults. Highlight all aspects of problems relating to awareness, understanding and action. Include severity ratings and recommendations.

Include details from the questionnaires. Produce a summary of the quantitative results. These will be used as a measure in subsequent iterations of the design to determine if and by how much the new designs are becoming better.

Useability evaluation report – an example contents page

EXECUTIVE SUMMARY
1   EVALUATION OVERVIEW
   i   *Evaluation objective*
   ii   *Evaluation scope*
   iii *Evaluation type*
   iv   *Evaluation considerations*
   v   *Report considerations*
2   REPORT ON EVALUATION OBJECTIVES
   i   *Team needs*
   ii   *Useability Goals*
3   USEABILITY RESULTS
   i   *Useability metrics*
   ii   *Task times*
4   KEY ISSUES
5   RECOMMENDATIONS

DESIGNER'S DETAIL REPORT
1   GENERAL USEABILITY ISSUES
2   DETAIL DESIGN ISSUES
3   EVALUATION DETAILS
   i   *Evaluation type*
   ii   *Evaluation scope*
   iii *Evaluation objective*
   iv   *Evaluation considerations*
   v   *Recruitment profile*
   vi   *Recruited profile*

vii *Evaluation context*
viii *Evaluation process*
ix *User Activities*
4 THE OPEN QUESTIONNAIRE
i *What were your first impressions of the system?*
ii *What were the most useful or attractive features of the system?*
iii *How much were your needs, objectives or expectations met?*
iv *What did you like?*
v *What did you dislike?*
vi *What would have been better for you and in what way?*
vii *What did you find surprising?*
viii *Do you have any other comments?*
ix *How do you feel about Nationwide after using the system?*

Give severity ratings

For each problem found under useability evaluation, it can be useful to allocate a severity rating. This can be done by one person – say the useability person – or by a number of people. If it is done by a number of people, it is useful to have a user (or a few users that are involved in the process as well as a business manager) who is clear about the business objectives – involve the key stakeholders.

Gitte Lindgaard's *Useability Testing and System Evaluation* classifies problems as critical, high, medium or low. Michael Levi and Frederick Conrad suggest problems as rating catastrophic, major, minor, cosmetic, or not a problem. Levi and Conrad have taken the logical step to account for using a number of people to allocate severity ratings; the classification of "not a problem," i.e. it is identified as a possible problem, but in my opinion there is no problem. Each is given a value, between 4 and 0, where 4 is critical and 0 is not a problem. Another way of scoring is to use a score between 1 and 7, where 1 is minor and 7 is catastrophic.

Lindgaard (with apologies to Gitte Lindgaard, the paraphrasings are mine) then suggests that each problem is assessed with regard to:

- impact on user performance – impact on the efficiency, correctness and error recovery for the user in obtaining their objective

- probability of occurrence – likelihood it will be encountered during the users activity (a function of how many users/testers encountered it)

- frequency of occurrence – is this problem likely to recur more than once.

I think it can be worth adding:

- usefulness – the degree to which the area of activity has useful value for the user or business

- satisfaction – the degree of impact on overall user satisfaction or happiness.

Each person's ratings are then aggregated and averaged. You could even work out the standard deviations as well to give some idea of the level of agreement.

Now, a number of problems arise. The first is the amount of time it will take to make all these value judgments or to record and assess all these items. This is a project management issue, and it is a question of looking at the cost in relation to the project budget, timescales and the benefits. It is a must to have some way of assessing the importance. So, you may have to decide to drop some categories.

Second, how do we aggregate these ratings to make a decision about what the overall rating is? Well, be clear about the purpose of the site, the business objectives, the profile of the typical users and the user's objectives. With this in mind you can give value ratings to the severity categories. Then you can decide which ones to omit, if necessary, and work out an aggregation formula for their importance to you in the context of what you are trying to achieve.

USE IS DESIGN

I am now going to look at two websites from a user perspective – Market-Eye and Blackwell's books – to bring many of the benefits home to you. I invited "domain experts" to use the systems. These users are being used as if they were taking part in a useability trial. As such they are stereotypical users.

I discussed what they hoped to achieve from the sites and we agreed a task scenario for them. I describe their situation and the task scenarios. Then I describe their "use experience." The user was asked to think aloud as they were using the site and this commentary was recorded; what appears here is an edited version of that commentary. The user's thoughts and comments are boxed, while my comments are set in italics. I haven't mentioned all the useability points, just enough to give you a feel for how much there is to learn from useability evaluations. Careful examination of the details can teach you a great deal about design issues.

Market-Eye

This useability evaluation was carried out between 22–24 February 1999, on the website at http://www.marketeye.co.uk as it appeared at the time. The principle of the issues remains unchanged – many sites still have similar problems.

The user's situation

- The user has medium-depth knowledge of investments. The user is interested in technical analysis and fundamental analysis of possible investment opportunities.

- The user would be using the website from home, periodically during the evening and periodically during the day on a 56k modem.

- The user was using Internet Explorer 4 as the browser, and the screen resolution was set to 800x600. While there are still users on 640x480, I considered this to be a reasonable baseline to carry out this "evaluation."

- The user currently has £5,000 cash to invest in the stock market. The user was interested to find out how the Market-Eye website may help him make his decisions about where to invest it.

- The user was interested in how the Market-Eye website may help him deal in his selected stocks and how it may help him manage his portfolio.

The user's activities

The user was given the following activity.

> Using the Market-Eye website, study a stock of interest to
> establish if it meets your investment criteria.

The user was advised they could stop if they felt the site could not meet
the task. The user was instructed to stay on site to complete the tasks.

The user's experience

My investment criteria are based on the fundamentals, current
equity price and the timing of purchase.
   I am looking for a stock with long-term, consistent growth over five
years of the share price, turnover, earnings and currently within
15 percent of its all-time high. I want to be able to check various
moving averages to test which way the price is moving. I want a
consistent quality over five years of EPS, Dividend Yield, Dividend
Cover, Total Assets, Current Assets, Current Liabilities, Stock, ROCE.
SOCE from which I will create some ratio indicators noted below. I
am looking for a current PE within 30 percent of the sector average.

Profit margin %(TP/TO) T>15%
ROCE% (TP/TA-CL) T>20
SalesCE% (TO/TA-CL) T>100
Quick Ratio ((CA-Inv)/CL) T>1
PE within 30% of sector avg.

So, the purpose is to obtain **the fundamental** *data and five years of*
share price *data and the* **sector** *data in order to examine it.*
He had three stocks in mind to check out: Cable & Wireless, Cable &
Wireless Communications and Gresham Computing.

He had already registered as an investor.

The user went in on the investor service, and was presented with the
screen shown here.

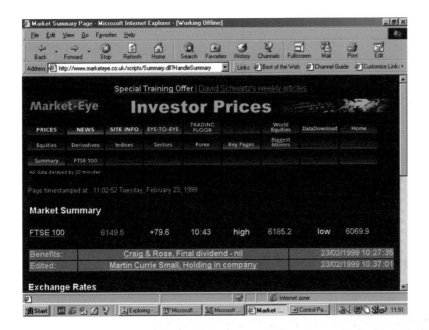

"Ah, this is headed 'investor prices,' but it is actually the summary of the key market prices with a 20-minute delay. Oh, right, the heading is in the middle left of the screen. There are a lot of items on the menu bar; I'm not sure what they all mean. I assume that the button Summary will get me to where I am and the button FTSE 100 will do the same as the underlined text of the same."

This has two headings apparently, and it seems the less noticeable one is correct. What it really means is confusing.

Headings should be headings – they are intended to clarify, not confuse.

What is below the fold is uncertain.

Make it obvious what comes next. Save the user time scrolling or clicking when maybe they don't have to.

The screen space is very poorly used with very little of it given over to useful information for the user.

Use screen space wisely.

The graphic display is unclear with a remarkable range of colors. The FTSE 100 price is in red and the market movement is up and shown in blue. Most people would assume red (negative, danger) is down and green (positive) is up. This has no relation to any normal color code that I am aware of. On a later version, they show the price in green and the market movement is shown as red for down. Better, but still, why is the price shown as green when it is down?

Make rational use of colors.

"I'm not sure what is the difference between prices and equities, or what key pages might mean. Maybe prices or equities is what I want. I'll try equities."

"Ah, equities means stock search."

The label on the button on the previous screen is different from the location he ended up on, headed "stock search" in white and centered, and "investor search" in orangey-yellow and also centered. Note, this is inconsistent with the first screen.

A button label is a signpost, make sure the user ends up
where the signpost says.

*The user first clicked "equity" without doing anything else,
misunderstanding that he had to enter a symbol and then press "equity,"
possibly because the button is so far from the field.*

Make actions close to the information to which they relate.

The user scrolled down to a list of every stock.

*Then, after scrolling down through the seemingly unending list he saw it
was the A equities, in alphabetical order by name. However, looking at the
last equities in the list he then realized they were not in alphabetical order
by name. Looking a little further he realized they were in alphabetical
order by symbol order, but the names appear first. He thought that was
strange and confusing that the data was organized by the second column
rather than the first.*

If you are going to provide something that looks like a sorted
list, put the sorting column on the far left to make it obvious
what is going on.

*So he went back on the browser and noticed the help message is below the
vision of the display.*

**If you are going to provide help, make it obvious how to get it
rather than hiding it away.**

The user then entered "Cable" under name and pressed search.

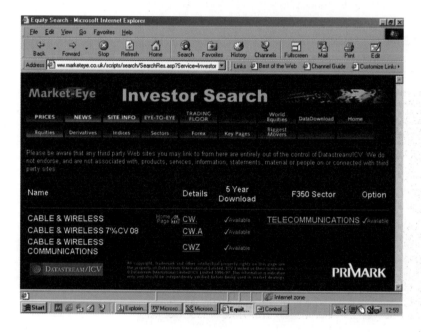

*He wanted to click on the name (since he had searched by name), but
couldn't so he clicked on the symbol under details column. Once again we
have an amazing mix of colors.*

Make the operation obvious and intuitive.

"I wonder if details will do what I want, will that be the same as
equity or fundamentals or something else?"

**If you are going to label buttons, make sure the meaning is
clear. If you are not making it clear, why bother?**

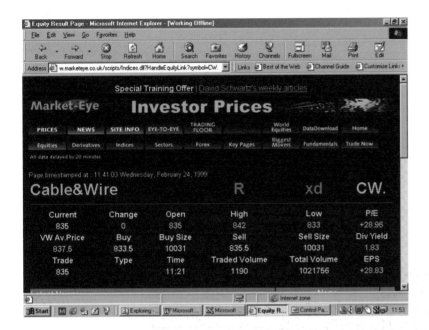

The system came back with a screen showing Cable & Wireless details about the share price and trading during the day, plus PE, Dividend Yield and EPS. Now the color of the price is blue, whereas on the FTSE 100 screen the price was green. Here the change is green, whereas it was blue before. Consistency and meaning of the "language" is not a strong point on this site.

Make good and consistent use of colors.

Below this, and invisible at this resolution without scrolling, is the share price graph and volumes for the last year, which are probably equally or more important to the user as the PE and so on, but is hidden from sight. As we know, all of this information can be comfortably put on one screen, even at 800x600.

Don't waste the screen space unnecessarily.

"Ok, I got the right screen, but I want to store the details for subsequent study. Since there seems no way to save the data in any other way, I'll use the browser to save as an HTML file."

There is little or no recognition of the user's scenario of use, so no provision for what a generic user might really want to do.

Make sure you find out what the use scenarios are, and that they are met at the right time.

The user then clicked on the "fundamentals" button and got the fundamentals. The heading has changed position yet again and the colors are now different; all values are now green and all headings are white. Since white draws the eye more than green on a black background, it would seem that Market-Eye want the user to read the headings and not the information (see below).

Make good and consistent use of position and colors.

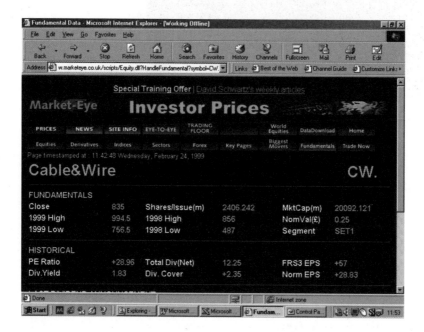

Once again the user wanted to store the details and did so as before.

"OK, now for the data download of CW."

The user then pressed DataDownload and got the following screen.

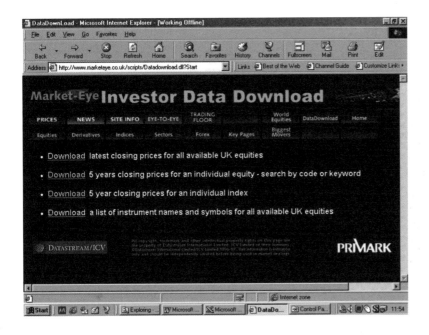

"Oh, what's this?"

It was inconsistent with the operation of the "fundamentals" button, in that the fundamentals went and got the data for the equity, whereas this didn't go and get the data for the equity.

Keep the operation of the system consistent and useful.

Also, it is now referring to closing prices, not fundamental data.

Make the signposting clear.

"I guess I had better do Download 5 year closing prices."

This step seemed totally redundant to him since he had already just pressed data download on the previous page.

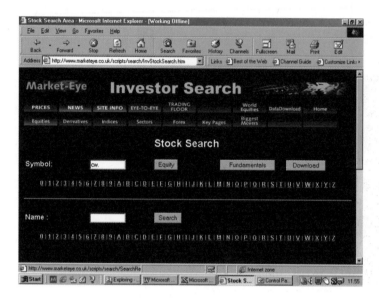

Don't force redundant steps.

> "I have already had this, what's going on? I feel I am in a loop here."

He went back twice on the browser to read the symbol name, since he had forgotten it, then forward twice to get back here.

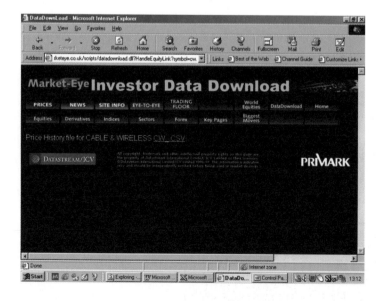

The system should always bring forward information
providing the opportunity for recall rather than memory.

The system should let the user do what they want to do, not
what they have to do – and this poor user certainly is having
to do a lot.

He then entered the symbol CW and clicked "download" for the third time.

"At last, we seem to be getting there."

*The system forced the user to press download three times, as well as some two
browser "backs" and "forwards!" Even now, he is forced into one more step,
press on the symbol (which he had three screens earlier) to download at last.
The user downloaded the data for subsequent analysis. Unfortunately, the
download only downloads price history, not the data he could see on the
screen when he pressed download.*

Keep the relationship between what the system purports to
offer and what it actually offers consistent and correct.

*The user then went back to stock search on CW and verified that he had in
fact got all the same details by using this process as were available from the
stock search buttons, and found he had.*

Don't provide two ways of doing the same thing – one will
usually do.

"Let's get the sector information now, I'll try sectors, and hope that
does it."

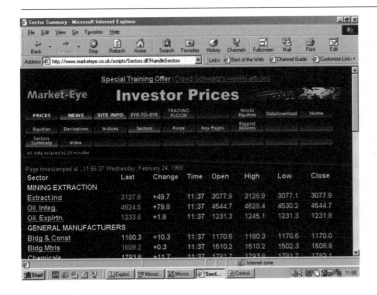

If you train the user to be uncertain and confused, that is
exactly what they will be.

"Right, I know CW is in the telecoms sector, though I don't
remember any of the earlier screens saying this."

---

*It did not say what the sector was on either the details or fundamentals
display for the stock.*

Don't rely on the user guessing how the information is
structured and what the structure is categorized by.

*There did not seem to be any natural way to see the sector from the equity
screen for the stock. The structure of the navigation is unsupportive of the
user task because the structure of the site is not based on the user task or the
information structure of the user's conceptual models.*

Understand the use scenario – again!

"Ah, it's called "Telecommtns", never heard of it called that before.
However, let's try the Telecommtns sector (for Cable and Wireless)."

Use a common "user-centered" language of communication.

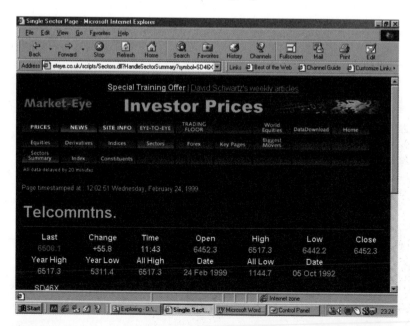

"This is useful. But I can't see the PE for the sector; I'll have to get that from the FT perhaps."

Provide the information the user needs. The use scenarios would have told the designers this.

"I like the intraday figures for the sector, that would have been useful on the equity price as well."

If you provide information in one place, also provide the same elsewhere, or you will raise or dash expectations.

"And as before, I cannot see any way of saving the sector data so I'll print off the screen."

Provide the actions the user needs.

"Ah, what's this? A "Sectors Summary" button as well as a "Sectors" button. Let's try that."

It did the same thing as Sectors. It seemed odd to have two buttons named differently on the same screen doing the same thing.

Don't provide two buttons on the same screen which do exactly the same thing.

It was not obvious to the user (nor to me) the way sub-menu choices appeared and disappeared, though perhaps there is logic to it.

"So what is the Index button for?"

Don't make the user confused and unsure.

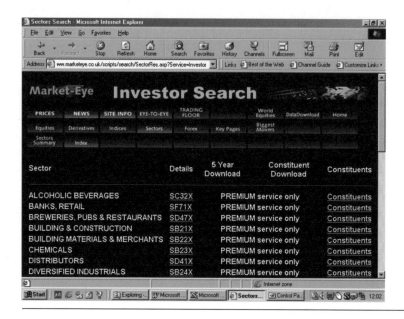

"Oh, it shows the sectors again, though laid out differently and not classified as had been previously, I wonder why the layout is different? I am confused about why sectors, sectors summary and index all provide roughly the same functionality. And this one has the option of seeing the constituents. Let's try that."

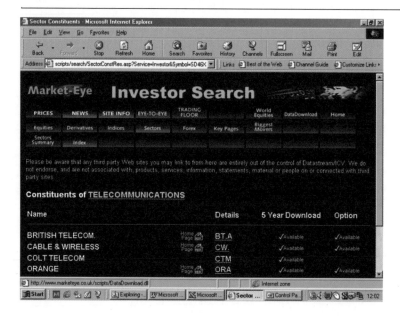

This must add to the cost of maintenance – three buttons and two layouts to do one job.

Keeping it simple saves money on development and maintenance.

"Right, so there are not as many shown here as the FT: I wonder why? Since it is different, perhaps I cannot use the FT sector summary as a meaningful source for the PE."

Keep consistent with industry standards, so the information is useful and relevant.

"And what does the Option button do?"

Pressing the "Option" button showed a fault in the system and an error "HandleOptionLink HTTP_BADREQUEST" message appeared.

Test the system.

The user then went off-line to study the information he had saved. He said that he began thinking about different ways of getting the information. The whole user task is bigger than the system-supported tasks, and that acts as a block to usage.

The outcome

The user managed to get a reasonable amount of information, but it was extremely hard work and confusing. It didn't really meet his needs. Key issues concerned:

- navigation systems – clues about what is what
- action support
- graphic design
- consistency
- clarity
- use of screen real estate.

The site needs restructuring and enhancing to support user tasks, and make it clearer what will happen when the user chooses any of the menu items.

Blackwell's Online Bookshop

The following think aloud useability evaluation was carried out on
15 March 1999, on the website at http://bookshop.blackwell.co.uk as it
appeared at the time.

The user's situation

- The user has experience of retail bookshops. The user is interested
  in buying two specific books – he knows the author of one and the
  first part of the title of the other.

- The user would be using the website from home, during the
  evening, on a 56k modem.

- The user was using Internet Explorer 4 as the browser, and the
  screen resolution was set to 800x600. While there are still users on
  640x480 and others on 1028x768 or higher, I considered this to be
  a reasonable baseline to carry out this evaluation.

- The user wants to buy a book by Bias on *Useability Cost Benefits*
  and one on print typography called *"The Non-designers..."* The user
  was interested to find out how the Blackwell's Online Bookshop
  may help decide whether to purchase it, and to buy it if he liked
  the look of it.

The user's activities

The user was given two tasks to complete:

1. Find out whether the Blackwell's Online Bookshop website
   can offer you the information on the books and what the cost
   might be.
2. Using the Blackwell's Online Bookshop website, purchase the
   books if you like the look of them.

The user was advised he could stop if he felt the site could not meet
the task. The user was instructed to stay on site to complete his tasks.
The user was advised to use my name and other details if necessary
during the process.

The user's experience

Task 1. Find out whether the Blackwell's Online Bookshop website can offer you the information on the books and what the cost might be.

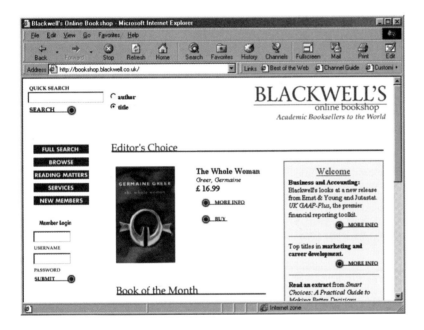

"This looks very clear; they are offering one special book they have called the editor's choice, Book of the month. I'm surprised they do not show more books, perhaps the top ten sellers or something like that."

In fact, the screen did show other books, below the fold, but they were not obvious.

The way the screen is used affects the interpretation the user puts on the information.

"I can immediately see that I can search for the title, and I am offered title or author search. Search button is a little twee. I am not sure what the blue buttons really mean – what is the difference between "Full Search" and "Browse," what does "Reading Matters" mean, what does "Services" mean, or member login (I thought they just sold books) and what does "New Members" mean?"

Make labels on buttons and elsewhere very clear and unambiguous, in the user's language.

Anywhere there could be a question in the user's head, provide a way to answer it.

The user was reluctant to press the buttons to find out, and the mouseovers had the same text in them as the buttons.

If you are going to provide help, make sure it gives more information than is already available.

"Anyway, it seems I just need to search. I'll enter the author, Bias, click on the button author, and then click on search."

The search went well, though performance was a little slow. On the search results screen, the search field was reset to blank and default title. As a result, the search expression no longer showed on the screen.

Bring information forwards to ensure the user knows what is going on and is reassured.

The search returned 47 results, in blocks of ten. Even so, the page needed to be scrolled through, and this may well have been a more efficient way for the user to browse all the results, than having to click "next ten" and scroll again.

Reduce user actions to the smallest number the user really needs to do.

None of the results seemed to be the author the user was looking for. Since the book was not located, the user reverted to the second search, which is described in more detail below.

Higher resolution would have shown this image so correcting the above misunderstanding about the Editor's Choice being the same thing as the

*Book of the Month. The misunderstanding could have been resolved by a
tighter graphic design at the lower resolution.*

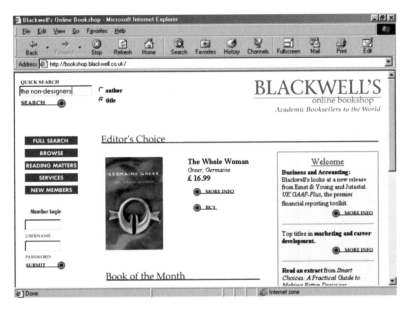

"I'll just enter the first part of the title and search."

Here, there was a good match with the user action.

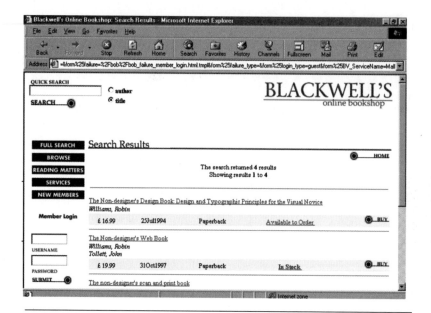

"Perfect, four results and the two I might be interested in straight away, and the first one looks more interesting for me. I am still not going to pay any attention to the blue buttons or the Member Login. Let's just look at the first book."

If there is no obvious and immediate value for the user in their activity, they will ignore it.

"There are more mouseovers on the buttons which could be used more effectively to explain to me what happens if I press the buttons."

"Right, this tells me only a bit more than the previous screen, and is nearly as much as I need as an online buyer if I don't want to find out more about the book, but I'd like to find out more."

Don't use two screens when one will do.

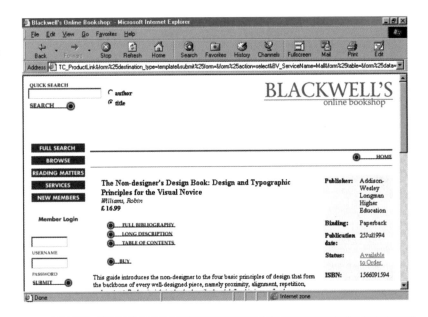

"It has some links for more detail, the full bibliography, a long description and a table of contents. I don't want to buy it without looking at it in more detail – shame there isn't a picture, or an example content page to look at, and perhaps some reviews."

The question here is what will make the reader want to buy it? In a conventional bookshop they would choose by the cover and leafing through the book pages to see the contents, layout and style. Perhaps that would help here.

Meet the user's needs (from the use scenario).

"Since it is the first item in the list, I will click on Bibliographic Information."

What you provide first is often what the user does, especially if they are uncertain.

"This is good and clear, though it is very dry and book centric factual, why do I want to know the weight in grams? I can't believe it is only 15 pages, perhaps that is wrong."

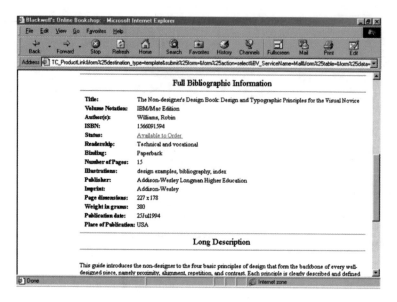

If one thing is wrong, other things will be doubted.

"Also, I have now lost the other menu items, so I will have to use the browser to go back."

The user went back the browser and forward again using the buttons until he realized this was doing the same job as scrolling. He scrolled hoping to find the buying form at the bottom of the page and it wasn't there.

Don't lose the user in hyperspace.

So, the top of this screen was using one icon to indicate two different operations – within page jumping and going to a new page.

Don't use the same "language" to mean two different things.

"The table of contents being laid out like this is not as easily accessible as I would like, though I like what it is suggesting is in the book."

If you are going to call something "a table," present a table, not a sentence.

The user scrolled back to the top.

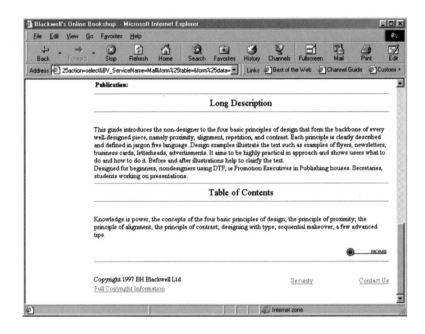

"I'll use the buy button anyway."

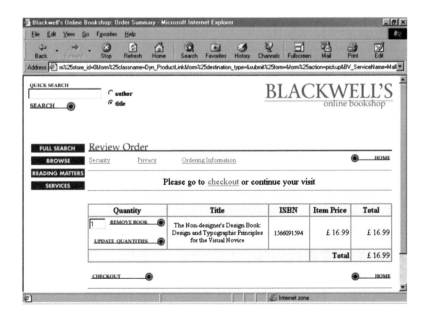

Liking the layout, the user wondered what was out of sight, but found nothing except another security button and then, wondered if there was a problem with security – not such a nice layout after all.

This layout could be improved to ensure that when there is only one book being ordered it all fits on one page. See the notes on Tufte about visual presentation and ChartJunk in Chapter 5.

Don't waste screen space, nor force unnecessary user actions.

"Let's find out about Ordering Information."

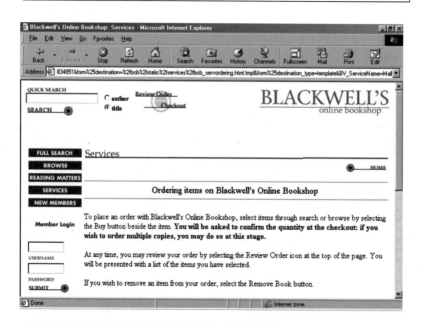

"Oh, I had hoped to find out mailing costs; I think I already know what to do to order, I'd expect to just go to checkout."

If your design is good, you should not have to "explain" very much.

Don't explain unless you have to, and consider all explanations as bad design, unless you can't find a better way.

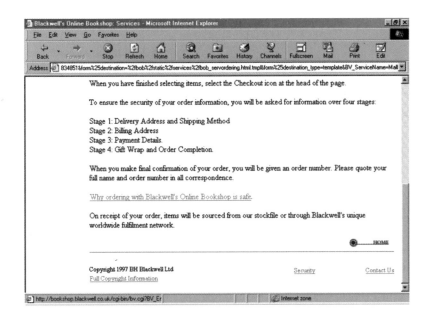

"I don't think this told me anything that I did not already know or expect, other than there is yet another reminder about safety. Is there a problem here I am not aware of? I'd expect it to be safe, or the service shouldn't be provided anyway."

The user is becoming worried about security now, whereas they weren't when they started.

Don't go out of your way to worry the user.

"Let's go back, and then go to checkout (since I can't see a way of doing that in one step)."

Make every action easy – at the right place and the right time.

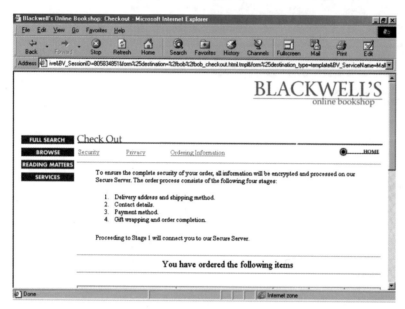

The figure repeats what the user had already seen under ordering information, and he then had to scroll down to see his order. What a waste of screen space. What the user wants is the salient information only.

Don't repeat information.

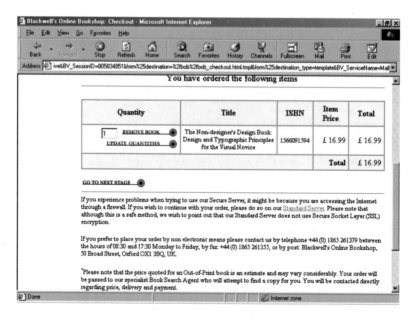

"Uh, huh. More about security problems – this is getting me worried. And the information is nothing new on what I already have seen on the previous page."

*The comment (if you experience problems) comes before any problems, why not only talk to the user about this if they have **had** a problem? This just seems to add to the user's concern, which they have gained through using the site and seen so much about problems which they just assume will not exist, but are now doubtful and beginning to expect problems. When things are safe you don't need to bang on about it, when they aren't, you do need to. (Those who are defensive are not good, those who are good are not defensive – Lao Tzu, Tao Te Ching 81.*

Potentially there is a lot on this site, because it is now mentioning "Book Search" and out-of-print books. But from a customer perspective, they simply want a book. They don't care in the first instance which sub-department of Blackwells it comes from if they have found the book they are looking for, whether it is books in print or from an out-of-print book search. This is putting an organizational structure on to the user that the user really doesn't care about at this time.

Don't give the user options they don't need at that time.

"The most important thing for me is to order the book, and I have been subjected to three pages of waffle. Let's go to the next stage. It says I am about to go secure, that's fine."

"So I have entered by name but now I have still to delete all the other text in the box – what a stupid idea! I'll have to clear down all these before I use them."

The user took this in good humor, but was actually most unimpressed by being forced to remove the descriptive text before being able to enter their own details. Also, the amount of screen real-estate is not being used effectively, forcing the user to carry out many additional scrolling operations to get his information in.

Make everything easy for the user.

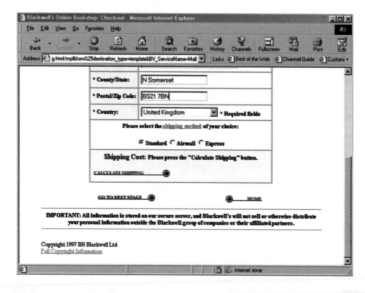

"The asterisked fields are required, but it looks like all the fields are required, so why tell me this in this way?

Uhmm. Standard, airmail, express.

Ah, Shipping Cost. Please press the "Calculate Shipping" button. Well why can't they just tell me what it might be rather than make me do this work? Is "calculate shipping" different from "go to next stage"? And do I have to do this before I go to the next stage?"

Don't confuse the user.

"And there's that message again about a secure server, they must have had a lot of trouble with it at some time, maybe they still do.

I'll calculate shipping then."

The user calculated this cost – but why did the user have to do anything? The calculation could have been done.

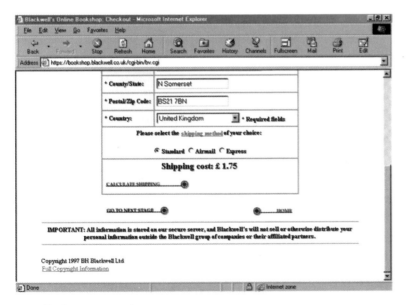

Reduce user actions.

"Let's go to the next stage."

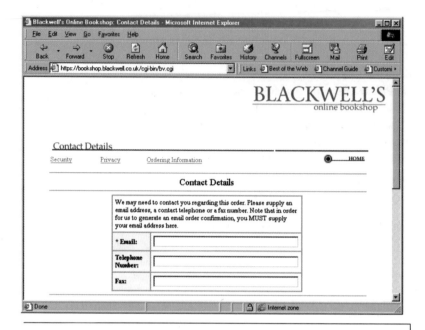

"We may need to contact you.... Why couldn't that have been done earlier when I was entering other personal information? I thought I had already given my contact details."

Because of the action "Calculate Shipping," the user has switched mode of thought from address details into costs and billing.

Keep like activities and like information together in the process.

"And they want a payment address as well, though we haven't done payment yet, I'm going to next stage and I'm ignoring payment address."

Keep like activities and like information together in the process.

Keep things in a logical order.

"Good, it seems happy about me ignoring my payment address, now payment type. Payment type? Oh, what kind of card, and other card details."

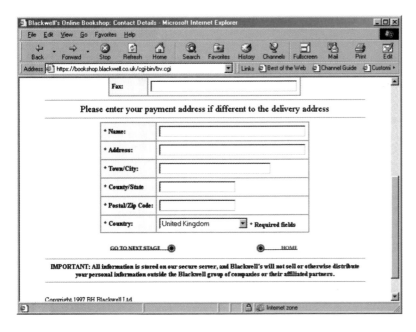

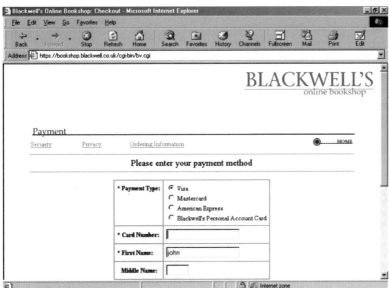

Use the user's language

This would have been right if they had carried out a card sorting exercise with representative users (see Chapter 3).

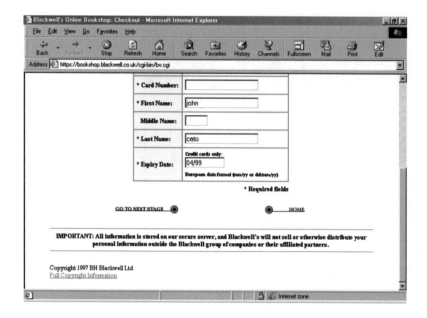

"First name, middle name and last name, why couldn't they get that before? And a pre-filled expiry date as well, Hmmm... let's do it and go to the next stage."

Don't prefill fields or radios or check boxes if you don't know the answer to at least a 80–90 percent probability.

The customer does not think of this as a payment type (though the accounts department might), they think of it as something like "please enter your card details." If anywhere, this is where they may need reassurance about confidentiality and security rather than earlier.

Use the user's language.

Three subsequent screen scroll downs summarized the details entered. The use of screen space for information is poor, less than 10 percent is used for useful information, and is wasting the user's time in scrolling down. A fourth screen finally allows the user to "complete order."

Don't waste screen space.

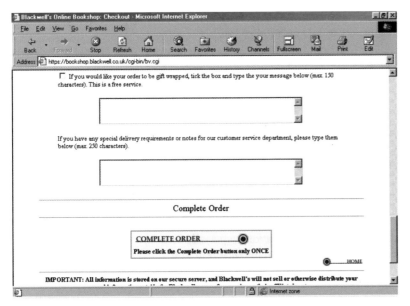

"Four screens' worth to scroll down. I won't bother with gift wrapping. Let's go to the next stage then, complete order. Please click the complete order button only once – gosh what happens if you do it twice?"

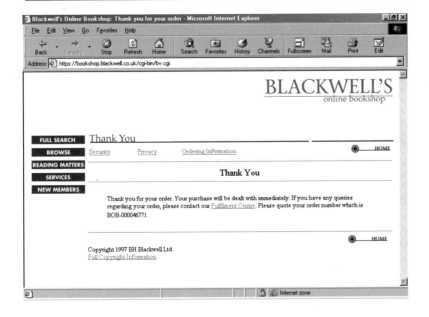

"Oh, that actually sent it off – I've just ordered it! I didn't want to order it yet, oh, what have I just bought? I thought "complete order" was going to take me to the final screen to complete the order. I didn't expect that."

The user was totally confused, and then laughed, taking the view that he could e-mail or phone (if he could find a phone number) to cancel the order. He decided to leave it, however. But part of the reason he was misled was because he had become so used to everything taking so many screens and processes, he didn't expect it to finish so swiftly (tempo and pace) and the terminology was misleading to him.

> **If you have a substantially different operation, especially a non-reversible one, make it look substantially different and non-reversible.**

The outcome

The user managed to order a book, but encountered many problems along the way. Overall, however, the Blackwell's site was better than the Market-Eye site. Key issues concerned:

- navigation systems – clues about what is what
- action support
- clarity
- language
- graphic design
- use of screen real estate
- consistency
- security and privacy.

The site needs work to make the existing system clearer, to restructure some information components in the order they are presented to the user, and to make it clearer what will happen when the user chooses any of the menu items. Use of screen real-estate is poor, although the underlying graphic design is pretty good.

Lessons to learn

I hope you can see how much we have learned from carrying out just one think aloud useability evaluation with one user. Doing it with four to six users would draw out enough information from the two systems described in this chapter to give a few weeks' worth of work. Many issues would be the same as the first, and you would get a number of new issues.

Make sure you follow the whole useability evaluation process described earlier. The questionnaires can also be very revealing, and you will receive users' feedback in their own words. They will, however, forget bits or misrepresent how "bad" the experience was. People often don't like to be overly critical, but the only way to get a really good design is to be aware of and sensitive to all the issues. The quantitative questionnaires will give you a measure of how well you are doing. This is useful as a benchmark for the next iteration.

LESSONS FROM USEABILITY EVALUATION

The key message is that an evaluation is just one part of an evolving process of design. As Koberg and Bagnall in *The Universal Traveller* said:

Evaluations are not conclusions; they are commencements. They end one journey and carry us on to the more knowledge-able beginning of another journey. Just as commencement means both to complete and to begin, so evaluation is a link between our problem-solving journeys.

Source: Reprinted by permission. *The Universal Traveller* by Don Koberg & Jim Bagnall, Crisp Publications, Inc. 1200 Hamilton Court, Menlo Park, California 94025.

There are many lessons to be learnt from a useability evaluation, even from the examples in this book that I have already discussed. What follows is a collection from the useability evaluations in this book. Some may seem obvious, some less so; but all of these have been forgotten or overlooked by one site or another – clearly they are not as obvious as one might think. Treat them as rules or guidelines.

However, I hate rules, because rules stifle creativity. So *any rule I give should be questioned by you*. Take it as a proposition, and test if it works for you. I propose you take it as a starting point and break any rule or guideline if you can find convincing arguments why the rule doesn't work in this case. Also, break any rule or guideline if you are deliberately trying to generate a discord – like the Jazz blue note.

Purpose

Purpose

Make sure what you say you do is what you really do. Keep the relationship between what the system purports to offer and what it does offer consistent and correct.

Needs

Make sure what you are doing meets the business needs and the user's needs.

Visions

Make sure you are clear about the organization's future visions, or you may be forced to design poor interactions.

Users

Make sure you know who your users are. If you don't know who your users are, and you don't know what they want, it is impossible to create a highly useable design.

Context

Make sure you know your user's context of use. If you don't know from where your users access the site, you will be unable to decide what facilities to provide for them.

Areas

Usefulness

Make sure the top level actions provided in the design meet the top level actions the user needs. Users want actions that meet their objectives as easily and obviously as possible. Structure the areas so they match the action patterns or the information patterns in the user's head. Understand the user.

Understanding

Ensure that the distinctions between the areas are clear and relevant enough to support the user's understanding of what they are doing (the action involved) or what they are understanding (the information that is being presented).

The action process

Usefulness

- Make sure the action process helps the user to do the right thing before you become too involved in the detail of the design. Keep the operation of the system useful. Meet the user's needs (from the use scenario). If there is no obvious and immediate value for the user in their activity, they will ignore it.

- Find out what the use scenarios are and confirm that the user's needs are met at the right time. The system should let the user do what they want to do, not what they have to do.

- Ensure that the rationale behind making a user perform a task (a user action) is clear and simple.

Consistency and clarity

- Keep the operation of the system consistent. Don't provide too many ways across the system to arrive at the same point: one name for one thing, one button for one action. Providing lots of ways to do one thing suggests the designer couldn't or wouldn't understand the user.

- Ensure button design has consistency and communicates the likely outcome.

- A button label is a signpost – the user should end up where the signpost indicates. The meaning must be clear, otherwise it is not working as a signpost.

- The user should always know where he or she is in the process and what comes next should be obvious.

- Do not worry or distract the customer with useless warnings and do not repeat warnings. The user is not dumb and will not like to be patronized.

- Keep the user informed, with information brought forward properly, but don't bore the customer with the same thing time and again. Keep a sensible balance.

Reduce effort

- Make it easy for the user to get to what they want – understand their use scenarios.

- The flow of action and feedback must be kept timely and clear.

- Keep actions in a logical order (from the use scenario).

- Make the action process as efficient and as error free as possible. Consider what is the easiest way for the user to meet their needs and reduce user actions. Don't make the user go round in loops or repeat steps. Make the screen transitioning and process clear and simple. Reduce the number of process steps.

- Don't use two screens when one will do. Reduce screen transitions. Don't waste screen space and force unnecessary user actions. If the subsequent screen has little additional information it can often be combined onto one screen, unless the additional information is a radically different mental concept for the user. For example, keep similar parts of the form filling task together.

- If the system can work for the customer, then it should – it is a computer after all. So, make sure the user doesn't have to work at anything physically or mentally (for example, making them do calculations in their heads or writing information down) unless you have consciously decided to make them work at it.

- Don't lose the user in hyperspace. Don't use interpage jumps unless it significantly adds value and is extremely clear what is happening.

Visual design

Space

Don't waste screen space. Provide a clean layout and graphic design. White space is good because it can aid clarity of understanding, but don't waste it unnecessarily. Think how you can make the best use of the screen "real estate."

Clarity

Make the graphic design simple and obvious. Aim for intuitiveness. Clear graphic design removes confusion and improves user understanding. Keep it clear and simple.

Layout

The way the screen is used affects the interpretation the user puts on the information, like the lack of "below the fold" signposting on the Blackwell's site.

Content

Use the available space for information the user wants, not what you think is cool or corporate (Schwab). Cut the sales waffle, the user believes it until you persuade them otherwise.

Usefulness

Make sure everything on the screen is purposeful, that is to say, everything from the largest image to the smallest word is useful to the user. Provide useful, concise, understandable and salient information only. Don't repeat information.

Consistency

Develop a consistency across screens of images and words. Maintain the consistency, unless you are trying to draw attention to something – then create a discord.

Color

Use of color should be subtle rather than brash, unless you are actively trying to be brash. Ensure the colors have similar tonal qualities, unless you are trying to *shout* something. Keep the number of colors used down to a minimum. Make rational, intuitive and consistent use of colors. (For example, green is positive, red is negative OR green is success, red is warning.)

Postioning

Use: Put actions in a logical, natural place on the screen (see the example which illustrates how Amazon "Proceed to Checkout," and "Use this address" were in the wrong place). Place actions close to the information to which they relate so the user doesn't have to hunt for it.

Language

Use: If you have a substantially different operation, especially a non-reversible one, make it look substantially different and non-reversible, unlike the sale closure on the Blackwell's example.

What's on a page – information

Usefulness

- Provide the information the user needs. The use scenarios will tell you what's needed and when.

- If the user thinks of information as being related, provide the information "together," rather than making them jump around the site to collect related information together. So, the conceptual modelling and card sorting will help you with that.

- Don't prefill fields or radios or check boxes unless you know the answer to at least 80 per cent probability.

- Do not worry the user unduly, like the site which banged on about security so much the user began to get worried.

- Ensure the information is correct at all times (see the Blackwell's example on p. 243 for an example of a mistake). If one thing is wrong, other things will be doubted by the user.

- If it is not useful and relevant, don't provide it.

Consistency

- Be consistent when you provide information. Don't force users to keep learning new phrases or new graphic layouts when they are essentially the same thing. The same is true for buttons, links, labels, etc. Re-use the design of information components, forms, dates, numbers, etc.

- If you train the user to be uncertain and confused, by using different words or phrases that mean the same thing, that is exactly what they will be.

- Keep consistent with industry standards, so the information is useful and relevant and immediately understandable.

Language and meaning

- Think about the way the user understands things. In this way you will understand the user. Use the terminology of the user and avoid being not tech-, team-, business-centered. Use a common "user centered" language of communication. Have clarity of meaning. Make labels on buttons and elsewhere clear and unambiguous, in the user's language. Don't use the same "language" to mean two different things, and don't use different "language" to mean the same thing. Do not confuse the user.

- Don't raise questions for no reason, unless there is absolutely no other way to design it. Don't put a question in the user's mind, without making it easy to answer. Any "question" on the screen must provide an easy way for the user to get an answer. Try to do this without being forced into using a help system.

- Make buttons buttony and links obvious.

- Headings should be headings – they are intended to clarify, not confuse, place them at the top of the item they are heading.

- If you are going to present a table, present a table, not a sentence.

- If you are going to provide something that looks like a sorted list, at least put the sorting column on the far left to make it obvious what is going on.

- What you provide first is often what the user does, especially if they are uncertain. So, take care over the first item in the list or the first thing the user will see.

Reduce effort

- Reduce mental effort for the user. Make everything clear to understand, don't make the user carry out mental arithmetic when the computer can do that more efficiently for them.

- Carry forward useful information. The system should always bring forward information providing the opportunity for the user to recall it rather than memorize it. Bringing information forward ensures the user knows what is going on and is reassured.

- Reduce visual scanning or searching. Place labels or text near to what they relate and align and justify appropriately.

- Reduce the text on the screen to make it easier to read and understand.

- Don't provide more concept than the human memory can handle (about seven).

Visual design

- Be consistent with how you present information.

- Ensure information is in the form the user needs it, at the time they need it and in the way they want it.

- Don't rely on the user guessing how the information is structured and what the structure is categorized by. Make it very clear.

- Make the information short and succinct, immediate. Be direct and to the point. Reduce the words, don't repeat a word or a word phrase unless you really have to. Make text clear and readable.

- Reduce ChartJunk. Think information, not junk.

- Show information in the most understandable way – graphs can be easier than numbers.

- Cluster information so it is easy to understand.

- Create a clear layout that communicates without ambiguity to the customer.

Action and interaction

Usefulness

- Provide the actions the user needs at the right time and make them obvious. Don't provide actions or options the user doesn't need at that time.

- Make the interaction easy – pulldowns vs. radios. Save the user time by reducing mental and physical effort.

- Use the AUA model to keep the interaction design clean and pure.

Consistency

- Don't provide two ways of doing the same thing, one will usually do.

- Don't provide two buttons on the same screen which do exactly the same thing.

Reduce effort

- Make the operation of the interaction easy, obvious and intuitive.

- Reduce physical effort – mouse movement, scrolling, clicks by thinking about the screen design and the interaction design.

- Reduce user actions to the smallest number he or she really needs to do. Think about the use of radio buttons when considering pulldown lists. Keep the interaction as simple as possible, it is not only easier to use but it also saves money on development and maintenance.

- If something is below the fold, lead the user into it.

- Keep like activities and like information together in the process, otherwise the user will have to switch thinking from one thing to another.

- Make everything easy for the user, but do not prefill entering fields if it is likely the user will clear them.

- The user should not be able to make any errors but, if they do, make sure he or she isn't made aware of the mistake. After all, if the user makes an error, your design was probably not good enough.

- Don't make the user press buttons to get information that could already be on screen, for example shipping costs could be automatically provided rather than making the user press "Calculate Shipping Costs" (see p. 251). Don't force redundant steps on the user.

Visual design

- Place action buttons next to what they relate to.
- Create useful, re-useable devices and components.

Help

- Don't explain unless you have to and consider all explanations as bad design, to be used as a last measure.

- If you are going to provide "help," make it obvious how to get it.

- Wherever there could be a question in the user's head, provide a way to answer it.

- If you are going to provide help, make sure it gives more information than is already available.

7 | SIDE TRIPS

CREATIVITY — BREAKING THE BLOCKS AND THINKING ANEW

What is "creativity"? There are many interpretations of the term, but for now, let's stay with the aspect of creativity that comes up with new ideas or new ways of looking at things. I am not describing the *physical* aspects of creativity (such as writing a program or building a pergola), but the *design* aspects.

> *"You employ stone, wood and concrete, and with these materials you build houses and palaces. That is construction, ingenuity at work.*

Le Corbusier

> *"But suddenly, you touch my heart, you do me good, I am happy, and I say 'that is beautiful,' ... you have established certain relationships which have aroused my emotions."*

Can anyone do it? While some people are more naturally creative than others, nearly anyone can learn to be creative. The old elitist idea "creativity is a rare skill" is now generally accepted to be false.

Koberg and Bagnall in *The Universal Traveller*, and Betty Edwards in *Drawing on the Artist Within* discuss this further.

> *"Solutions which merely work are not creative.*

> *"Creative solutions lead, inspire, provoke, advance, delight; turn us on to their correctness, obviousness and simplicity.*

> *"Creativity is beyond the norm, or abnormal."*

Koberg and Bagnall

Creative people have a number of behaviors in common. They are more spontaneous, habit free, non-conformist, aware of many different things and self-confident. They read a lot, discuss a lot, play a lot. They generally do better when they have people who trust them, believe in them and give them physical and emotional space. They are capable of moving between a detached view of the "problem" and a highly involved, immersed view of it. They become fascinated; they speculate, tease and explore possibilities, often in a playful, unconventional or extreme way. They can suspend practical constraints and be wild and intuitive with ideas while also being able to snap back to logical, analytic reality. To be truly creative takes more exploration time; this is repaid by new and innovative ideas.

> *"The formulation of a problem is often more essential than its solution,*   A. Einstein
> *which may be merely a matter of mathematical or experimental skill.*
> *To raise new questions, new possibilities, to regard old questions from a*
> *new angle, requires creative imagination and marks real advances."*

Creative people generally have the "left-brain" competencies (analytic and problem-solving, memory and recall, practical and constructive) combined with the "right-brain" competencies (spatial and pattern-matching, intuitive and insightful). Their skills often join the speculative with the analytic and the verifier. They go beyond the norm and this often means they are not the detail specialist, but the highly competent, keen learners of new things, more widely skilled.

Informality leads to creativity, but how should we manage it? It seems that there needs to be an informal environment, in which there is top-level, credible management sponsorship, environmental and behavioral support, and – especially for those new to it – some facilitated structure to aid creative thinking, and to provide for the formality of the analytic and testing out of ideas.

Creativity – your behavior and attitudes

Fear

Fear is a *blocking* emotion. It prevents movement and roots you to the spot. Fear constrains and rejects risk taking. Fear may be the greatest enemy of creativity and can take many forms. Have you ever feared:

● making mistakes

● being successful

● criticism

● losing security, money or status

- wasting time or going over budget

- being disliked or not being accepted

- being true to yourself?

Try making a list of your fears. Do it *now*, while you are thinking about them. These fears are your compass. Practice facing your fears and "walking into them," releasing them. Try with small fears first to get practice and then develop. Keep pushing at the edges, gently, of your fear envelope. Take a risk a day.

Curiosity

Children are innately curious – everything is new, fascinating, to be explored. They touch, taste, feel, push, grab, squeeze, react, laugh, cry, grimace or smile without inhibition. They are totally curious and spontaneous. Everything is an exploration, a testing ground of experiment.

This is how children learn. They see patterns and they make sense of the world that sometimes is the same as ours, and sometimes is not. That is often their delight, and so we should delight in "oddball" people and ourselves when we are being curious and experimental.

My daughter, when she was five, on seeing a man with a road drill, asked me what he was doing. "He's drilling the road," I said innocently. "Oh, he's going to put a screw in it," she said. Curiosity and wild patterns. This thought could lead to a totally new more efficient way of putting up road signs.

So, be curious and fascinated, delight in what you see and who you meet, be free from false pride, be free from the expectation of others, be involved and 100 percent present, be active and playful, explore, be a truth seeker and an experimenter. Again, take a risk a day.

Belief in yourself

If you don't believe in yourself, who will? And if you don't, you will probably fail. Everything in the world began in the mind. Nothing that was ever created by humans did not exist first in the mind. Everything comes from your thoughts. We create the world we live in. So, if we don't believe in ourselves, we create an outcome that matches that. Equally, if we believe in ourselves, we create the outcome that matches that. OK, it's about probabilities really, nothing is ever guaranteed, but it's good to put the odds in our favor.

How can you believe in yourself? Start with little things – find something new to stretch yourself and commit 100 per cent to achieving it. Make it more than you've done before, but not too much more. You may be surprised at how successful you can be. As you achieve more, you believe more. As you believe more, you create more.

Notice someone who seems to be full of self-belief. Notice how they behave. Notice their positive characteristics. Learn to mirror them and see how it feels. See that you too have many positive characteristics. Develop your own ego strength. Accept compliments; don't deny your strengths but allow yourself to say what you are good at. Be strong enough to be vulnerable, open to making mistakes and recognize that a mistake is only a way of exploring what works and what doesn't – a mistake is a creative act.

Make a commitment to stretching, thinking positively about yourself, believing in yourself and your creativity. Once more, take a risk a day.

Constructive discontent

If everything is "fine," you are probably not trying to improve. And if you are not trying to improve, you are not creating anything new. And if you are not creating anything new, you are dead; you are on a life support machine.

> **Discontent is a prerequisite for problem solving. Discontent is one of the most creative emotions. Discontent must be honored and respected for its value.**

I was working as a consultant in an organization where they were going to dismiss a young man on the project because he was always discontented. I spoke to that man and found out why. It was because he could see a better way of doing things so we could all do what we did more effectively – he was very bright but frustrated. He did not have the skill to communicate his discontent constructively. I spoke to the management and invited them to see another point of view. They listened, heard the man, kept him and the productivity increased.

If you want to get creative, practice some constructive discontent. Get rid of all the mantras, "Let sleeping dogs lie," "Keep your head down," "Don't rock the boat," "Just do what you are told," "Don't criticize." However, remember that you must be *constructive* with your discontent – learn to communicate fully what you are thinking in a constructive, open and positive way. Take a risk a day.

Wholeness

A sense of wholeness is a sense of roundedness, a sense of being able to see and feel from many different viewpoints. We are generally either more right-brain oriented (non-verbal, spatial, visual, feely, perception, intuition) or left-brain oriented (logical, analytical, verbal, writing, mechanical, detailed). It is said that most women tend to be right-brain oriented and most men left-brain oriented. Try watching the behavior of the opposite sex and try acting out their observed behavior patterns. Try doing things you don't often do, like painting and drawing, or dancing, or listening to other kinds of music, or going to museums or art galleries you haven't been to, or eating in unfamiliar places, or involving with people outside of your own familiar cliques or genres. Try acting out others' points of view, arguing against your own.

Consider whether you feel you are more sensing, feeling, intuitive or judgmental, whether you have a predominant style. Try acting out the least predominant style and find out what that feels like.

On a project, it is good to have a mix of people (right/left brained, sensing/feeling/intuitive/judgmental, positive/negative, calm/fiery), who can make the team whole by bringing the mix of characteristics together. But try for yourself to make yourself whole also.

Control habit

There is a belief that there are "good" habits and "bad" habits. Good habits are those that move you in the direction of your vision and values. Bad habits are those that move you away from your vision and values.

However, habit with awareness and thought is neither good nor bad, it is just a habit, and habit is not creative. Habit is what we do when we don't think. It is engrained in us from past experience. It has proved useful in the past. It does not mean that it is bad, but unthinking habit is not creative, original, new or fresh. It is stagnation.

No famous creator ever followed the path of their peers; they all broke new pathways. Einstein did not come up with the theory of relativity by following group habit, he did it by creative active visualization. Feynman did not find the cause of the Challenger disaster by following habitual pathways, he did it by going where the others would not. Jung did not break new ground in understanding the unconscious by following his peers or predecessors, he did it by following his deepest "heart" emotions.

Dare to be original, dare to be different, dare to be true to your own self. Creativity demands listening to yourself. Consistently, creatively break habits. Stop conforming, become unique, be prideless, fearless, adventurous, self-believing truth seekers. Take a risk a day.

If everything in your life is totally sorted and totally at ease, you're probably not taking a risk, you're probably not being creative, and you are probably not being true to yourself (unless of course you really have got it all sorted out?).

How do they do it?

W. J. J. Gordon described four paths to creativity.

- *Involvement and detachment.* Looking at things from an involved inside view and also looking at things from a detached outside view of the problem.

- *Deferment.* Don't jump to the first idea, look at more than one way and explore and examine.

- *Speculation.* Be prepared to speculate, even wildly, have fantasies and visualize in the mind.

- *Autonomy.* As a design takes shape, it begins to take on a life of its own, e.g. Lara Croft of Eidos software.

Creative thinking needs two approaches according to James Sowrey – association and analysis. Also, much current research suggests there are two modes of thinking, right brain and left brain. Usually, we are predominantly more one than the other. Betty Edwards (*Drawing on the Right Side of the Brain*) and Guy Claxton (*Hare Brain, Tortoise Mind*) both discuss creativity and the left brain/right brain issues. Accordingly there are two primary classes of technique for creative discovery.

- *Associative* – speculative, intuitive, spatial, emotional – right brain.

- *Analytical* – factual, logical, linguistic, rational – left brain.

Associative thinking tends to be *divergent*; it uses speculation to generate a wide range of ideas and possibilities. Analytical thinking tends to be *convergent*; it uses logic to work with ideas and facts determine the best solution. We achieve our best when we have a balance between the two.

Associative techniques

Synectics

Begin looking at unusual relationships.

James Webb Young explained in his book *A Technique for Producing Ideas* that "the ability to make new combinations is heightened by an ability to see relationships."

"Synectics" (William J.J. Gordon in his book *The Metaphorical Way of Learning and Knowing*) looks at analogies between two seemingly unrelated things. It invites us to ask how x is like y.

For example, at random, how is a financial information system like the contents of an icebox? This may cause us to think about how we organize the icebox, and indicate how we might organize a financial information system differently. We may decide to categorize items by frozen, liquid, fresh vegetables, renewable, and thus have financial information stored by a similar connotation.

Free association

Take a word, phrase or idea, and list everything that comes to mind when you think of that word. Take the first thoughts that come up, however random they may seem. Be visual, aural, verbal or kinesthetic. It is similar to the use of synectics, but differs in that you are making a subconcious association, rather than something that seems dis-associated.

Getting inside the problem

This idea involves visualization in a different way. Here we imagine we are actually the design or part of the design, and see what it feels like being that part. For example, we may imagine that we are the PE of a share and notice that we keep getting changed by small amounts each minute, and every now and then we get changed by a large amount, highlighting the relationship between the share price (minute-by-minute changes) and the earnings per share (annual changes). We may notice that we change nothing so far as we can tell. This may lead us to structure the visual design of the financial information by the categories of highly dynamic changes and periodic changes.

Of course, for this example, we could come to the same conclusion by data analysis and structuring techniques, but we may not have such a visual sense of how we might portray it to the users.

BRAINSTORMING

Brainstorm process – how to do it

Get a group of people together, with a facilitator. The ideal group size is 10–12, though brainstorming can be done with less, even with just one person. The facilitator looks after the timing, suggesting, encouraging, balancing views, clarifying, co-ordinating while not taking control of the ideas, leaving ownership with the group.

Brainstorming is generally carried out using a whiteboard or flipcharts to record suggestions. A way that I find most useful is one I adopted in 1989 using small PostIt notes. Each PostIt is restricted to one idea. I find the best method to be a three-stage process.

1. *Brainstorm on PostIts as individuals.* Each person works by themselves for a small period of time, say five minutes, or until it looks like the volume of ideas is slowing down.
2. *Share and develop on a table in small groups of three or four.* Begin to develop a structure and a sharing on a table in smallish groups, allowing time for each person to share and discuss – do this as a two-stage process, first laying out and developing more, then developing and discussing.
3 *Share and develop on a wall in the whole group.*

Categorization

Share and develop on a wall set up to collect the PostIts in whatever structure you are working to. The structure may be: the six hats; organizational objectives; user, task, object; or any other of the discovery structures in the book. This can take around ten minutes or so.

Rationalization process

Collect all similar ideas together. This is a facilitated stage, where the facilitator is looking after the ideas of all, and clarifying meaning. It is good if members of the group help actively with the clustering. Keeping duplicates together helps to achieve a sense of the collective sense of importance of an idea. If something is mentioned many times, it is clearly important. Equally, if something is mentioned only once, it may be unimportant – or it may be a previously unthought of brilliant idea. Judgment is still deferred until later.

Prioritize

This stage requires organizing ideas by perceived value. With the whole group working together, begin moving the PostIts into positions on the work wall that signify their importance by some value judgment. Be clear about the criterion of the value judgment. This may be urgency of investigation, perceived worth to the company or design, ease of implementing and so on.

This can be done more than once by different criterion. Each organization should be recorded.

Re-brainstorm

Bring the whole group together the following day to add to any of the ideas and discuss the issues and ideas further.

Analyze

Create an action plan, allocating responsibilities and timescales to investigate the ideas further. This may be to check feasibility, validate the risk, investigate the facts, further structure and analyze and so on.

Brainstorming rules

There are some basic rules in brainstorming.

- *Criticism or judgment is not permitted.* We are looking to expand our thinking at this time; judgment and criticism stops the wildness, volume and spontaneity of ideas. Analysis takes place after the initial brainstorming is finished.

- *Be intuitive, immediate, wild.* Just get it down. Don't use your logical analytical mind at this stage. Take responsibility for your own feelings. Just do it, if a thought occurs, get it down.

- *Go for quantity.* The more you can get the better. There is time later to reduce.

- *Encourage the silent ones.* The facilitator should use their skills to be aware of what is going on and find ways of encouraging the silent, quieter members of the group. They often have things of great value to add. Working on PostIts helps because they don't feel overwhelmed by the more vociferous, since the vociferous are also working privately at this time.

- *Do it now – don't wait for others.* Don't be a sheep, be a lion. Go for it yourself rather than waiting for the flock.

- *Build on others' ideas.* If an existing idea sparks off an idea of yours, write it down, don't hold back. This is most likely to happen during group sharing.

Recognize the limits of brainstorming

Brainstorming is just that. It is the seed of ideas, not the final answer. A friend of mine thinks brainstorming is a waste of time. In checking why, it is because he perceives people think it is the answer, whereas I see it as the question.

> **See brainstorming as the question, the start of an investigation, rather than the answer.**

The six hats technique was introduced by Edward de Bono. It is used to explore a variety of perspectives on a problem. It can be used privately as well as in group working.

I have used it successfully in consulting to blue chip clients at the early stages of the project, and working with project teams. It can be illuminating, frustrating, enjoyable and ultimately of enormous value. Doing this with an experienced facilitator working with a team from all levels of the organization can draw out many unspoken fears and expectations, dreams and visions.

It is not for the manager who is faint of heart, who has a fear of failing; they usually block it and say it is not appropriate for their team. These are the ostrich managers, head in the sand and don't want to face the truth; they usually end up failing later, when it is too late, with their team holding them in low esteem.

The "mountain lion" manager, however, will love this technique – it will enable them to face the true realities and opportunities head on, to put right what is wrong and make the most of what is right. Their team will respect them for it. The procedure is described below.

What are the six hats?

There are six perspectives from which to view a problem.

- *White* – facts, information, neutral.

- *Red* – pure emotion, don't rationalize, feelings.

- *Blue* – control, organizational issues.

- *Black* – negative logical, why it can't be done.

- *Yellow* – positive speculative, benefits, why it will work.

- *Green* – creative, new ideas, added value, visions.

The facilitator introduces the principles of the six hats, then poses the problem to the group. The problem is expressed in terms of the project the group are working on. For example:

"Our project is to produce a website which will provide up-to-date financial information to private and corporate investors. We aim to be market leaders and to be recognized as the authority on financial information in the most useful way possible for our clients. We want our website to pay for itself within nine months and our clients to feel our charges are repaid twice over within six months of use."

The facilitator asks the group to work initially by themselves, brainstorming on PostIt notes. (See *Brainstorming* earlier in this chapter.)

Then the facilitator guides them, e.g. "With this project in mind, do a personal six hats brainstorm about all aspects of the project."

The group will normally spend 10–15 minutes writing down everything they can think of.

The facilitator can walk about and be available for non-leading suggestions and answering any questions that might arise.

Then the facilitator will invite them to place their PostIts up in a shared space such as a work wall. Everyone should then read everything that has been said, and to add any more that other thoughts might spark off. Duplications or extensions are fine. That is the point; to get a fuller feeling, like a collective unconscious about all aspects of the project expressed and out there.

By having the thoughts expressed on PostIts, there can be a degree of anonymity and thus greater freedom of expression. Managers and team workers alike can vent their anger or frustrations as well as their visions and desires. This is why "ostrich" managers hate it.

The whole process will take about 45 minutes before the group energy begins to wane. At this point, while it is still fresh, it is possible to work on organizing, prioritizing and allocation of responsibilities to deal with issues. However, sometimes it is better to leave this on the shared workspace and come back to it at the end of other exploratory work. An experienced facilitator who also knows the business of software systems development can decide which to choose.

An example of a six hats brainstorming

An extract (the actual output was six pages of A4 created in 30 minutes) of a six hats brainstorming created by a team I facilitated who had worked on other projects in the same organization came out with the following. In this case, most concern was with project development problems, and so not much attention could be given to visionary design. But, this at least gives management a clear understanding of the issues to address and those to support before excellent design can be undertaken.

Facts (white)

- Interfacing with other business systems need to be considered early in the project.

- Scope of project will change.

- External influences will delay the project.

- Timescales of project will change again.

- I don't know enough about the subject.

- It is not a widely understood process.

- Only one person to start process.

- Hard to get team motivated with constant change in plan/timescales.

- No clear management steer!

- What will users expect from the system?

- It will be an easier system to use.

- Customers expect something soon.

- There is snow outside!!

Logical (black)

- Management are being unrealistic in expectations of delivery timescales.

- Politics are not letting the project progress!

- Overtime – I don't want it!!

- Not enough time.

- How can we implement "visionary" screen designs where the business dictates brevity and speed?

- Current system constraints.

- Interfacing with systems which are written in other languages!

- Only one person on analysis not enough. Insufficient resources.

- The users are going to want something more than just information.

- What is the main direction of project?

- Behind schedule before we even start!! Project has to deliver something – soon!!

- Development method not clearly defined.

- There is no method fully explored to move analysis to design to implementation.

- Where do we start!

- Why are we doing this workshop now? (We should have done it a year ago!)

- Not enough knowledge of the user's process.

Positive/speculative (yellow)

- Get more users involved.

- We have a large skill set. We have good ideas/knowledge within team.

- This is potentially going to add benefit to customers making a difficult task easier.

- Use the database information system to advantage.

- We have a strong team and great team spirit.

- Good team skill levels.

- This type of brainstorming/analysis should have been done a long time ago.

- We have really good socials.

- It has to work.

Emotions/feelings (red)

- Good team spirit (social).

- Management controlling timescales are either unaware or ignoring the extent of detail and changes involved in each deliverable.

- Our site is going to be the best!

- Passion is preventing logical thinking.

- What happens to us if we don't deliver; if we fail, where do we go then?

- Very complicated. This area is too complex!

- The team consists of a number of intelligent and creative personnel who have yet to spend a long time period on design and development – how is morale going to hold up?

- We don't have the right personnel resources. Who is it going to involve?

- Feel we are "putting off" doing the harder parts of the site.

- I don't want to do overtime. I want to go skiing.

- This is an exciting project to work on.

- Maybe we've missed a much easier/quicker way of doing this project.

- It seems we are short on creative input until something has already been done. Suddenly, everyone's got a view (usually different from what you've done).

Control/direction (blue)

- Not enough thought has been put into how the project is organized – who does what – methods, etc.

- We don't know the plan or timescales, can it be done in time?

- No direction – always in replanning!

- More positive direction/support is needed from senior management.

- Management view/politics may prevent delivery in time.

- Too many people jumping on bandwagon and preventing project moving forward.

- Conflicts with other systems.

- What can we reuse?

Creative/visions (green)

- Guide the user through a process from a high level.

- Improved streamlined process will impress customers.

- Give information associated with change in share price trends.

- It should have the "look and feel" of money.

- Integration with existing systems.

- Reduce support staff work load.

- Personalize with portfolios and personal interest news feeds.

- We can split up the development in smaller parts and share round responsibility more.

- We should talk to users early and get involvement plus a marketing advantage.

Summary

The actual percentage of comments per category were:

- White – 16
- Black – 21
- Yellow – 11.5
- Red – 23
- Blue – 13.5
- Green – 15.

These results indicated an overall feeling of emotional concern and negativity or fear. Each of these issues should be assessed, prioritized and addressed.

CITY IMAGE, NARRATIVE AND INTERACTION DESIGN

Introduction

Kevin Lynch's book, *The Image of the City*, written in 1960, discussed the elements that make a city dweller's environment understandable and navigable. It seems to me the ideas that spring from this are paralleled in hypermedia interaction design, and there is a relationship with narrative also.

I look for practical ideas that may help with design strategies of an interactive system. Anything that can give me models for design that work in a commercial or industrial environment must be useful. This is one of them.

For some years now, since 1989, I have been exploring the idea that Lynch's book may be used as a source of inspiration and a model for a design thinking strategy for interactive multimedia systems. Since then, I have been presenting these ideas at conferences and design workshops to perhaps 1000–2000 people, sowing seeds in the audience's mind and also in mine. For me, the original seed idea came from a conversation with Bill Verplank.

City image inspires

The following text was first presented at a workshop on "Narrative and Hypermedia" in Brighton, April 1997.

Hypermedia interaction design

Hypermedia applications are typically used for marketing, communication, point of sale, education and self expression. We have to consider how to give them character, make them conversationally interactive and create emotional responses rather than simply informing.

So, perhaps the first level of conversation takes place in the mind; interactivity is increased by generating emotion in the user.

We can try to design a character and a tempo by flowing and weaving around the main aspects of what emotions we are attempting to invoke and convey, such as comfort and tension, interest, involvement, intimacy, professionalism, humor, excitement and fear.

This creates an environment which has a feel of its own, one that speaks to the user in its own distinct way with its content and appropriate image and develop a stylistic unity.

About this paper

I suggest in this essay that we can improve the quality of that interaction by learning from Lynch's frameworks and being creative in how we apply them to our own design problems.

I describe components of Lynch's framework, with an introduction and the give a brief discussion from three perspectives:

- city image
- narrative
- interaction design.

Overview of the concept

Lynch identified the city image or form as a key to the city dweller understanding of the city. He summarized the form as an archetypal structure, recognizing that in navigation of villages, towns and cities, or indeed any physical space there are five conceptual aspects of understanding.

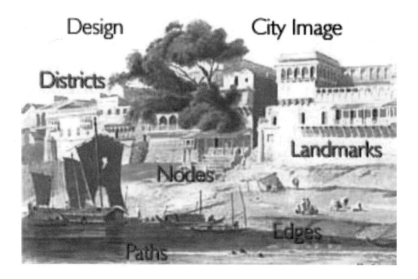

The primary notion is one of "paths," the connecting principle. And, in order to understand the city form and to carry out useful work, the following four further concepts are uppermost in a person's mind: the nodes, edges, districts and landmarks.

Now, within each of these primary concepts, I will write about them from three separate points of view, city image, narrative, and interaction design. I hope to show how there are interesting lessons to be learned from them.

CITY IMAGE

> *"We have the opportunity of forming our new world into an imageable landscape; visible, coherent and clear. It will require a new attitude and a physical reshaping of the domains which entrance the eye, which organize themselves from level to level in time and space."*

About Florence, Lynch says "every scene is instantly recognizable, and brings to mind a flood of associations. Part fits into part, The visual environment becomes an integral piece of its inhabitants lives. It is by no means perfect, even in terms of imageability... but there seems to be a simple and automatic pleasure, a feeling of satisfaction, rightness and presence..."

NARRATIVE AND STORYTELLING

It is by narrative that we can begin to describe the character of a space the story takes place in, we develop the tonal quality of what we portray. We can do this by manner, presentation, tempo, color, believability, involvement, attraction, attention, surprise, familiarity, recall, symbolic gestures, shorthand, and so on.

INTERACTION DESIGN

We should attempt to create an involving, attractive and enjoyable interactive environment, one which encourages us to use and delight in our use. Perhaps we can create an interactive environment where people, our users, will say the same as Lynch says of Florence. An interactive space, multi-dimensional and rich in artefacts, yet at the same time some essential underlying simplicity that communicates and draws us in.

Paths

Paths are the primary framework for understanding an environment. They are the physical manifestation of process, and provide the framework for a person's action. A person generally wants to achieve their own goals as effectively as possible, and the paths should be created to effectively reflect the users' goal. If their goals are work-orientated, they will wish to make effective use of time; if they are leisure-orientated, they may wish to take time and meander through a fascinating landscape. Effectiveness is an objective issue.

CITY IMAGE

> "The paths, the network of habitual or potential lines of movement through the urban complex, are the most potent means by which the whole can be ordered. The key lines should have some singular quality which marks them off from the surrounding channels, a concentration of some special use or activity along their margins, a characteristic spatial quality, a special texture of floor or facade, a particular lighting pattern, a unique set of smells or sounds... these qualities should be so employed as to give continuity to the path."

Lynch found that actual distances travelled are often misunderstood, they relate to the quality of the journey as much as the physical reality.

NARRATIVE AND STORYTELLING

Indicates paths to be followed and lead and re-incorporate concepts, fragments, symbols from the past to delight and surprise the listener or reader. These fragments are revisits of characters and situations, actions and outcomes that we begin to know and become familiar with. The storyteller leads the listener from one space to another developing tempo, delight and humor, dark moments and archetypal myth.

INTERACTION DESIGN

The designer's goal is to improve the quality of the journey. Paths are identifiably distinct within themselves, but also they join and cross boundaries of district, pass through nodes and pass by landmarks.

The way we navigate is based on our intuitive understanding or remembered sequence of the collective space we inhabit. "Go to the banking area, and get some cash" and we can generally find it. "Go to the file menu and save the file" is equally easy. "Go to the yellow cave and locate the gold" is a time-consuming adventure.

If our use purpose is a highly functional objective, the last task is particularly frustrating. However, "Find the story about Abbe Don's grandmother" is simple, once you know the URL, but without the URL is particularly difficult.

Our navigation devices should be made as natural and as easy as possible.

Paths are made real by their imageability. Their imageability is increased if the collective imageable space of districts, edges, nodes and landmarks is distinctive. Navigation is enhanced by clearly visible landmarks and other signposts.

Nodes

Nodes are where paths converge; they may be thought of as places, and often they are locations of activity, of decision, of dynamics. The traveller may find a market place as a node, and a landmark and a district. If all three are combined, this can create a powerful location for the traveller and a highly memorable image. Reassurance and sense of orientation can be heightened and delightful.

CITY IMAGE

> "Nodes are the conceptual anchor points in our cities, the first pre-requisite for such perceptual support is the achievement of identity by the singular and continuous quality of the floor, walls, detail, lighting, vegetation, topography and skyline of a node."

> "The essence of this type of element is that it is a distinct, unforgettable place, not to be confused with any other. Intensity of use strengthens this identity, and sometimes it is this very intensity of use which creates the visual shapes which are distinctive."

> "If a break in transportation or a decision point on a path can be made to coincide with a node, the node will receive more attention. The joint between the path and the node must be visible and expressive. The traveller must see how he enters the node, where the break occurs, and how he goes outward."

NARRATIVE AND STORYTELLING

We lead our listeners into decision points, perhaps looking to the audience to guide our way forward, a narrative is a two way street, and we give out what we take in. So it is, with these special places in the story, we sense the space we have arrived at and choose which way to go next. What we sense, is in part the quality of the story and also in part the quality of our audience. Here lies a decision space.

INTERACTION DESIGN

These are often the decision points in a user's interaction. They must therefore be very clear, allowing the user time to think and providing clear direction as to what to do. They are signposts, menus if you will, to what to do next.

Places can be improved by providing cues, pointers, indications – perhaps by way of landmark visibility – so to make the user's task simpler, and the more memorable the node is the more it becomes a focal point of the user's orientation and attention.

Edges

Edges provide a useful orientation for making a move from one district to another and can be hard or soft. Hard edges make a sharp clear boundary between two spaces, making it eminently clear where the spaces change but can be shocking as well as reassuring. Soft edges can make the transition more gentle, but may also lead to indistinctness, and an indistinct edge can also be both supportive and unsettling. How the edge is designed affects the emotion of the traveller, the designer must understand the subtleties of the edge, and create the edge to support the desired emotion to satisfy and enthral the traveller.

CITY IMAGE

> "Edges are boundaries between two districts. They are lateral references. Edges may be barriers which close one region off from another, or they may be seams along which two regions are related or joined together. An edge gains strength if it is laterally visible from some distance, marks a sharp gradient of area character, and clearly joins two regions. When two strongly contrasting regions are set in close juxtaposition, their edge is laid open to view and visual attention is easily concentrated."

NARRATIVE AND STORYTELLING

We draw the listener beyond the borders of the known into the unknown, sometimes surprising, sometimes telegraphing and building anticipation for the next move of the story. We make transitions from one domain to another, leading our listeners into familiar territory, or introducing them to the new, but with, perhaps, some familiar anchor points to grasp hold of.

INTERACTION DESIGN

Edges are like the transitions we make in interactive systems, from one page to another, or one domain to another. They can be very disconcerting in interfaces, but in my experience, this is usually because the user is unaware that the dramatic transition is about to be made, so it comes as an unwelcome surprise. We can do two major things about this. We should attempt to make such transitions more of a clear change, in a way which is involving and enjoyable (unless we are deliberately attempting to shock), or we can telegraph the change to the user so as to prepare them for it, building expectation and satisfying expectation.

It can make it a line of exchange rather than a cliff edge.

Districts

Districts are areas of common feel, a place where one can rely on some notion of consistency, be it a Jewish community or a mountainous landscape. They provide an anchor of reliability and reinforcement for the traveller, a space of reassurance or a space of tension, it is an identifiable unified space.

CITY IMAGE

"A district in its simplest sense is an area of homogenous character, recognized by clues which are continuous throughout the district and discontinuous elsewhere. The homogeneity may be spatial characteristics, building type or feature, continuity of color, texture or material or of floor surface, scale, facade, lighting or silhouette. The more these characters overlap, the stronger the impression of a unified region. It appears that the thematic unit of three or four such characters are particularly useful in delimiting an area."

"The district may be structured within itself as well, subdistricts internally differentiated while conforming to the whole, nodes which radiate structure by ... patterns of internal paths. A structured region is more likely to be a more vivid image, telling its inhabitants not only you are somewhere in X, but you are in X near Y."

NARRATIVE AND STORYTELLING

We draw the listener into spaces of the mind, half remembered, but remembered by all, we create images of the spaces by speech pattern, vocabulary, tonal quality, facial expression, involvement and unity with the listener, both speaking and responding, not passive, an interaction where we are guide and god, perhaps like the god in the machine. We create spaces and subspaces in the listener's mind, giving structure by developing detail in the space.

INTERACTION DESIGN

It seems to me we can consider the parallels of typography, layout, color, sound and stylistic unity as ways of reinforcing a domain's thematic unity. For example, we may consider the use of a font, the leading, the spatial layout of the typography as one dimension of unity. We may also consider the use of color and similar color tones to reinforce the immediate feel of knowing where one is and to give it a character that works for the domain theme, a financial space may use typical English £20 note colors to give it a feel of richness and unity. Perhaps typical sounds may be played, perhaps some classical piece that associates with money, played light and gentle, a refined piece.

Within this framework, it may be possible to illustrate where within the domain the user is, perhaps by subsequent color gradients or by appropriate typography or even sound.

And, we must not forget the nature of space:

> "We pierce doors and windows in the walls of a house, and it is on these spaces, where there is nothing, that the utility of the house depends."   Lao Tse

The nothingness as well as the fullness adds to the user's experience of space.

> "Space constantly encompasses our being, through its volume we move, see forms and objects, hear sounds, feel breezes, smell fragrances of a flower garden in bloom."   Francis D. K. Ching

Landmarks

A landmark is highly memorable, an object of beauty and difference. It may be large and imposing, or small and delightful in its beauty. It is distinctly different, like a fascinating woman or man; wonderfully

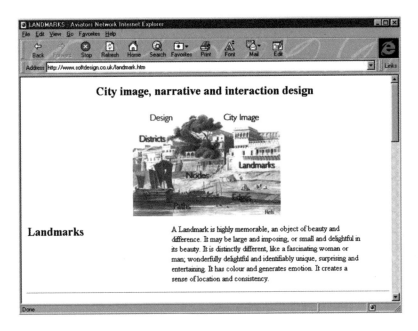

delightful and identifiably unique, surprising and entertaining. It has color and generates emotion. It creates a sense of location and consistency.

CITY IMAGE

> *"The essential characteristic of a viable landmark is its singularity, its contrast with its context or background. It may be a tower silhouetted over low roofs, a bright surface in a drab street, a projection in a continuous facade. Spatial prominence is particularly compelling of attention. It is also more remarkable if it has clarity of general form, as does a column or sphere. If, in addition, it has some richness of detail or texture, it will surely invite the eye. A landmark is not necessarily a large object, it may be a doorknob as well as a dome. If it is visible from near and afar, ... it becomes a stable anchor for the perception of the complex urban world. The bestowal of a name and what is associated with it, once it is known and accepted, has power."*

NARRATIVE AND STORYTELLING

Landmarks in narrative, are often revisited places, sometimes of phrase fragments, sometimes of described locations, sometimes characters, and they become reinforced in the listener's mind, as landmarks in the

story. Sometimes they are conjoined with a decision space, sometimes
not, but they remain with the listener long after the story is told. Mostly
they are not the background, the story's backdrop, but key components
of powerful imagery, that move, delight and haunt long afterwards.

INTERACTION DESIGN

One of the questions I ask when carrying out useability evaluations is
about what users found most memorable, sometimes they describe
pages, sometimes activities (functional devices), sometimes a visual
form. What is clear, they can remember the landmarks well and this
increases the imageability of the interface and the interaction, they act
as locating points within their environment and can be used by them
as targets of their interaction, especially if describing how to use a
product to another. Users begin to name such landmarks.

   When designing, we should aim to make our landmarks visible from
afar, to aid navigation, unless, of course it is our intention to challenge
and confuse. We can perhaps make the landmarks useful as a compass,
as in the Duomo and its campanile in Florence. Can we create interfaces
with visible landmarks which aid navigation and orientation?

   Landmarks can also have a marked effect on the feel of the product,
acting as a defining characteristic, so the mood generated by the landmarks
is of great importance to the overall feel a user may have of the system.

Relating city image to this book

- Districts are like our *areas*.

- Edges are the separation of and making the transition from one
  area to another.

- Paths are the *action processes* and *navigation*.

- Nodes are the primary locations, where *information* is provided
  and decision making and *action and interaction* can take place.

- Landmarks are the *specials* – memorable things, helping to keep
  us oriented.

DESIGNING FOR WAP PHONES

WAP phones are a different kettle of fish. Compared to Internet websites, they are like going back into the dark ages. This is both bad and good. It's bad because they are currently very difficult to design a good interface for. It's good because it focusses the mind and makes you reduce everything to its barest minimum.

WAP is set to take off. In the UK, for example, it is estimated that people change their cellphone on average between 12 and 18 months. They will go for newer versions, and all the newer versions will be WAP enabled.

Market research and predictions from the major research houses suggest the following growth profile.

	2000	2001	2002	2003	2004	2005
no. phones	1452k	5804k	13,158k	21,832k	29,327k	34,216k
%ge pop.	2	10	22	37	50	58

Screen size

The Nokia 7110 is one of the most popular models in the UK, and is shown overleaf. On this particular phone, you have 95×65 pixels of screen space. You have five lines of visible text, of which the first line is the title of the card (a card is like a page). An image can only take up one line. You can't mix text and images on the same line.

Memory in the devices is small, so the decks of cards have to be designed to be small and tight also.

Discovery – users and use

You have to be very careful thinking about the users, their context of use (on the move, in busy places, want to be very quick), what their needs are and what will be truly useful for people on the move. Then as before, be very clear and "tight" about their use scenarios and the effectiveness, efficiency and satisfaction they are aiming for.

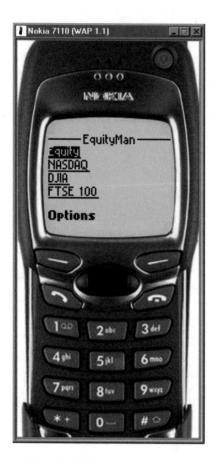

You should integrate everything so it fits with your existing business and all cultural norms. Your aim is to have to "teach" users as little as possible about how to use it, so everything must be designed to touch the instant recall of the users' minds and cause as little thinking as possible. You must also cut everything out that is unnecessary.

Think about the value they can get from what you are providing. Question what they will want while on the move. They are likely to want services providing dynamically changing information or information that will help them in some other way while they are on the move.

Typical use might be to access bank accounts and credit card details online, to save using an ATM or to ensure or transfer funds prior to purchasing in a shop. Another use might be for travel information – train and flight times and so on. Another might be share prices and a fast deal service.

Design

Areas

Keep the number of areas low – you can get four navigation points on a screen at once – scrolling is accepted as a standard action, but the short-term memory becomes an issue, much more than seven is unwise.

You can have sub areas, but don't go too deep, or the user will get lost. Aim to make the site a maximum of three layers deep, with useful information on the third layer if not before. The third layer can be a process, and the process should not be more than about five steps long, less is better. Indicate which area the user is in using the title.

Make sure you design the areas in keeping with the user's action structures and that you provide the most-used actions first in the list.

Navigation

Navigation is provided by clicking on a link. Links are indicated by underlined text and are reached by scrolling and selecting. Links can only be by themselves on a separate line. That's all there is to it – the guidelines under *Areas* above apply.

Everything must be easy to move forwards and back. The structure is likely to be largely hierarchical.

Make sure they can get back home easily, and they can get out easily at all times. You want them to revisit the site, and if they get lost, stuck or uncomfortable, they are unlikely to.

The link "signpost" must bring them to where they expect, so the title on a subsequent card should include the language on the text link, just as it should for a website or any design, although here it is especially important.

Information

Tables are not supported and available fonts are minimal. The display space is very small, so all information must be reduced to the absolute minimum while staying understandable. Right now, if the user wants lots of information, they will come to your website. So, this must be crisp and dynamically useful information. It must be up to date.

The language you use to communicate is going to be critical. Use short, tight meaningful phrases rather than long ones and keep words short. Use culturally obvious ubiquitous words or phrases rather than ones that take thinking about. Consistency is crucial. Abbreviation can be used if it is clear and obvious.

Everything must be tight and clean. Make everything as clear as possible and avoid having to provide help. As I have said before, if you have to provide help, you have probably got the design wrong.

Use graphics sparingly. They will generally be small, but still they use bandwidth and take time to download. So, use them when the purpose is compellingly useful for the user, or for you (your logo or identity perhaps).

Images can be bigger than one line, but they will scroll up or down. Generally, you should not use images bigger than one line.

Menus can be provided by a multi-selection list, rather like a drop down. Here we don't have the option of radios, so you will have to think carefully about how you are going to provide this menu-like facility. It may be better to stay with a list of links rather than a multi-select.

Action and interaction

Interaction is limited to scrolling up and down, entering values using numeric keypad numbers or text (like SMS) and selecting.

The data entry side of things is very poor in the current versions of WML – the number of keystrokes is high and tedious. A typical interaction is "scroll down to input box," select input box to bring up a new "page" for data entry (make sure you bring forward necessary information to this "page"), enter the information, use the OK (a different key from select, and often this is confusing), scroll down again and select the "accept" option and so on. Presently there seems to be no way round this. A facility also exists for hiding password text.

Numeric entry is not so bad, but text entry is tedious and requires many additional "keystrokes."

Using "back" takes the user back to the previous card, but to the top of the card, i.e. the context the user was in on the card is lost. This also is bad for interaction design and must be considered in the design of the information. It points to the 7+-2 issue again and keeping cards small.

In essence, you must design each part of the interaction so the user can use selectable links (like menus) as far as possible.

There is an on-timer facility which enables you to present one "screen" first and then make an automatic transition to another screen. If you are going to use this, then question "Why?" What is the use? It must have a compelling purpose.

When scrolling a list, when the user reaches the bottom, it will scroll round to the top again. This might seem confusing, but it is a culturally understood thing with cellphone menus already, and this is generally not a problem.

On the Nokia, there a facility called "use number." This can be an effective way of linking the user on the move, examining say a train timetable or a stock price to dial in and book the ticket, or to buy or sell a stock.

EquityMan example

I made up a quick example of how a system might look for examining equities (see here).

Scroll down one and then click to see the result.

Keep it tight, keep it clean, keep the user oriented. As always, make sure you do useability evaluations, do them early, start with paper prototypes and work your way up.

The future

The major players in the cellphone market are thinking how to overcome the limitations of the device, and are coming up with new ideas. WML will be upgraded to a variant of XHTML and much more flexibility in layout and interaction will be here soon. The constraints of the small screen and the poor input options will be improved and resolved. The figure below shows how these phones might look.

Possibly in 2001 or 2002, a pen and voice-based interface might be here and our interaction design problems and opportunities will change. It will give much more flexibility in the design and is likely to make a major impact on the market and the use of the internet.

With mobile devices, people will not have to go home and power up their PCs to get online. They will be able to do it when they want to, wherever they want to, and potentially much quicker. The change could be tremendous.

APPENDIX

Dynamic equity information – day/minute

Name – Equity Name and Ticker symbol – identifier
Sector – information – identifier

Financial

PRICE SUMMARY
  Current Mid Price
  Price Amount Value Change
  Percentage Change
  Buy Price
  Sell Price
  Day Open
  Day High
  Day Low
  Day Close
  12 month High
  12 month Low
  All time High
  Percentage of All time high

RATIOS
  PE
  Div Yield
  Dividend cover
  Earnings Per Share
  FRS3 Earnings per share
  Gearing
  Shares in Issue
  Market Cap

VOLUMES
    Volumes Traded
    Volume Buy Trades
    Volume Sell Trades

Historical equity information

Name – Equity Name and Ticker symbol – identifier
Sector – information – identifier

PRICE SUMMARY
    OHLCV values
    5 year graph
    Moving averages

RATIOS
    Average PE
    Div Yield
    Dividend cover
    Earnings Per Share
    Gearing
    Shares in Issue
    Market Cap

Changing company information – irregular

Name – Equity Name and Ticker symbol – identifier
Sector – information – identifier

RESULTS (ANNUAL/INTERIM)

P&L
    Date
    Turnover
    Trading Profit
    Pre tax profit
    Post tax profit
    Dividend

Reserves B/Fwd
Reserves C/Fwd
Ord cap, reserves
Shares in Issue
Mkt capitalization

CASH FLOW

ASSETS
Intangibles
Fixed assets
Fixed investments
Current Assets
Stocks
Debtors
Cash, securities
Total Assets
Current Liabilities
Creditors short
Creditors long
Prefs, minorities
Net Assets

SHARE PRICE SUMMARY
Current Mid Price
Price Amount Value Change
Percentage Change
Buy
Sell
Open
High
Low
Close

RATIOS
PE
Div Yield
Dividend cover
Earnings Per Share

FRS3 Earnings per share
Gearing
Shares in Issue
Market Cap
ROCE
Quick ratio
PEG

News

Name – Equity Name and Ticker symbol – identifier
Sector – information – identifier
   Date
   Annual Results
   Profit Warnings
         Positive
         Negative

Announcement dates

Name – Equity Name and Ticker symbol – identifier
Sector – information – identifier
   Dividend Ex Div Date
   Dividend Payment Date
   AGM Date
   Half Year Results Date
   Annual Results Date

Company summary

Name – Equity Name and Ticker symbol – identifier
Sector – information – identifier
   Activities
   Registrars
   Auditors
   Main Shareholders

Dynamic sector information – day/minute changes

Sector – information – identifier

PRICES
Price
Price Amount Value Change
Percentage Change
Day Open
Day High
Day Low
Day Close
12 month High
12 month Low
All time High
Percentage of All time high

RATIOS
PE
Yield
Div Cover
Earnings Per Share
FRS3 Earnings per share
Gearing

SECTOR INFORMATION – IRREGULAR
As above, per year
Composition – what equities are in it

USER INFORMATION
Equity
Investment criteria
User specified equity match criteria
Portfolio

Information detail discovery

Now we can begin examining the details of each object.

Choosing the first objects

Just as with choosing tasks worthy of unpacking first, we should choose objects worthy of unpacking. Here, it is good to choose ubiquitous high level objects, ones the user is going to find most useful. An obvious couple are equity price and equity day summary.

How to proceed

We want to detail the purpose, attributes and life history.

OBJECT PURPOSE
Every object must have a purpose. Try describing in words what its purpose is. If you can't, try asking yourself why. If you get stuck, move on, try another object and come back to this one later. Never let yourself get bogged down, flow and action is the key here.

OBJECT ATTRIBUTES
Try detailing all the attributes of the object. Once more, don't worry if you feel you haven't got them all yet or if you can't detail it all yet. Design is iterative, it is important to start (a journey of 10,000 steps begins with the first step). The attributes may also give you further insight into the purpose of the object.

LIFE HISTORY METHODS
Objects have a life; thus they have a life history. It follows that a good way of proceeding is to identify all aspects of the object's life. All things (and objects) must be:

1. Created – or they can't exist
2. Destroyed – or they live for ever
3. Used – or they have no purpose.

And they may be

4. Changed – because we know all things change.

All aspects of an object's life involve an actor in a role carrying out an action. So, this forces us to close the loop by asking what role or action is taking part in this object's life. This may tease out further understandings of the system and the actors, roles, actions and objects in it. Once again, it is an iterative process.

An example

OBJECT   Equity price

PURPOSE   Contains the summary of the current mid, buy and
          sell price.

ATTRIBUTE	*Type*	*Constraints*	*Functions*
Mid price	Money	$0..\infty$	
Buy price	Money	$0..\infty, >$Mid price	
Sell price	Money	$0..\infty, <$Mid price	

Invariants, Constraints
Validation
Value ranges
Event trigger
Pre-conditions
Postconditions
Derived
Format, Display forms
Item, importance to user, derived from,
used by, computable function, attribute
characteristics (text, char, num, float, etc.),
display forms

LIFE HISTORY METHODS	ROLES	ACTIONS
Created by System on system initiation	System	Equity Price Create
Destroyed by System on system closure	System	Equity Price Destroy
Used by System on dependent value changes, User on Equity Price analysis	System, User	
Changed by DataFeed on Price value change	DataFeed	Equity Price Change

OBJECT   Equity Day Summary

PURPOSE   Contains the summary of the equity price and
          volumes for the day

ATTRIBUTE	Type	Constraints	Functions
Date	Date	Date	
Open Price	Money	0..∞	
High Price	Money	0..∞,>= Open Price	
Low Price	Money	0..∞,<= Open Price	
Close/Current Price	Money		0..∞,
		>= Low Price & <= High Price	
Amount	Money		==Close Price – Change Close Price(Date –1)
% Change	Number		==Close Price – Close Price(Date – 1)/Close Price(Date – 1)*100
Volume Traded	Number	0..∞	
Buy Trades	Number	0..∞, <= Volume Traded	
Sell Trades	Number	0..∞, <= Volume Traded	

LIFE HISTORY METHODS	ROLES	ACTIONS
Created by System on system initiation	System	Equity Day Summary Create
Destroyed by System on system closure	System	Equity Day Summary Destroy
Used by System on dependent value changes, User on Equity Price analysis	System, User	
Changed by DataFeed on Price value change	DataFeed	Equity Day Summary Change

And, there is more, which is well outside the scope of this book. For a technical viewpoint, see Fowler, *UML Distilled* and Cook, Daniels and Coleman, *Object-Oriented Development, Fusion,* and Jacobson, *Object Oriented Software Engineering,* and Meyer, and Wills and Graham and the rest.

BIBLIOGRAPHY

Books

Author	*Title*	*Publication details*
RG Bias and DJ Mayhew (Ed)	*Cost-Justifying Useability*	1994, Academic Press
Fredrick P Brooks, Jr	*The Mythical Man-Month*	1982, Addison-Wesley Publishing Company Inc
Francis D K Ching	*Architecture: Form, Space and Order*	1979, Van Nostrand Reinhold
Derek Coleman et al	*Object-Oriented Development, The Fusion Method*	1994, Prentice Hall
Steve Cook and John Daniels	*Designing Object Systems: Object-Oriented Modelling with Syntropy*	1994, Prentice Hall
Betty Edwards	*Drawing on the right side of the brain*	1986, William Collins; 1993, Harper Collins
Martin Fowler	*UML Distilled*	1997, Addison-Wesley Publishing Company Inc
Don Koberg and Jim Bagnall	*The Universal Traveller*	1973, William Kaufmann Inc
Brenda Laurel	*Computers as Theater*	1991, Addison-Wesley Publishing Company Inc

Gitte Lindgaard	*Useability Testing and System Evaluation*	1994, Stanley Thornes Publishers Ltd
Kevin Lynch	*The Image of the City*	1960, The MIT Press
Tom de Marco	*Controlling Software Projects*	1982, Prentice Hall
Muller et al	*Participatory Heuristic Evaluation*	ACM Interactions, 1998
J Nielson and RL Mack (Eds)	"Heuristic Evaluation" in *Usability Inspection Methods*	1994, John Wiley & Sons
Donald A Norman	*Psychology of Everyday Things*	1988, Basic Books
Sogyal Rinpoche	*The Tibetan Book of Living and Dying*	1992, Harper Collins
Edward R Tufte	*The Visual Display of Quantitative Information*	1983, Graphics Press
Edward R Tufte	*Envisioning Information*	1990, Graphics Press
Edward R Tufte	*Visual Explanations*	1997, Graphics Press
Ben Schneidermann	*Designing the User Interface*	Addison-Wesley, 1987 and 1992
James Webb Young	*A Technique for Producing Ideas*	1994, NTC Business Books

Journals

Article title	*In (publication)*	*Publication details*
"A Heuristic Evaluation of a World Wide Web Prototype"	*Interactions*, 1996	ACM 1996
"Hat Racks for Understanding"	*Communications of the ACM*	Marc Rettig
"Pros and Cons of Co-participation in Useability Studies"	*Useability Interface*, Vol. 4, No. 4, April 1998	Chauncey Wilson
"The Use of Think Aloud Evaluation Methods in Design"	*SIGCHI Bulletin*, January 1991	Peter C Wright and Andrew F Monk

Other

"Cost-Benefit Analysis of Iterative Useability Testing"	CM Karat, from proceedings of Interact '90 Conference
ISO 9241	International Standards Organization (ISO)

Index

software environments, choosing 31, 44–5
sorted lists, order of 227, 263
sound effects 156, 157, 159
Sowrey, James 272
space on screen, using 115–23, 141–51,
    184, 188, 225, 229, 260–1
  WAP phones 293
special effects 167–70
stakeholders 24
standards
  importance of 145
  ISO standard for useability 6, 26
storm cloud development, presentation of
  152
storyboards
  use in design 78–83, 83–93
  use in testing 203, 206–8
structuring
  actions 77–83, 89–90, 92–3, 259–62
  areas 73–6
  information 61–7
style
  arty style 108
  choosing 114–15
  entertainment websites 112–13
  graphic designer style 109
  magazine style 107
  mixed styles 110
  newsprint style 106–7
  purpose and 111–12
  TV and film websites 113–14

tabs, use in design 131, 132, 134, 156–7
  alternatives 137–40
target markets, scoping 24
  example scope 30
Tatami floor mats 118–19
Tate Gallery website 108, 122
teams, composition of 271

Teire, John 103–4
testing
  analyzing results 219–22
  AUA evaluation 219
  benefits of 6
  choosing testers 193–4, 195–6
  cost-benefit analysis of 6, 195–6
  example tests 181–4, 185–8, 222–57
  heuristic evaluation 214–18
  lessons to learn from 257–65
  methods 13–14, 195, 205–6
  paper prototypes 206–8
  procedures 197–204
  questionnaires, use of 208–13
  remote 206
  timing 191–2
  what to test 192–3
thinking
  analytical 273
  associative 273–4
  brainstorming 35, 274–82
  creative 267–74
timetables, presentation of 151–2
touchscreen systems 193–4
Tufte, Edward R. 143, 151–3
TV and film websites, style of 113–14

update facilities 164
urinals, design of 153
use scenarios 48–54, 74
useability
  definition of 3–6
  setting targets for 26–7, 31
  testing see testing
user-centered design, benefits of 6–7
users
  involvement of 17, 26, 41–2
  roles 33, 35–6, 37, 38–9
  satisfaction 27, 70–2, 76–7
  user profiles 40–1, 42–7